# Mary Garden's Story

Mary Garden To-day

# Mary Garden's Story

by MARY GARDEN &
LOUIS BIANCOLLI

*London*
MICHAEL JOSEPH

*First published by*
MICHAEL JOSEPH LTD.
26 *Bloomsbury Street*
*London, W.C.1*
1952

*Set and printed in Great Britain by Tonbridge Printers Ltd., Peach Hall Works, Tonbridge, in Baskerville eleven on thirteen point, on paper made by John Dickinson at Croxley, and bound by James Burn at Esher*

# Contents

# Illustrations

*To*

JEAN TENNYSON

*in loving appreciation*

*of our long & loyal friendship*

# Aberdeen to Chicago to Paris —with stops

I MADE my first public appearance when I was five years old, in Aberdeen, Scotland, one afternoon when I sang for my grandmother's friends who had come in for tea. I was thought to be something of a prodigy at the time, and everybody wanted to hear little Mary sing. So little Mary was brought in and perched on top of a table. With all the confidence in the world, I sang 'Three Little Redcaps Growing in the Corn.' What else I sang that afternoon I don't remember, but I do remember that as I sang that song I twirled my fingers around the top of my head.

If there was one thing I did as a child that was in any way theatrical, it was my habit of pretending. I was always pretending. When my sisters were doing anything I didn't like, I just fainted away on the floor, and that would scare the liver out of them. They would go running for Mother, and there I was roaring with laughter inside.

Other than that I remember nothing in my childhood that pointed to a dramatic career. I never once said I was going to do this or that—I just did it when it came. I hadn't the remotest thought of becoming an opera singer and never in any way trained for the stage. As a child I knew only that I wanted music, and the older I grew the more I knew I would never be happy without it.

Of course, in those days there wasn't very much in the

way of concerts in Aberdeen, and of grand opera there was nothing at all. I was still a tiny child, however, when I was taken to the Music Hall in Aberdeen to hear a singer named Marie Roze. The hall still stands there, and even to-day I never go into it without feeling the thrill of that first contact with a stage personality.

Mme. Roze was a very handsome and majestic woman, and I shall never forget the way she sang 'Ocean, Thou Mighty Monster.' It was as if a new world had suddenly been unlocked for me. Many years later, when I met Marie Roze's son in America, I remember how excited he was to hear that his mother was the first person I had ever heard sing in public.

About an hour's ride from Aberdeen my grandfather had a beautiful country place where we usually spent a good part of the summer. My sisters and I would go out there and roam all over the lovely fields and forests. I remember we had peacocks on the property, and what wicked brutes they were! One of them jumped up one day and pecked at my sister's eyes, leaving her with scars to this day. Behind the property we had an enormous hill where bagpipers would come and play for us.

At that time my grandfather had fine horses and a set of dogcarts. One day I remember a party was given in the house, and I was permitted to come. I wore a white silk dress, honeycombed all over, of which I was proud indeed. I was sent up to bed early, and I remember that as I entered my aunt's bedroom, I saw one of my grandfather's dogs lying on the bed. When I said, 'Hello, Oscar!' he jumped at me with a growl, and before I knew what was happening he sank his teeth into me just above my throat. I was so terrified I couldn't move or cry out for help. But my aunt had heard Oscar growl, for she suddenly burst into the room and shouted, 'Oscar!' and he let go of my chin.

By then my white silk dress was one mass of blood, and I

can still see myself walking out of the room and down the stairs into the drawing-room, where everyone stopped and stared at me in horror, and all I could say was, 'I think the dog bit me.' The party immediately broke up, and I was carried to the doctor, who cauterized my chin. Oh, I had a pretty face for months! And what an awful to-do in the house over that accident!

When I think what might have happened if that vicious brute had taken me just a bit lower down—at the throat. . . . He was jealous, you see, because he thought I was coming into my aunt's bed. I still carry the marks of his teeth. I was about eight years old then, and it was shortly after my meeting with Oscar that we left for America.

'We' were Mamma, my two sisters Agnes and Amy, and myself. Papa had gone on ahead of us to establish himself in business. We left Scotland on the old *Anchoria*, and during the fifteen days of the crossing I had my first real taste of liberty. My mother was ill all the time and during most of the voyage did not come up on deck, and my sisters and I just ran riot all over the boat. The stewards gave us raisins and oranges, and we rolled all over the floors. The captain, who was a fine old seadog, would grab me and hold me over the rail and say, 'Shall I drop you in the ocean?'

The captain adored my mother and confessed it quite openly. Toward the end of the crossing he would carry her up on deck in his arms. She was in an agony of seasickness, and he took every care of her. One day he said to her, 'Now, Mrs. Garden, if your husband doesn't meet you in New York, I'll take you all back to Scotland for nothing.'

And, sure enough, when the *Anchoria* docked in New York, Papa wasn't there to greet us. Mother sat her three little girls on a tin trunk and said, 'Don't you move till your father comes.' That was our first taste of America—waiting for Father. We were all beginning to feel very sad and forgotten, when suddenly we saw a man rushing towards us with his hands in the air. It was Papa. After we all scolded him for being late we had a grand reunion, and he took us in a carriage with two horses to our first home in America—on President Street in Brooklyn.

I remember it was a beautiful street, with large gardens on the side opposite our home, and a fountain in front of our window from which water went streaming gaily. My sisters and I were quickly in love with our new home, but though Mother was happy to find the whole family together again, she was soon homesick, oh, how homesick! I shall never forget how she would sit at the window for hours and wait for the postman for word from her beloved Scotland. And how she cried!

When we left Brooklyn we moved to Chicopee, Massachusetts. There my sisters and I passed the happiest days of our childhood. In the spring and summer we went bicycling all over the beautiful countryside, and in the winter there was skating and tobogganing.

Father gave us dancing lessons once a week and took us for long walks in the woods. Being an athlete himself, he tried to make athletes of the rest of us. He even gave us boxing lessons, but I'm afraid I never learned much about this manly art because I laughed all the time.

Then Father would organize running races, with a prize of twenty-five cents for the winner. I never won that prize. And once a week we had our literary evening. Father would select a poem by Byron, Burns, or Shelley or a stanza from Scott's *Marmion*. There was always a prize for that, too, and that prize, because of my good memory, I always won.

It was in Chicopee that my third sister, Helen, was born, and it was there that I first sang in a public building. I was about ten. Mrs. Murkland, the wife of the minister who was our next door neighbour, heard me sing at home one day.

'What a lovely voice your little girl has, Mrs. Garden!' she said to Mother. 'Couldn't we have her at the church festival?'

'It's entirely up to Mary,' my mother replied. 'I shouldn't mind at all.'

'Oh, I'd love to, Mrs. Murkland!' I cried.

'Very well, then,' she said, 'you come to my house and we'll begin working on a song.'

So I began studying my song at the minister's house, and when the day of Mrs. Murkland's church festival arrived I climbed up on the platform and sang it with great éclat. That was the beginning of my public career, and the name of the song was 'The Birds Were Singing in Every Tree at Five o'Clock in the Morning.'

My desire for music became stronger every day, and I soon decided I wanted to play the violin. So Father got me a teacher in Springfield. I was given a box and a fiddle that were several sizes bigger than I was, and I remember that whenever I marched down the street to my lesson everybody looked at me and laughed. My teacher was a sweet old gentleman named Phelps. One of his legs was shorter than the other and he used an iron support under it. I studied with him for about a year, till I was ready to appear once more at Mrs. Murkland's annual church festival, this time as a violinist.

I believe I was quite a little fiddler by then, and I was told by everyone that I played very nicely on Mrs. Murkland's programme. My selection was something from *The Bohemian Girl*, with all the variations. That was my first and last appearance in public as a violinist. After that, the violin ceased to interest me, and I soon gave it up. I had never really cared for it much, and it wasn't giving me what I was looking for in music. I can still recall my last conversation with Mr. Phelps.

'Mr. Phelps,' I said, 'how long will it take me to become a good violinist and how good will I be?'

'Mary,' he replied, looking at me very solemnly, 'you will probably become a good amateur in twenty years.'

I couldn't face that.

Some time after I gave up the violin I went back to Scotland for what was intended to be a brief visit. I remained four months, during which time I took up the piano, and that was a far more serious matter. To begin with, I promptly fell in love with my teacher, who was a man named Smith. To impress him, I used to work and work, often five hours a day, till everybody in the house was wild. But I was very much in love with my Mr. Smith, and my piano lessons continued.

That was my first real flutter. I am sure Mr. Smith never knew, for he never paid the slightest attention to me except as a pupil. But *I* knew—I was in such a state of excitement every time I came for a lesson; but my Mr. Smith never noticed it and to the end was as correct as a metronome, and as cold.

About that time Mother sent us to a private school. I was a very bad pupil. Geography and history were the only things I really cared for. Arithmetic was and has remained a complete mystery to me, and I was perfectly dreadful in drawing. I remember I could never grasp perspective. My drawing teacher would get furious with me and rap me over the fingers because I distorted every object in my sketches.

That private school still exists in Aberdeen. Not so long ago they asked me to come to their prize-giving to give awards to the young ladies enrolled there, and I was very happy to go. Before making the awards, I gave a little talk, recalling my experiences in their school many years before.

'I am sure it could not have been my achievements in arithmetic or drawing,' I said, 'that prompted the governors to honour me with this invitation.'

Although I was not proving a great scholar at the school I did make remarkable progress at the piano in a short time. I loved Chopin and Grieg, and those precious months in

Aberdeen provided a wonderful basis for the long, long hours of work with operatic scores that came many years later. But I didn't like the piano very much. Again I knew instinctively it would never give me quite what I wanted.

When we next returned to America we went on to Chicago instead of going back to Chicopee. My father was now connected with the Pope Company, a Chicago firm that made bicycles and was later famous for some of the small early automobiles. Chicago became my home till I left for Paris. We had not been there long when I found myself very restless. I was groping and wasn't sure toward what. I felt a constant drive to be doing something or preparing to do something. My father had begun to notice this restlessness of mine, and it worried him. Being a great athlete and sportsman, he hit on a plan that was to prove helpful to me throughout my career.

'Mary,' he said one day, 'why don't you take up fencing?'

'I think that would be lovely,' I cried. 'But with whom?'

'There's a magnificent fencing master named Yates right here in Chicago. Why don't you go down and see him?'

Well, I went to Yates and took fencing lessons with him. He was a slippery little man, very deft with the foils. We fenced and fenced, and it was great fun. The movements have to be so swift in fencing that it made me very quick. I must have been fifteen then. I can still see myself going at him with my foil in my hand. I just loved it.

In his last years Father became a great golfer. We used to play many games together on the courses in Switzerland, until one day he turned to me and said, 'Mary, would you get me a pair of very small opera glasses?'

This surprised me, because he had never complained of his eyesight. 'What do you want with opera glasses, Father?' I asked.

He took a deep sigh and said, 'I can't see the flags any more, Mary.'

I believe I was just sixteen years old when my father's employer, Colonel Pope, visited us in Chicago. After dinner the Colonel asked me to sing. I did, and he congratulated me very warmly. Then he turned to Father: 'There's a lady here in Chicago named Mrs. Robinson Duff, who teaches singing. Why don't you take Mary down to see what she thinks of her voice?'

A few days later I met Mrs. Duff and found her handsome, tremendously charming, and oh! so French in manner; and of course I was quite captivated. She was *so* everything that I had dreamed of, and never seen in my life. After I had sung for her, she came up to me, seized my hands in hers, and said warmly, 'Oh, but I must keep you as my pupil!'

So Father let me study with Mrs. Duff for about a year. I took two lessons a week with her.

I owe much of my vocal success to Mrs. Duff. I was very young and very emotional, and I had a long pigtail down my back. At first I was bored by the exercises she gave me. I couldn't see why we had to spend so much time on breathing. Now I realize what it did for me. My first advice to a girl who is starting to study singing is: avoid an incompetent teacher.

After we had been working together for some time, Mrs. Duff had me sing at one of her pupils' concerts in Chicago. I sang '*Una voce poco fa*' from Rossini's *Barber of Seville*. I wasn't a coloratura—God, no, I wasn't that!—and I never had the slightest desire to be one. I was evidently something of a success, for Mother long treasured a newspaper review of that concert. Just one line of it was devoted to me, but he must have had second sight, that gentleman who wrote it: 'I think the girl who sang "*Una voce poco fa*" has a future.'

One day Mrs. Duff came to see Father.

'Mr. Garden, may I take Mary to Paris with me?'

'I'm very much in favour of her going, Mrs. Duff, but it's an expensive business and I'm not a rich man.'

'I don't mean right away,' Mrs. Duff said, 'and I think I know how it can be arranged. I have a pupil who is married to a very wealthy man in Chicago. He might be interested in sponsoring Mary's studies in Paris.'

Shortly after that this gentleman and his wife came to Father and in a perfectly friendly way said, 'Mr. Garden, we shall be happy to help Mary continue her studies in Paris for three years.'

We had now been some years in Chicago when Father's business again took the family back East. This time they went to live in Hartford, Connecticut. I stayed on in Chicago to study with Mrs. Duff, and my sponsors had very kindly asked me to live with them until I left for Europe. From time to time I would visit my family in Hartford. I remember one of our neighbours there was Hayden Eames, brother of the great American singer, Emma Eames.

Mr. Eames knew that I was studying singing and for hours he would tell me wonderful stories about his sister. And I remember how much impressed I was by the sacrifices he told me his sister made to gain the place she did. Those hours with Mr. Eames were perhaps my initiation into the fascinating world of opera.

It was while visiting Mother and Father in Hartford that I met a handsome young man named Peter Parker, of a prominent Boston family. I think I was about seventeen at the time. The house next to ours in Hartford was then occupied by four or five naval officers, which made it quite exciting for my sisters and me. One of these men, Peter, attracted me, and we became very great friends. He and I would go out in the winter in sleighs, skate, and do all sorts of beautiful things. There was lots and lots of snow everywhere.

Then one say I decided it was time for me to go back to Chicago for my last lessons with Mrs. Duff before leaving for Paris. Pete and I spent that last day together. We took a sleigh and went for a long ride. Our only companion was Pete's dog Jake, a gorgeous Irish setter that both of us were extremely fond of. During the ride Pete suddenly grew serious.

'Mary,' he said, 'I'm desperately in love with you. Will you marry me?'

'I'm very fond of you, Pete,' I replied, 'but I'm not in love with you and I won't marry you.'

We rode on for a while in silence.

'Pete,' I said, 'if it's any comfort to you, I shall never marry.'

'I don't understand.'

'I've already made my choice,' I said. 'I know it's got to be one or the other, music or marriage; it can't be both. And I've made up my mind. I've decided I want music. I'm perfectly reconciled to what I'm going to miss, and I know there will never be room in my life for marriage.'

Just then our horse took fright at a trolley that was coming our way, swerved violently to one side, and turned over the sleigh. Pete and I were thrown into the snow, and before we could get back on our feet we saw Jake, blinded by the light of the trolley, dash in front of it. He was killed instantly. Pete rushed over and brought him back in his arms. Then he put him down gently in the bottom of the sleigh, and we both sat and cried all the way home. We never once thought of saying good-bye.

That was the last time I saw Peter Parker. The following day I went back to Chicago. We exchanged some correspondence for a while, and soon that faded out too. I heard nothing more about Peter Parker till ten years later. By then he had become just a faint wisp of a memory. . . .

Later, in Chicago, I heard Nellie Melba for the first time. That was in the great Auditorium. The opera was Guonod's *Roméo et Juliette*, and I shall never forget that performance because during the balcony scene a man dashed out on the stage and aimed a revolver at Jean de Reszke, who was singing Romeo.

Before the man could fire, two stage hands rushed from the wings and dragged him off the stage by the hair. I remember how thrilled we all were by de Reszke's calmness in the face of mortal danger. He never made a move, but stood looking up at Juliette's window with his back to the audience, and as the excitement died down he went on singing as if nothing had happened. It was a lesson I never forgot. I had seen a great artist face death with cold disdain.

Ten years later, in Paris, Jean de Reszke and I talked over that narrow escape of his.

'Weren't you frightened at all, Jean?' I asked him. 'He might easily have fired that shot.'

'There was nothing I could do but hope that he would not fire. I hadn't a moment's fear.'

'How about Melba?' I asked.

'She remained behind her shutters on the balcony, screaming like a lunatic. She kept shouting backstage:

' "Ring down the curtain! My voice is gone!"

'And then I lost my temper for the first time and called up to her:

' "For God's sake, keep quiet, Melba, and open the window and come out!" '

And Jean told me that to his surprise Nellie Melba, looking as meek as a lamb, did as he commanded her, and the evening ended in a triumph for them both.

Well, I finally sailed away with Mrs. Duff to begin a new life. I never saw America again until I came back as an established artist.

## Paris and Sybil Sanderson

MRS. DUFF and I arrived in Paris at three o'clock one morning, and as we passed the Opéra she clutched my arm and exclaimed:

'Look, Mary, that's where you're going to sing some day!'

I remember being impressed not at all by her remark, perhaps knowing how utterly unlikely it was that anything so wonderful could ever happen to me.

A few days later we began to call on the professors of singing who had been recommended to Mrs. Duff.

'Now, Mary,' she said to me, 'I want you to use your best judgment in picking out a teacher, because if you don't like your teacher you'll never succeed.'

Our first visit was to a small elderly man with a nervous and excitable manner. I remember that the moment I opened my mouth he rushed up to Mrs. Duff with his hands waving wildly above his head. All I could get from the torrent of French that poured from him was the one word, *jolie!* repeated again and again. I didn't know a word of French, and I wanted to know what all the excitement was about, so I asked Mrs. Duff.

'He thinks you are very pretty, Mary,' she said.

'Oh, but what about my voice?'

'He's certain he can put you on the stage of the Opéra in twenty-six weeks.'

'But who wants to go on the stage of the Opéra in twenty-six weeks?' I cried. 'I certainly don't—and won't.'

And with that we left the studio.

Our next visit was to a gentleman who advertised himself as the teacher of the great Jean de Reszke. I don't remember what he said about my voice, but I shall never forget the rest.

He began by making me hum scales through my nose. And of course all he succeeded in doing was to tie my voice into knots.

Then he told me to unbutton the front of my dress. What he was looking for I can't imagine, possibly my method of breathing. Mrs. Duff and I left the studio roaring with laughter.

It was then that Mrs. Duff suggested I go see Mathilde Marchesi. This celebrated teacher was then in her seventies, but her reputation as a coach was greater than ever. Everybody went to her. So we too went down one day, and were admitted into one of the most magnificent homes I have ever seen. I found Mme. Marchesi an old, curt, haughty woman who came forward like an empress and just deigned to bow to you—almost didn't bow.

'We want you to hear this young lady sing, Mme. Marchesi,' Mrs. Duff said.

Mme. Marchesi gave just the faintest nod.

'Would you like to hear her sing now?'

Mme. Marchesi nodded again, and I sang for her.

'I shall begin by giving you exercises for high notes,' she announced, without any other comment.

'But, Mme. Marchesi——' I began.

'We shall make a coloratura singer of you,' she went on.

'But I don't want to be a coloratura!'

She frowned haughtily.

'That is the only beautiful singing there is, young lady,' she said coldly.

I didn't like her at all, but Mrs. Duff urged me to try her for a while, and I stayed with Mme. Marchesi three weeks. Every lesson I took with her was for coloratura singing. I hated it, and I knew it was not for me. Then Mrs. Duff asked me to accompany her to Karlsbad, where she wanted to take the cure. We returned to Paris about a month and a half later.

'Now, Mary,' Mrs. Duff said to me, 'you've got to go back to Marchesi.'

'But I have no desire to be a coloratura,' I said.

'Still, she's a great teacher, perhaps the greatest in the world, and it can't do you any harm to take a few more lessons with her.'

'Very well, Mrs. Duff, I'll make one more try,' I said.

I went back to Mme. Marchesi and found her sitting on her throne in that palatial drawing-room of hers.

'Here I am again, Mme. Marchesi,' I said.

'I've never seen you in my life, young lady. Who are you?'

'I studied with you for about three weeks some time ago. My name is Mary Garden, and I'm the girl who didn't want to become a coloratura singer.'

'Oh, yes,' she said slowly, with just the slightest trace of remembrance in her voice.

'Shall we begin again?' I asked.

Mme. Marchesi gave me a date for the following week, but as I closed the door on the empress in her throne room I said to myself, 'Mathilde Marchesi is never going to get any more of my money.' So I sat down and wrote a letter telling her that I would not be at my lesson, that I had decided not to continue my studies with her, and that I still didn't want to be a coloratura. A few days later I got a reply.

'Mary Garden,' it read: 'A rolling stone gathers no moss. Don't cry till you come out of the woods. Mathilde Marchesi.'

Her Majesty certainly remembered me the day she sat down to write that letter. I never went back.

Mrs. Duff was now growing desperate. No one seemed to

satisfy me as a singing teacher. There was one more name on her recommended list, a professor named Trabadello. When we entered his studio, Trabadello put me immediately at my ease with his first remark.

'Sing for me in a normal, natural way,' he said, 'as if you were singing by yourself at home.'

I wasn't being asked to sound like a freak. I turned to Mrs. Duff and said:

'This is my teacher.'

Look out for teachers with freak methods! I have always cautioned young singers against them. The chances are they are making you one of their experiments. No voice teacher has ever found anything superior to giving simple scales and exercises sung upon the syllables 'lah,' 'leh,' and 'lee.' With a good teacher to keep watch over the breathing and quality of the voice, one can feel perfectly safe. It was that way with Trabadello.

I have always believed in a great many scales and in a great deal of singing florid rôles in Italian. That language is invaluable for the singer. It doesn't matter whether you intend to sing in French, German, English, Russian, or Hebrew, you will gain immeasurably from practising in Italian. That, too, Trabadello taught me.

Our next problem was to find the best and quickest way of studying the French language. It was decided that I should go to live with a French family, and after some hunting around Mrs. Duff found a pleasant and musical family named Chaigneau in the Clichy quarter of Paris. She entrusted me to their care and returned to America.

M. Chaigneau was a painter, noted at the time as a member of the Barbizon school. There were three daughters, all excellent musicians: one a pianist, another a violinist, and the third a cellist.

The Chaigneaus called their home La Villa des Fleurs. For almost a year, twice a day, I sat down to eat with the family—father, mother, grandmother, the three daughters, and one son—and spoke nothing but French.

After six months with the Chaigneaus, I found myself reading, with great ease and still greater pride, *L'Abbé Constantin.*

I was finally compelled to leave this charming family because their home was too far from my work. I next moved into a *pension de famille* on the Avenue Marceau, near the Arc de Triomphe on the Place de l'Étoile. There I met several American students all hoping to make a name for themselves in opera some day. One of them was Herbert Witherspoon and another Clarence Whitehill. There was also a beautiful young girl named Greta Hughes, later to become Mrs. Witherspoon.

We spent many amusing evenings together. Each of us was certain he or she had found *the* perfect professor of singing in Paris, and for hours we would argue the merits and demerits of all others. Then I entered the Yersin School to perfect my French diction.

I had been studying in Paris for about a year and a half when a bombshell fell on my head.

Once a month I went down to the office of my sponsor's financial representative to get my money. This had continued for about a year and a half. Then one day the blow fell. The man who had been paying me looked at me coldly and said, 'Miss Garden, there is no more money for you.' I must have looked stunned. 'Those are my orders.' I didn't say a thing. Absolutely bewildered, I walked out of his office and returned home. I was then studying with two great teachers—Trabadello and Lucien Fugère. In a daze I went to each of them and said, 'I can't take any more lessons with you, Monsieur. I haven't any more money.'

They were perfectly wonderful about it.

'It makes no difference at all that you cannot pay, Mlle. Garden,' they assured me. 'Pay us when you are ready.'

Fugère was graciousness itself. 'Never will I take any money from you,' he said.

They didn't even think of letting me go.

The studios of both my professors were in Montmartre. Every day I had been walking there for my lessons from my pension near the Arc de Triomphe, and walking back again. So that day I returned to my little room feeling that I was not altogether friendless. I was young and youth knows no obstacles. But conditions got worse every day. My room and board were costing me sixteen francs a day, and it was getting so that I couldn't even pay my landlady. Father sent me a little money, but I was becoming pretty desperate. I still had no idea why the payment from my sponsors had stopped so abruptly, and one day I sat down and wrote them a letter telling them they could keep their money and that my only hope was that some day I could pay them back every penny they had given me.

Just about that time I was introduced to a very rich count, who wanted me to go off with him to his château in the north of France. I had laughed at him each time he made the proposal, pretending to believe he wasn't really serious, and secretly scandalized. In my desperation, I began to feel strongly tempted to go.

I was pacing the floor of my room one day, feeling very lonely and hopeless, when there was a knock on the door. I opened it, and a woman stood there.

'Miss Garden?'

'Yes?'

'I have been sent by your sponsors in Chicago.'

'Won't you come in, please?'

She came in, quickly surveyed the room, and sat down.

'Miss Garden,' she said finally, 'I am very much interested in finding out just what prompted your sponsors to stop the payments.'

'I haven't the faintest idea,' I said.

'We have been hearing stories about you . . .'

'What sort of stories?' I asked, beginning to sense something ugly.

'About your private life.'

'Please go on,' I said coldly.

'We have been getting anonymous letters about what you are doing in Paris.'

'And what have I been doing in Paris?'

'Just about everything—except work.'

'Will you be more specific, please?'

'They said you had lovers.'

'So that's it,' I flung at her. 'You can see for yourself the way I am living. Does it look to you as if I have lovers, or that I am not serious about my work?'

'Also, that you've had a child . . .'

I stood up, opened the door, and said to her, 'Will you please go at once?'

I should like to add that some years later my father paid back the full sum advanced by my sponsor, with compound interest. Shortly before he died I asked him how much it had come to.

'Something between twelve and fifteen thousand dollars, Mary.'

I found out later, from a friend of my sponsor's, that he referred to the day he received the cheque from my father as the blackest day of his life.

I had been living in a tiny room on the fifth floor of a pension on the Rue Chaldrin. Everything I needed was in it—my piano, my dressing-table, my bed, my writing-table, my clothes, and music. Outside my window there was a charming little balcony. I often walk by there now, just to look up and say, 'So that's where I lived as a student!' The irony of it all is that I have always lived that way, simply, almost ascetically. I know people have had fantastic notions of what my living quarters looked like. They have thought of me as a mysterious woman with the habits of a sybarite. They have pictured me treading on deep, plushy rugs and eating out of gold plates. The truth is I have always been able to get along on very little.

I was now more desperate than ever. After that lady left I said to myself, 'I'm going to take a walk in the Bois and think over what in God's name I should do.' It was then late in November and all the leaves were falling. I walked in them, thinking, 'What shall I do—*what* shall I do?' The thought of the rich count and his château crossed my mind . . . and as I was thinking, there passed me by a lady in deep mourning, with great crêpe veils that were dragging all the dead leaves behind her. I can still hear the rustling of those dead leaves. And with her were five little white terriers. I knew the dogs. I had seen them at the house of the great American singer, Sybil Sanderson, for whom Massenet wrote the opera *Thaïs*. I recognized the heavily veiled lady by her terriers as she passed me by and walked on. But I gave no sign of recognition. She went a little way, turned, and came back, and we were soon face to face.

'Why, Mary Garden!' she exclaimed, lifting her veil. 'What are you doing out at this time of day?'

It was about eleven in the morning. Following Mme. Sanderson was a beautiful carriage and pair.

'Oh, I'm trying to work out something very tragic in my life,' I said.

'Well, come into the carriage and have a drive with me.'

When we got in, Mme. Sanderson put her hand very gently on mine and said: 'What is the trouble?' That was the first kind word spoken to me in my moment of panic. I burst into tears and told her the whole story. When I had finished she threw back her head, a gesture which was very characteristic of her.

'You call *that* trouble?' she said.

'Well, Mme. Sanderson, it's trouble for me, because I don't know where to turn.'

She looked at me gravely.

'*I* have trouble, my dear, but my trouble will never be settled . . . I have lost my husband.'

And then she began to cry too, and we both sat there in the carriage on that cold November morning, holding hands and crying our hearts out. Then Mme. Sanderson turned to me.

'You're coming home to lunch with me,' she said.

Mme. Sanderson then occupied a magnificent apartment on the Champs-Elysées. While we were eating we again discussed my situation.

'Where are you living, Mary?'

'On the Rue Chaldrin, No. 15.'

'Do you owe them anything?'

'A month's rent on my room. I have no money at all, and the landlady said to me this morning, "You'll have to pay or go."'

Mme. Sanderson rang for the butler.

'Will you please go to the Rue Chaldrin, No. 15?' she said. 'Pay the woman what this girl owes and bring all her belongings here to my house.'

The butler did as he was told and was soon back with my things. I was given a beautiful room in Mme. Sanderson's apartment.

'Now, Mary, you stay here as long as you wish,' she said, adding, rather sadly, 'I have been living here all alone and it's much too large for me.'

From that moment on, my life, which had become one black horrible worry, was sunshine again. Mme. Sanderson took an interest in everything that concerned me. When I think of her it is as a sister who never failed me till the day she died. I have never known anybody with such a divine sense of loyalty. Tragedy of all sorts clouded her short life, but she never lost her innate grace and courtesy. And that woman's beauty was perfectly fabulous. I was told that when she made her début at the Paris Opéra in Massenet's *Esclarmonde*, and removed the veil that covered her face, there was a gasp of adoration from one end of the house to the other.

The day after I was installed in Mme. Sanderson's apartment, I sang for her.

'Mary, you're good!' she exclaimed. 'How would you like to sing for M. Carré?'

'The director of the Opéra-Comique?'

'Yes; I know him quite well.'

'But wouldn't he regard it as an imposition?'

'Not at all. We'll have him over for dinner and let him discover you for himself.'

# I Start at the top in *Louise*

ALBERT CARRE was then about forty-eight years old. He had been made director of the Opéra-Comique two years before and remained at his post till 1912. The dinner at which I met him for the first time must have occurred early in January, 1900. Charpentier's *Louise* was then in rehearsal at the Opéra-Comique. At table M. Carré looked at me through and through till I was thoroughly embarrassed.

'You know,' he said, turning to Mme. Sanderson, 'that's a very special kind of girl. I have a feeling she will make an interesting Louise.'

I was so overawed I could do nothing but stammer a few words of thanks. You see, I had come from a Scottish family where everything was planned and parcelled and life went on in an orderly and unchanging way. What was happening to me now was unlike anything I had ever known before. I was speechless. M. Carré and Mme. Sanderson did all the talking and I listened. M. Carré then turned to me:

'Who are your teachers in Paris?'

'Trabadello and Lucien Fugère.'

'None better. How long have you been studying with them?'

'About two years, M. Carré.'

'I'd like very much to hear you sing.'

'I'd like very much to sing for you.'

'I haven't time now,' he said, 'because we are rehearsing

Early days in Paris

MARY GARDEN : ALBERT CARRÉ (*left*) and GUSTAVE CHARPENTIER

*Louise* Act IV

*Louise*, and we are all very busy. But when *Louise* is given, you'll come down and sing for me.'

Mme. Sanderson looked as happy as if this had all been happening to her, and not to me. She thanked M. Carré warmly and gave me a radiant look.

'Could I take Mary with me to a rehearsal, Albert?' she asked.

'By all means; come down to-morrow. It might be a good thing for both of you.'

At two the following afternoon, Mme. Sanderson and I went to the Opéra-Comique and watched *Louise* being rehearsed. We sat there, and I was just drunk, as if I had taken wine. As I listened to this magnificent music, I was in a dream. Suddenly I heard someone speaking to me.

'Well, how do you like it?'

I awoke from my dream. It was M. Carré.

'Oh, M. Carré,' I cried, 'what a wonderful opera! What gorgeous music and drama! How I'd like to study it!'

'Very well,' he replied. 'I'll get you a score.'

He rushed off and soon was back with a copy of *Louise*.

'Here's the music,' he said, putting the score in my hand. 'You can study it if you want to.'

So I took *Louise* home with me, and from that day I spent every waking hour studying the score by myself. One morning Mme. Sanderson said to me: 'Good gracious, Mary, why did I ever take you to the Opéra-Comique? Will you never tire of *Louise?*'

'Never!' I answered, and I went back to the piano, till I got every note and word of that opera into my mind and body. I was never away from my beloved *Louise*, not for very long.

A short time after we attended that rehearsal of *Louise* Mme. Sanderson was taken ill. On the advice of her doctor, she went to the south of France to rest and recover. As she was shutting up the apartment on the Champs-Elysées, she said to me: 'Mary, we're going to find a little place for you to stay in while I'm away. You'll be able to work there till I get back.' And she got me a little room in a pension and paid six months' rent in advance.

'I don't want you to have any more trouble,' she said to me before she left, 'and, Mary, you've nothing to pay.'

For six months I was absolutely tranquil. I thought only of work, and work meant *Louise*. After the brilliant *première* of February 2nd, 1900, M. Carré would send me tickets for the Opéra-Comique. I would take my score with me, and with a pencil jot down everything I could learn from the performance, all the details of acting; where everybody stood, and what happened on the stage at every moment. I put it all in my score. Then I would go back to my little room and act it out. I never had any kind of audience—individual or collective.

M. Carré was as good as his word. One day I received a message to come down and sing for him. I went and sang two numbers, '*Ah, fors' è lui*' from *La Traviata*—in French—and the Saint-Sulpice scene from Massenet's *Manon*. When I finished, M. Carré asked me to step into his office.

'Garden,' he said to me, 'I like your voice and I like you. I want to keep you in the Opéra-Comique, but at present I have no place for you.'

'I see, M. Carré,' I said, puzzled and somewhat disappointed.

'However,' he continued, 'I want you to accept a contract.'

'Yes?'

'Dated seven months from now, in October, at 250 francs. Is that agreeable?'

'Oh, completely, M. Carré!'

My mother still has the cable I sent her that day, announcing the proud news that I had been engaged by the director of the Opéra-Comique for the month of October for a sum which was the equivalent of fifty American dollars.

Then came Friday the thirteenth, April, 1900. I was in my little room at the pension, working as usual at the piano on *Louise*, when there was a knock on the door. A messenger boy was there with a letter from M. Carré. I opened it excitedly.

'Come to see me in my office the moment you receive this,' it read.

So, I on with my hat and down I plunged the five flights of my pension. I had no idea what was in the wind, and I don't believe I even knew *Louise* was on that evening. It was being called by M. Carré that excited me. I arrived at the Opéra-Comique and went straight up to the director's office.

'I believe you told me, *ma petite* Garden,' were M. Carré's first words, 'that you know *Louise*.'

'Yes, M. Carré—every bit of it.'

'You're not exaggerating?'

'I know every note, every step,' I assured him. 'I have lived with *Louise* for weeks, M. Carré. I have been to almost every performance, and I have mutilated the score you gave me with hundreds of pencil notes.'

'Very well, you've convinced me,' he said, laughing. 'Now listen carefully. I may need you to-night, because Mlle. Rioton, the young lady who created the rôle, is ill. Will you help me out?'

'With pleasure!' I cried.

'You are certain you can do it?'

'I'm positive I can, so positive, M. Carré, that your orchestra could be playing the *Marseillaise* and I would still sing *Louise*.'

'*Bon!* Now, this may not be an emergency. Mlle. Rioton may be all right, after all.'

'I understand.'

'But I think I'd like to have you in the house to-night. Do you mind?'

M. Carré then opened the top drawer of his desk and took out a ticket to a seat in the orchestra.

'This is your assignment for to-night, *ma petite*,' he said. 'Be back at the opera house at 7.30, and don't move from that seat till the final curtain. I hope you are not superstitious.'

I looked at the ticket. The number was 113, and this was Friday the thirteenth! It was now four o'clock. I said good-bye to M. Carré, and rushed back to my little room. I immediately got out my score, and for the next three hours I studied *Louise* all over again. I couldn't make myself realize that I was finally going to do it. You see, I had been going my way alone. I had studied the rôle all by myself. I was independent. And yet I never doubted for a moment that I could do it, and do it without missing a note or syllable. I was ready.

When the curtain went up that night I was in seat 113. The house was jammed, as it had been every night that *Louise* played. Then it began. The first act went all right; Mlle. Rioton showed little sign of trouble, but there isn't much singing in the first act. When the curtain fell at the end of the second act, I saw a man with spectacles looking around in one of the orchestra aisles. When he came straight toward seat 113, I knew the moment had come.

'Are you Mlle. Garden?' he asked.

'I am, Monsieur.'

'Will you come with me.'

I was taken behind the curtain on the stage of the Opéra-Comique. Never in my life have I seen such absolute confusion. They were all running around like chickens with their heads cut off, electricians and wigmakers, musicians and members of the chorus, scene shifters and officials. From this chaos emerged M. Carré.

'*Eh bien, ma petite* Garden,' he said, seizing my hand. 'Can you finish *Louise* for me to-night?'

'Certainly, M. Carré!'

It seems that Mlle. Rioton had run out of the door and

down the street and that the man who had been sent after her hadn't been able to find her. No one else in the company could sing the rôle of Louise. The opera had been running since February 2nd, and while they make it a point to have understudies for the major rôles, there was none for Louise. It was all very curious. Other than Mlle. Rioton, I was the only person in Paris that night who knew *Louise*—and nobody knew me!

Suddenly everybody stopped to look at me. 'Who is this girl?' they asked. They were all standing there in the middle of the stage and their eyes were all on me—just an unknown little Scotch girl. André Messager, who was conducting the opera, came up to M. Carré. Sensing what was in M. Carré's mind, he pointed to me and, with what he thought was great sarcasm, said:

'Who is this?'

'This is Mlle. Garden,' M. Carré calmly replied.

'And what do you propose to do with her?'

'She is going to finish the opera for me to-night. Do you mind?'

M. Messager began to protest violently. He said he was scandalized at the idea that some little nobody whom he had never heard of and whom no one else had ever heard of should be going on the stage of the Opéra-Comique without a rehearsal in one of the company's greatest triumphs in its history.

'This is outrageous!' he fumed. 'Give them back their money! *Louise* will fail to-night if you let this child sing, this Mlle. Garden whom nobody knows.'

For a moment M. Carré said nothing. I just stood there, looking at all these people, and suddenly the whole thing seemed unreal.

'Make an announcement from the stage!' M. Messager went on, assuming that M. Carré was about to yield. 'Give them back their money!'

Calm as ever, M. Carré said, 'Mlle, Garden will finish *Louise* to-night.'

M. Messager flung out his arms in despair. He came up close to me and shouted:

'Very well, young lady, but don't you lose your head!'

'I never lose my head, Monsieur,' I retorted. 'Don't you lose *yours!*' Ironically, he did a few weeks later, but that is another story. . . .

We had to work fast now, since intermission time between the second and third acts was drawing to a close. They took me upstairs to the dressing-room, and there they dressed me in a beautiful long blue silk gown that had nothing whatever to do with *Louise*. I then weighed ninety-eight pounds. I was so small they could find nothing else to fit me. So they pinned me into this dress and brought me downstairs again. They put me in the front part of the stage behind the chair where my lover Julien was supposed to be sitting, waiting for me. Then everybody on the stage went into the wings, hundreds of them, all waiting to see this unknown person rise—or fall. I wasn't a bit nervous. I have never been nervous in all my life and I have no patience with people who are. If you know what you're going to do, you have no reason to be nervous. And I knew what I was going to do. . . .

There was a short orchestral interlude as the curtain went up, and suddenly I was looking out into the auditorium. My first feeling was one of fascination at all the gorgeously dressed people out there. I was especially struck by the white shirt fronts of the men. With the electric lights on them, they looked like beautiful white penguins. I couldn't think of anything else at that moment, and I remember how it amused me. When it was almost time to begin '*Depuis le jour*,' I turned my back to the audience and walked up the end of the stage, looking at Paris. 'Now is your chance!' I said to myself. And I came back and put myself behind the chair where I had to sing that beautiful aria, and I sang it as if I had been on the stage for a hundred years. There I was, a little Scotch girl, singing before the most critical audience in the world in the government theatre of a foreign country in a language that wasn't my own . . . and what a triumph!

After the third act, I remember Messager made the whole orchestra stand up in recognition of what I had done. 'Messieurs,' he said dramatically, 'on your feet!' And by then everybody in the audience was asking. 'Who is she? Where does she come from?' I have never seen such enthusiasm as I did that night when I finished. There were curtain calls and curtain calls, and they all shouted and threw their programmes and little roses and handkerchiefs on the stage. Because, you see, they didn't know who in the world I was. Charpentier was in the house that night and he came down to Carré, wild with excitement. 'That's the temperament I want in my opera!' he exclaimed.

'*Eh bien,*' the director replied, 'keep calm and perhaps we shall arrange it for you.'

The following day every newspaper in Paris said that they had never seen anything like it. 'A new artiste emerged last night in a dramatic *coup de théâtre* in *Louise*,' they wrote. Then everybody began writing and talking about me, and I found myself *the* person of Paris. I went on living in my little room, and I was surprised to discover how it didn't change me a bit. It is very curious when I think of it now. I took everything as it came. I didn't become pompous or arrogant. I have always taken everything in a perfectly simple way. My way of living was that way at the beginning, and it is that way now—simple. If I told every detail of my life—the way I really lived—nobody would believe me, it was so absolutely plain.

Well, that was Friday night, April the thirteenth, 1900. My career had begun. On the following Wednesday night they put me on in *Louise*, this time for the entire performance, and in the eight years that I was with the Opéra-Comique I sang the part one hundred times. I began my career at the top, I stayed at the top, and I left at the top. When, many years later, the time came to leave it all, I did so without any hesitation. I always wanted people to say to me, 'Aren't you going to sing at the opera?' I preferred that to having them say to one another, 'Oh, the poor thing, she's trying to do her best, but . . .' I never permitted my audience to say that of me. I had heard them say it of too many others. . . .

Sometimes, just for the fun of it, I think of *Louise*, and I'm always astonished to find how it's all there in my mind. I was in bed not so long ago and went over every note of it as if I had sung it yesterday. It's there, every detail of it, imprinted on my brain as on a photographic plate. And so is every note of *Carmen*, *Faust*, *Pelléas*, and *Salomé*. They are there in my brain to stay, and they are there because they are great music—and only because they are great music. But I created the Hélène of Saint-Saëns, and I couldn't do—or recall—a note of it now. It's all faded from my mind, and I suppose that is the difference between what is great music and what isn't.

I have been asked again and again how I 'interpreted' Louise, and my answer has been and still is that I didn't 'interpret' her. I just walked on the stage as Louise. I wasn't Mary Garden, I was the Paris *midinette*. I think M. Carré must have seen that creative something in me at that dinner at Mme. Sanderson's. I have no other explanation for the courage and certainty he showed in putting me on in *Louise* without my ever having been on any stage before.

Louise was the only rôle of the twenty-three I sang in which I wore my own hair. Every other rôle I sang with a wig of the period. *Louise* is a modern thing; that girl still walks the streets of Paris to-day, and they don't wear wigs to-day. It is her own hair you see—or should see.

The morning after my début, they took me up to the dressmaking department of the Opéra-Comique. They made me three dresses for the full performance I was to do the following Wednesday night. I had nothing to say about what had been designed for the part; it was their decision, not mine. Later I used ideas of my own in costuming my rôles, but for Louise I submitted like a lamb. The dressmakers were all enchanted with me, because I was so tiny. Fitting me was the easiest job they had ever been given. For the first act they gave me a simple dress with a white shirtwaist and a big black tie and, of course, a hat. I wore the same outfit in the second act. For the third act they put me in a beautiful muslin dress, small décolleté, with roses—it was summer—and a pale pink sash. In the fourth act I wore a lavender gown, very *collant*, very tight, with a collar that was pale lavender, because most of the last act was passed in the moonlight. And I wore black button shoes with buckles.

About my shoes I should like to say something special. I was always very proud of my feet, and I used to put aside twenty francs out of my pay for the day when I thought I needed a new pair. That was my only extravagance in *Louise*—an extra pair of shoes. Whenever I thought my shoes were getting, oh, just a bit shabby, I would go and acquire a new pair.

The day they costumed me I signed a new contract with M. Carré, this time for a thousand francs a month, four times the salary of the old contract. The contract was to run for five years. Mlle. Rioton never sang *Louise* again at the Opéra-Comique. The rôle became exclusively mine, and I never found out if they had an understudy for me. All I know is that I never missed a performance. Later they gave the rôle of Hansel to Mlle. Rioton, and she was perfectly enchanting in it.

At the fiftieth performance of *Louise* we gave an enormous lunch for Charpentier at Montmartre, where he had written the opera. . . .

Charpentier was one of the proudest men I have ever

known. Before the success of *Louise* he was desperately poor. No one could offer him a thing, he was so proud and sensitive. Charpentier wrote both the words and music of *Louise.* Some years later he said to Messager: 'The success of *Louise* gave my mother a beefsteak every day for years.' So she must have been in a pretty bad way, too, before *Louise* brought fame and fortune to her son.

It was at that old haunt of Charpentier's, the Moulin de la Galette in Montmartre, that the company gathered one day to honour the genius who had brought such glory to the Comique. We were all there, the entire company of musicians and singers and conductors and handymen. Everyone sang, and there were toasts galore, and we had a grand time. We all felt we were living out Puccini's *La Bohème*, when all of a sudden, in the midst of that gaiety, Charpentier collapsed at his table. Everybody rushed to his side, and he was quickly taken away and the party broke up on a note of sadness.

From that day Charpentier was always a sick man, suffering from some kind of anæmia that must have begun in those black, hungry days of his youth in Montmartre, when he fed on nothing but his hopes for the opera *Louise*. I can't blame him for having been very cautious with his money in later years. I met Charpentier once in Cannes. I was playing roulette one day when I looked up and there he was . . . with his five francs. I went up to him. 'So, Monsieur, I've caught you!' 'Oh, yes,' he said meekly, 'but only five francs, as you see!'

I had the good luck to meet Charpentier recently at the thousandth performance of *Louise* at the Opéra-Comique. We talked of the great days fifty years before, when *Louise* was a new thing and all Paris was asking who this young composer was that had written the libretto of his own opera.

'I had always meant to ask you this, M. Charpentier,' I said to him. 'How did you happen to think of that libretto?'

'Well,' he replied, 'when I was a very young man I had

a romance with a little dressmaker named Louise. Then she disappeared, and I got the Prix de Rome and left Paris.

'The day arrived when I began to think of writing an opera. I asked my publishers to look around for a libretto for me, and I advertised everywhere for one.

'I couldn't get what I wanted, so one day, while in Rome, I asked myself, "Is there anything in my own life that I could make a libretto of?" '

'And you thought of your little dressmaker.'

'Precisely. I decided to call my opera *Louise* and to build the story around my own romance with her.'

'It must have made her very proud and happy when your opera proved to be such a triumph,' I said.

Charpentier shook his head and smiled sadly.

'I never saw the real Louise again,' he said. 'I looked everywhere, but I never found her.'

## My Romance with André Messager

❁

WHILE I was a student, living in my little room on the Rue Chaldrin, I met a young doctor who came to the pension for his meals. We became good friends and often went out driving in the Bois. I found him a man of great personal charm, and the relation continued on a very pleasant basis—until one day he began to talk about marriage. Now I knew nothing about 'romance' at that time, and I certainly hadn't the remotest thought of marrying anyone—then or at any other time in my life. Well, my young doctor became perfectly wild. He not only wanted to marry me, but to marry me right away. 'Become a doctor's wife?' I said to him. 'I'm interested in only one thing—my career. Why can't we go on being friends and enjoy the spring together?' It was no good. My young doctor was obsessed by the thought of marriage.

Well, he went home one day and told his father he was in love with me, and the next thing you know his father came to see him. What followed struck me as so parallel in many ways to the scene in *La Traviata* that I have to laugh every time I think of it. The great difference, of course, was that *la dame aux camélias* was giving up the man she loved, and I wasn't.

'My son,' said the very distinguished gentleman, who was prominent in government circles, 'has a great career ahead of him.'

'I don't doubt it, Monsieur,' I said. 'You have every reason to be proud of him.'

'Then you understand why it wouldn't do to have him married to you?'

'Monsieur,' I said, flabbergasted, 'you have no need to worry. I don't love your son and I have no intention of marrying him—ever.'

Shortly after that meeting, my young doctor asked me to have tea with him. He then lived in a small apartment right off the street level, with the windows opening over the pavement, as so many of them do in Paris. I went to his flat, and as soon as I entered he locked the door behind me and put a revolver on the table. I had never see him look so determined.

'Now, Mary,' he announced, 'you're going to marry me or die with me.'

I had to think fast, and I wish now I could remember just what it was I said that made him leave the room for a moment. In my fright I might have promised to marry him, and asked him to get me a drink. . . . But leave the room he did, and just as he did so I opened the window and jumped out into the street and ran home. When I arrived, breathless, at my pension, instead of going to my room I went into the one next to it, which was vacant, and locked the door. A few moments later I heard him racing up the stairs, force open the door to my room, and walk around in it for a while. Then all was quiet for a moment, and soon I heard him slam the door behind him and dash down the stairs.

The following day I had a frantic call from his sister.

'Mary, my brother has just shot himself!' she cried.

'Oh, how dreadful! Is he . . .?'

'Thank God, he's alive, but he's in great pain. He keeps asking for you. Won't you come to see him?'

'No,' I said firmly. 'That would only make matters worse. We must never see one another again.'

'But he loves you so!'

'He thinks so now. He'll get over it much faster than you think.'

I never saw my young doctor again, but that wasn't the end of the story. His family sent him to Biarritz to recover and there he remained to become very successful. Five years later I was invited to come to Biarritz to sing, and my sister Aggie went along with me. Returning to the hotel one day, I found an enormous basket of flowers in the middle of the floor. They were from my young doctor. With them was a little note: 'I have a little villa just outside Biarritz. Won't you pay me a friendly call?'

'I'm not going, Aggie,' I said to my sister.

'Mary, I think you should go.'

'No. I remember the last time too vividly.'

'Oh, he's got over that, I'm sure. Respectable physicians don't carry revolvers and threaten to kill girls who won't marry them.'

'Well, if you're so brave, why don't you go yourself?'

'I think I shall. I want very much to meet your mad young doctor.'

'It's your funeral.'

My sister found him sitting in the garden of his beautiful villa, waiting for me. When she explained that I couldn't come, he was very gracious about it.

'Would you like to see the inside of my villa?' he asked her.

'I should be delighted!'

As the two of them strode into the house, the doctor turned to Aggie and said:

'Miss Garden, there are three things I love—horses, dogs, and your sister.'

And there on the walls of his villa were his three loves—a picture of me, a picture of a horse, and a picture of a dog, and then all over again, a picture of me, a picture of a horse, and a picture of a dog. Aggie came back looking very wistful.

'I have never seen such a beautiful love, Mary,' she said.

'Nonsense, Aggie, you're just being sentimental,' I replied. 'I'm sure he got over it a long time ago. He'll marry soon, and that will be the end of it. Watch and see.'

'I wonder.'

The story of my ardent young doctor ends in Aberdeen, Scotland, in 1940. A letter arrived one day from a lawyer in Paris, informing me that the doctor had died and that he had left me something in his will which was being sent to me by parcel post. When the package arrived, I opened it, and what do you suppose it contained? Five little volumes of manuscript, neatly written and bound by hand, all five of them about love, and every line of it all written by my young doctor. I read them and shook my head. 'Mercy, what nonsense!' I said to myself. He had never married, and I suppose he thought himself in love with me to the end, and perhaps he was. For me it had been just youth and fun, no sex, and no romance.

That was the first time I saw what love could do to a human being, the first time any tinge of madness entered my life, and it had frightened me to death. I was in no way responsible for the way he felt about me and the way he brooded his life away over me. Men can make such fools of themselves. Yes, I suppose he never married because he loved—or thought he loved—me. But, then, he loved his horses and dogs, too. I leave it to others to understand such men. I'm afraid I don't, never have, and never shall. I can truthfully say I have never felt that way about any man.

My first real romance was with the man who had warned me not to lose my head—André Messager. It was only a few short weeks after my debut as Louise that he proceeded to lose his. . . .

Soon after I signed my second contract with the Opéra-Comique, I noticed that Messager was taking more than a professional interest in me. Our great love for Charpentier's opera had brought us close together, and I suppose I was dazzled by the fact that a man of his position in the world of music should be taking a fancy to me. Besides being a conductor of distinction, Messager was successful as a composer of operas and operettas. At the time we met he was just forty-seven. He had a son of eighteen by his first wife and was then married to his second, a gifted English composer of songs named Hope Temple.

Messager's interest in me soon turned to love. But let me say this and emphasize it strongly: I never really loved him. I was enchanted, perhaps, but never in love; I was never that way with anybody. I never lost my heart, and I always knew what I was doing, with Messager and with those who came later. I never knew what it was to have that mad passion, where you say mad things and sometimes do them. I can't explain it. Some years before her death, I discussed it with my mother, who told me she had been like that herself. 'You know, Mary, I never loved anybody in my life.' 'Didn't you love Father?' I asked. 'No; I liked him.' I think I understood what Mother meant, only because I felt the same. Neither of us ever really 'loved' a man, and neither of us ever lost her head. The great difference between us was that Mother married, and I never did.

My intimacy with Messager lasted two years, and this is how it started. I signed a contract to go to Aix-les-Bains for the summer. One day Messager arrived—and remained. The country around Aix-les-Bains was very beautiful, and we would take walks together. And one day it began. . . . He was so much in love, and in my own strange way perhaps I was, or thought I was, just a bit. I found him a charming and delightful person, but mercy, there wasn't any thought of a *grande passion* or marriage or anything like that. As I said, he was married, and his wife was very fond of me. I suppose I liked him and was very fond of him, but that was all, really.

One afternoon, while at Aix-les-Bains, Messager and I

went up to the top of Mont Revard, and there in the salon of the lovely house perched high up there we had our first contact with the music of Claude Debussy, the man who was to become such an important figure in the lives of both of us. There was a piano in that salon, and while I sat down before it and idled over the keys Messager strode over to a table upon which was lying a copy of the French magazine, *L'Illustration*. Opening it, he came upon some music that immediately excited him, for he shouted out:

'My God, Mary, here's a composition by Claude Debussy, and it's perfectly beautiful.'

I came over to look at it, and it was the song, *Extase*, and the more I examined it the more it seemed to be mine, so near were its mood and idiom to me.

'Oh, how I want to possess that song!' I cried out to Messager.

'Perhaps you shall some day—and its composer, too,' said Messager.

'André, you're jealous!' I laughed. 'Of a few bars of music!'

Later, after we produced *Pelléas et Mélisande*, I told Debussy that it was the song *Extase* that had first brought us together, which explains why he then dedicated the song to me. It wasn't until some years later that I discovered that the same song had also brought Debussy and his first wife Lily, together. She, too, had seen the song in *L'Illustration* and said to herself: 'I'd like to know the man who wrote this song—I've *got* to know him.' Lily would say to me, 'Mary, I fell in love with Claude through that song, didn't you?' and I would answer, 'Only with his music, Lily.'

It was at Aix-les-Bains, incidentally, that I sang Thaïs for the first time. Massenet had written that opera for my good friend, Sybil Sanderson. Sybil had a beautiful château at Aix-les-Bains, and she was with me for my first performance of the rôle she had created at the Paris Opéra in 1896.

'Mary,' she said, 'Thaïs must have pearls.'

And she threw around my neck millions of francs' worth of her marvellous pearls. Decked out in this pagan splendour, I paraded before my director. He became extremely nervous.

'Do you realize what a fortune you have around your neck?' he asked. 'What if something happens? They will hold me responsible.'

No one in the whole company was really at peace until Sybil came into my dressing-room after the performance. The pearls were put around her own beautiful throat once more and taken home. Everyone breathed easily again. . . .

Also in the house that night was my good friend, King George I of Greece. He came down from his box after the performance and said to me: 'Mademoiselle, that's going to be one of the greatest successes in the world.' It was from that conversation with King George that I was determined, a few years later, to make my debut in New York in *Thaïs*.

A few months after that my romance with André Messager led to some difficulty in my relations with Albert Carré, the director of the Opéra-Comique.

As my next rôle, M. Carré gave me the part of the heroine in *La Marseillaise*, an opera by a composer named Lucien Lambert. It was all about the man who wrote the great French anthem, Rouget de Lisle. I was Rouget de Lisle's fiancée in the opera, and the central episode had to do with the first performance of the hymn in the château where Rouget de Lisle composed it one night. I played the piano as Rouget de Lisle's friend, the man who was my father in the opera, sang it. Rouget de Lisle stood there beside me at the piano. When I suddenly stood up from the piano and shouted, '*Je suis française!*' everybody in the Opéra-Comique laughed—because, you see, I still had an accent and have always had a little bit of one. After that, the opera was given only on Bastille Day, when all the theatres are open and the people are admitted free of charge.

And so it went. There was nothing in my life but work, work, work—and André Messager. I was at the theatre almost every day. And soon I began to work on my next creation—Gabriel Pierné's *La Fille de Tabarin*, based on the book of Sardou. That was the first time I met the great Sardou. He was then a small, elderly man, and he wore a black velvet coat and black velvet beret. He had an enormous white silk handkerchief that he used to pull out of his pocket and cry copious tears into . . . he was so overcome by his own words.

Well, we gave *La Fille de Tabarin*, and even Sardou's tears couldn't save it from being a failure. I never cared much for the music of Pierné. Lucien Fugère, one of my teachers, was in that opera with me, and he was a great artist, but the rôle of Tabarin didn't suit him one bit. In *Louise* he was one of the greatest fathers ever seen on the stage of the Opéra-Comique, and the rôle stayed with him till he died.

My next opera was a revival of *La Traviata*. M. Carré dressed it up in new costumes and scenery and made some intelligent cuts in the score. And he staged it as drama, good theatrical drama. Violetta was one of my favourite rôles, but I sang her only in Paris and Brussels, never in America, and the reason was this. The American brand of Violetta was a coloratura, a healthy, robust nightingale with a high E flat finishing the first-act aria. If she ever missed that E flat, heaven help her! Now, as far as I was concerned, that had nothing whatsoever to do with the lady of the camellias. So I left my lady in Paris.

Soon after I created Pierné's *La Fille de Tabarin*, I sang Massenet's *Manon* for the first time, and that proved to be my second real triumph in Paris. It was through this success that I was approached for the first time by Covent Garden, and my career of bad luck in London began.

I signed a contract with Covent Garden, arrived in London, settled at the Hotel Cecil, and began rehearsals for my debut in Gounod's *Roméo et Juliette*. That was to be followed by *Faust* and *Manon*.

Rehearsals went very smoothly. Then it began. Two days before my debut, I was sitting at an open window, admiring the boats sailing down the Thames, when Ernest Van Dyck, the celebrated Wagnerian tenor, came in to see me, and the first thing he said was:

'Mary, get away from that window! No singer can do that in London and not pay for it.'

I laughed and paid no attention, being certain that nothing, not even the London air, could harm me. So I thought.

Well, the morning of the day of my début, while practising, my voice completely failed me. Not one high note came out of my throat! I was desperate. I remained quiet all day and, finally, at about seven o'clock, I went over to the opera house. I waited and waited—wondering what great disaster lay ahead for me.

When the moment came for me to sing Juliette's great waltz, panic seized me. I was about to run back and lock myself in my dressing-room, when Pol Plancon, who was also in the cast, caught me.

'None of this,' he said to me in French. 'Your place is out there.'

And he pushed me on to the stage, and I had to sing the waltz. What a debacle, that whole first act! Every note above A had to be imagined by the audience because there just wasn't any note. Then a curious thing happened. My throat suddenly became warm, and my notes were free again, and so I finished the opera much better than I had begun it.

The next day I was taken to a doctor, who confirmed the awful truth. My vocal chords had suffered a severe attack of rheumatism. Van Dyck had been right—I was now paying for admiring the Thames through an open window.

For two weeks I was not allowed to sing or talk. I just sat in my room in complete despair and silence. And then I was well again, and able to finish the season. But my mind was so stamped with the horror of that début that for many years it was impossible for me to sing Juliette anywhere. Not till a decade later did I sing the rôle again. That was at the Opéra in Paris, and I enjoyed a great success in it. The mental block was now completely gone.

It must have been shortly after the production of *La Fille de Tabarin* that Albert Carré called me to his office one day.

'Mary,' he said, 'you know that I'm a free man again.'

'Yes, M. Carré.'

'Will you be my wife?'

I was stunned; I knew M. Carré admired me, but I had never suspected that he loved me. As for myself, I had tremendous respect for him, and a deep devotion to him for all he had done for me. I worshipped him for the confidence he had always had in me. He believed in me completely, and whenever I went to consult him about any of my rôles, he would say, 'Just do it your own way; you can do no wrong.'

I was, of course, very flattered by M. Carré's proposal.

'M. Carré,' I said, 'I'm very fond of you, but I don't love you and I never intend to get married.'

'We could accomplish a great deal together here at the Opéra-Comique.'

'But we are together, M. Carré.'

'Yes, but I love you and want you as my very own.'

'I'm sorry, M. Carré, but there is someone else in my life.'

'May I ask who?'

'André Messager.'

That seemed to sober M. Carré for a moment. He looked at me fixedly for a few moments, and then said:

'Very well, let's both forget about it.'

But M. Carré didn't forget about it. Two days later he

proposed again, this time by letter. Ignoring what I had told him about Messager, he asked me whether I might change my mind and reconsider marrying him. After all, he was a free man, and Messager wasn't. . . . I sat down and wrote a reply that was audacity itself. When I think of it, the nerve I had at the beginning of my career, defying the man who could break it so easily! I wrote back telling him I could never love him because I was in love with André Messager. I boldly underlined this statement—I clearly remember putting two lines under it, not one.

So M. Carré called me to his office again, and the moment I entered I saw there was trouble in store for me. Furiously waving my letter at me, he jumped from his chair. Then he pulled open a drawer of his desk, took out my contract, tore it up violently, and flung the pieces into a wastepaper basket.

'You're through!' he shouted. 'Now you can do what you like and go where you like and with whom you like!'

When he said that, he looked very, very miserable, and very, very angry. My God, was he angry! I was heartbroken. Without a word, I got up and left his office. By a convenient coincidence I had received a tempting offer a few days before my clash with M. Carré. A man from the publishing house of Heughel had come to ask me if I would be interested in creating *Louise* in Italian at La Scala in Milan. I had not given him an answer. So when I returned home from M. Carré's office I sat down and wrote Heugel that I was ready to accept their offer. The request, it seems, had come from Giulio Gatti-Casazza, who was then managing La Scala and was later to become general manager of the Metropolitan Opera House in New York.

So, I got myself a score of *Louise* in Italian and began to work on the language. Then I wrote M. Carré that I was very sad at what had happened, adding, in casual way, that I was going to sing *Louise* at La Scala. As soon as he got my letter he sent a messenger over to my house to come down to see him at once. When I walked into his office, he came over to me, calm and smiling now, and said:

'*Ma chère petite* Garden, please send your Italian score back.'

'But I've already told them I would sing it.'

'Never mind. I will never let you go.'

I didn't say anything. On his desk was a new contract, and he put his arm around my back and said, 'Sign that,' and I signed it, and I didn't go to Milan. M. Carré became one of my greatest artistic friends.

Then came my break with Messager. The truth is my romance was getting me down. I was never really emotional about sex, but perhaps the only time that my emotions almost got hold of me was with Messager, at least in the early stages of our relation. I was young; it was my first romance, and the first of this thing always seems wonderful. But I soon began to see another side to my lover. He had a fearful temper. For no reason at all, he would say the most savage things to me. Each day his language became more and more rude. And then he was jealous, frightfully jealous. All the men in my life were jealous, but perhaps Messager was the meanest of them all in his jealousy. I never gave him any cause. It was all in his mind.

After two years, I felt I was getting ill from this relation with him. I remember—it was just about the end—one day he came to my apartment and he got out of his pocket a great roll of money which he had just received as royalties from his compositions. Twisting his lips meanly, he flung the bills into my lap. 'This is for you!' he shouted. I took the money and threw it right in his face. 'You get out of my house!'

I was so young and so proud, and that kind of life was unknown to me. That man just broke me, trying to dominate me all the time, saying wretched things to me. I thought I was going to lose my mind. Whatever feeling of tenderness I had once had for him was dead in me.

One day I saw him approaching in the street, and a great feeling of loathing came over me. I was literally nauseated at the thought of his being there in my apartment with me again. I saw him come to the street door. I quickly rang for my maid and told her that when the gentleman called he should be told that I was not in. It had taken me a long time to make that decision; I had been humiliated more than any woman has a right to be, and all at once I knew it was the end. I knew that I just couldn't go on any longer. Physically and spiritually, he was destroying me, and I said to myself, 'It's got to stop now!' And it did. Messager knew I was home, and he knew it was over. After that, apart from two brief encounters, we saw one another only as artistic colleagues.

Ironically enough, it was after Messager and I had broken that M. Carré and he had a violent quarrel over me—a quarrel that, according to him, led to his resignation from the Opéra-Comique. One day Messager asked me to come down to his office to receive an autographed copy of his light opera, a lovely thing called *Véronique*. So I went down to the Opéra-Comique, and while Messager was inscribing the score at his desk, I went fiddling around the office, looking at things and touching them, and I suppose without knowing what I was doing I found myself near the door, and my fingers were soon playing with the latch. You know how you fidget when you're idling around, waiting for someone to finish something, not even realizing what you're doing with your own hands. Well, without being in the least aware of it, I had somehow locked the door. Why I did it, and how I did it, I have no idea. Then there was a knock, and Messager, who was still writing, said to me, 'Pay no attention.' Again, I have no idea why he said that. There was no reason for secrecy or concealment. There was another knock, and whoever it was tried to open the door by turning the knob, and of course it was locked. Then it was silent in the hall outside.

Messager finished what he had to write on the score. I thanked him, said good-bye, and opened the door, and of course there was M. Carré, looking very serious indeed. He stepped into the room and angrily came up to Messager, and I heard him say: 'How dare you lock your door to your director?' I put my score under my arm and went away. Later I found out they had had a dreadful fight over that locked door. M. Carré accused Messager of all sorts of things, and Messager quite rightly denied everything, calling M. Carré every name he could think of for suspecting anything of the kind. Finally, Messager shouted, 'I cannot remain here any longer, I resign!' And M Carré shouted back, 'I accept your resignation!' A short time afterward Messager went on to London, where he became director of Covent Garden.

I was coming back from Florida for my first Town Hall lecture late in 1949, and I was twenty-seven hours on the train, and many things came into my mind, among them Carré's proposal of marriage. I said to myself, 'I wonder why I didn't marry Albert Carré?' Not for love, of course, but for ambition. I still wonder why I didn't. Because, you see, with his genius for the theatre and my genius for creation, and his admiration for my work and mine for his, together we would have made the Comique the greatest opera house in the world. But there you are; I didn't marry him, and I know now, as I knew then, that I could never marry any man. I never lost Carré's admiration, and he was always looking for something new for me to create. It so happened that he married a young singer and had a daughter by her called Jennie. I'm afraid the new Mme. Carré wasn't a very good influence at the Comique, and besides she loathed me—why, I'm not sure, unless she knew or surmised how Carré had once felt about me. Shortly after his marriage, I left for America. I learned later that when I departed, Mme. Carré went into my dressing-room and ordered everything thrown out—curtains, furnishings, everything.

'Take all that rubbish away and burn it,' she ordered. 'The Scotch girl that kept this room for eight years was tubercular.'

I must say I had never bothered Mme. Carré in any way. Well, she succeeded in pulling down the Opéra-Comique. M. Carré was helpless in her hands. She didn't like anyone but herself to sing in her house, and she took over all my rôles and everybody else's rôles, but she never gained a great name. By a strange coincidence, I was reminded again of M. Carré after my Town Hall talk in New York in 1949. A handsome young gentleman came up to me when I had finished and said, 'I married Jennie Carré.'

'What a delightful surprise!' I said. 'I knew Jennie's mother.'

Very solemnly he said. 'So did I.'

I said a moment back that I had had two short non-professional encounters with André Messager. The first one occurred when I was stopping with some friends at the Carlton Hotel in London shortly after Messager was made director of Covent Garden. One day my friends had to go down to the river to lunch and I was left alone. I went down to the grill, and as I descended the stairs, there was Messager coming up. We met on the stairs, and he said, 'Mary, I've got to see you again,' and an astonishing thing happened to me. As he spoke there was all that desire, or sex, call it what you will, all over again, and I had thought myself completely cured. All I could say was, 'Yes, André, we will see each other again.'

'Will you lunch with me to-morrow?'

'Yes, André,' I answered mechanically.

Later my friends returned to the hotel.

'Do you know whom I ran into on the stairs to-day?' I said.

They couldn't imagine.

'André Messager!'

Their faces fell.

'And I'm having lunch with him to-morrow!'

And in one voice they said, 'No, you're not, Mary! That's all ended. You're going back to Paris with us to-morrow.'

And I went back to Paris, and I didn't lunch with Messager. But had I lunched with him, I feel certain that that something which had made me ill might have all come back again, and that infatuation, or whatever it was, of which I had thought myself cured would have started all over again. I couldn't have been completely cured if I had said 'Yes' to him that day on the stairs. And I recalled how that thing had begun to pull me down. I knew my health was beginning to go . . . I might have met a different man, perhaps more like myself, friendly, kind, yet independent. I might have had my great romance with him. I might even have married him, but he would have had to be an extraordinary person to make me change my mind about marriage and love.

And it came to me again how curious it was that something that had begun as a lovely and charming idyl had become a thing of bitterness and cruelty and nausea, till I hated it and him. And yet, there on the stairs of the Carlton Hotel in London, long after I thought it was ended, I was ready to see him again. I can't understand it.

But for one more meeting I didn't see Messager again till he invited me over, many years later, to sing for him at the Opéra in Paris. We became great friends then. We never once spoke of the past. What had happened between us was dead and buried, and one would never have suspected that there had been a moment's ecstasy between us, or a moment's bitterness. He was a great worker, and so was I, and in the end that saved us.

It was some time in May of 1903 that I got the dreadful news that my good friend Sybil Sanderson was dying. They had brought poor Sybil home from Cannes, where her mother had sent her for treatment of an incurable disease. Then one day her maid telephoned me.

'Miss Garden,' she said, 'will you please come at once? It's very urgent. Miss Sanderson is very, very ill.'

I went up to Sybil's apartment, and when I walked into the room, I had a strange experience. I had not seen Sybil for a month or two, and now I suddenly saw the death mask on her face. I had never seen a death mask before in my life, but as I stayed with her it slowly disappeared. Then there was a man sitting in a corner, smoking a big black cigar in the bedroom of a dying woman.

Poor Sybil had baskets over her because she couldn't stand a sheet touching her body, which was all swollen and discoloured. And I remember her maid came in to feed her. She had pieces of raw meat covered with salt, and the maid opened Sybil's lips, because her lips were as hard as wood, and put these little pieces of meat between her teeth with little toothpicks. That was all she ate.

Then I turned to this man sitting in the corner with his cigar and I said, 'Don't you think you should smoke somewhere else?'

And I saw Sybil making a gesture to me, and I went over and put my ear to her, and I heard her say, 'No, Mary, let him smoke; he's my fiancé.'

So I went home, feeling very wretched.

Two days later—it must have been five in the morning—my bell rang. I heard a great argument going on in the hall between my maid and a voice I didn't know. I jumped out of bed to see what it was all about. And there was a Hearst reporter telling me that Sybil was dead.

'That can't be true!' I cried, stunned.

'It *is* true, Miss Garden,' he said. 'She died at two this morning.'

So I put on my things and we got a taxi, the Hearst man

and I, and I went in with him. The moment the maid saw me, she said, 'Miss Sanderson is dead.'

And the Hearst reporter turned to me and said, 'You see, Miss Garden, I was telling you the truth. We know everything.'

And I said, 'All right, now will you kindly leave me?' and he did.

'Would you like to look at her, Miss Garden?' the maid asked.

'No, I would not.'

And she looked relieved and said, 'I'm glad, because she's frightening to look at.'

Later I went back to the house to see the doctor.

'Was Sybil conscious when she died?'

'I don't know,' he answered. 'Her screams were so frightful, I couldn't tell whether she was conscious or not. I hope she wasn't.'

Now Sybil, who had been a Protestant, had become a Catholic when she married Tony Terry. But she left orders to be cremated, and cremated she was. I shall never forget the funeral. I was sitting next to the coffin, with Sybil's sister. I've often heard people say, and I have read it in books, 'My heart is breaking,' and it always seemed such a silly exaggeration to me. But while I was sitting at that service next to the coffin of that great dear friend of mine, I said to myself, 'I understand how a heart can break.'

I thought I never would get out of the church for pain and sorrow. I could feel something tearing and tearing within me. Her valet went up to her before they took her body away and removed a small diamond bracelet that Tony had given to her, which Sybil had never taken off, and he brought back to her mother, who was ill at home.

After Sybil was cremated, they put her ashes in a box, and they put the box into the wall of the Paris crematory. Then they gave her a number, and there we leave my beautiful friend in her thirty-ninth year.

## Debussy and his Mélisande

IN telling about Charpentier's *Louise* I remarked how the whole fabric of that music has remained with me because it is great music and all great music has the quality of lingering with one. What is not great music has a way of leaving one's brain—mine, at any rate. I had this sad experience with an opera that M. Carré assigned to me some time in 1902. This was *La Reine Fiammette*, by Xavier Leroux. The book was by the poet Catulle Mendès, a very beautiful book, and in many ways it was a very beautiful opera. But I didn't care too much for the music, and I suppose because I didn't I put my whole soul into it to make it a success. Soul or no soul, *La Reine Fiammette* was not a success. We sang about ten performances, then put it away for good.

I had the strangest experience with that opera some years later. While I was in America, there was talk in the newspapers of the Metropolitan giving *La Reine Fiammette*. I couldn't believe my eyes, for I had supposed the opera dead and forgotten. So, when the performance was announced, I got myself a ticket and went over to the Metropolitan to hear it. There I sat in a daze of bewilderment. I couldn't recognize a single note of it! 'Did I ever really sing that?' I kept asking myself. 'Was that what I sang at the Opéra-Comique? Did I act that rôle?' I sat there and heard the whole opera and never once 'knew' that I had ever sung it. I no longer possessed the music, because it wasn't good music and it couldn't stay with me. The notes had gone completely out of my brain, and along with them the words. It was just as if I had never sung it.

*La Reine Fiammette* didn't have a long life in America either. Again, it shows what a difference great music will make. Here was *La Reine Fiammette* wiped clean from my mind in a few years, and there, on the other hand, is *Pelléas et Mélisande*. It is now fifty years since I first heard that divine music of Debussy, and if anybody said to me now, 'Mary Garden, you're going to sing Mélisande to-morrow,' I wouldn't need a single rehearsal. Every note of that opera is in my head for keeps. And the reason is that it is the music of a genius, not of a talent.

Well, it was just after *La Reine Fiammette* that Claude Debussy walked into my musical life. That was late in 1902, and there I stood before something! One day M. Carré let us all know about this new opera, and after he had finished talking about *Pelléas et Mélisande* and its composer, he began assigning rôles to each of us. Then one afternoon we were all invited to M. Messager's home. We were there only a short while when the door opened and in came Debussy. We were all presented to him, and he spoke the usual words of greeting. Without another word, he sat at the piano and played and sang the whole thing from beginning to end.

There we sat in the drawing-room—M. Carré, and M. and Mme. Messager, and the whole cast—each of us with a score, heads bowed as if we were all at prayer. While Debussy played I had the most extraordinary emotions I have ever experienced in my life. Listening to that music I seemed to become someone else, someone inside of me whose language and soul were akin to mine. When Debussy got to the fourth act I could no longer look at my score for the tears. It was all very strange and unbearable. I closed my book and just listened to him, and as he played the death of Mélisande, I burst into the most awful sobbing, and Mme. Messager began to sob along with me, and both of us fled into the next room. I shall never forget it. There we were crying as if we had just lost our best friend, crying as if nothing would console us again.

Mme. Messager and I returned to the drawing-room just as Debussy stopped. Before anyone could say or do anything, he faced us all and said:

'*Mesdames et messieurs*, that is my *Pelléas et Mélisande*. Everyone must forget that he is a singer before he can sing the music of Debussy. *Oubliez, je vous prie, que vous êtes chanteurs!*'

Then he murmured a quick '*Au revoir*' and, without another word, was gone.

We all went home and began studying our rôles. The first two acts of *Pelléas* I found a little difficult for me—just a little bit—that is, difficult getting into Debussy's very individual way of writing. It was all so different from anything else any of us had ever sung. I went into the third act, and that I found a great deal easier. When I came to the death of Mélisande I discovered I had absolutely nothing to study. I just knew it. How, I haven't the slightest idea. Debussy himself later said to M. Carré: 'I have nothing, absolutely nothing, to tell her. In some mysterious way, she knows or senses everything.' There was nothing for me to study at Mélisande's death. Why? Because, I suppose, I just died. When I sang the opera at Oscar Hammerstein's Manhattan Opera House many years later, a doctor, whose name I have forgotten, came backstage and introduced himself.

'Miss Garden,' he said, 'may I ask you what may strike you as a very strange question?'

'You may, Doctor.'

'Where have you seen death?'

'I have never seen it.'

'But that's incredible!' he said. 'Because you die in the last act as I have never seen anyone who did not actually die do it.'

M. & Mm. Maeterlinck with Miss Garden after a performance of *Pelléas et Mélisande*, January 27, 1920

Chrysis in *Aphrodite*

'I have never seen death at any time in my life,' I repeated, and the doctor went away shaking his head.

One of the greatest compliments of my career was paid me by that fine artist, Alexander Kipnis, and it was in connection with this same scene.

Kipnis was the old King Arkel in my performances of *Pelléas et Mélisande* in Chicago. He was a born king, this great singer known the world over, yet he came up to me one day and said, 'Miss Garden, I'd like to study Arkel with you.'

And Kipnis came every day to my studio and studied the rôle of the King, Arkel, and he gave the most magnificent interpretation I have ever seen.

Well, Kipnis told a friend of his, who told me, what happened to him in the last act of *Pelléas*. There was this devoted old king who never left Mélisande's side, and he came to me with my baby in his arms.

Kipnis said that when I died he couldn't sing . . . because of the lump in his throat.

That was typical of all my creations. I never saw where Salomé lived. I never was with that great dancer of Egypt, Thaïs, but I knew her. I knew them all. That sort of thing was always happening to me—the feeling of being someone else and having been somewhere else. I never knew anything about the lives of these women of opera. I had them all in me, in my very flesh and blood. If only someone could tell me about that. I must confess it has always been a mystery to me. They were just there, and they had nothing to do with me personally. Absolutely nothing to do with Mary Garden from Aberdeen, Scotland. Was it a sixth sense? Maybe. I just don't know. All I do know is that when I finished any performance of mine—Louise, Salomé, Mélisande—and went home and had my glass of milk with ten drops of iodine in it, I never remembered that I had sung anything or that I had been impersonating anyone. Never, never, never. I was always myself again.

So you see why I say, over and over again, I never 'studied' any of these rôles. I never had to rehearse, really. They were always there, in me, in my body and soul, when I sang. It made no difference what country or period it was, it was always the same, an extraordinary thing that I shall never understand. I have never thought about it quite as much as I do to-day, and I wonder more than ever just what the answer to the riddle is. Yet I am sure that I could tell another person, another singer, how to do it—if she had any imagination. I could *make* her do it. I could put it into her brain so that she could *see*, let us say, the genius of those two men, Debussy and Maeterlinck.

No, I had nothing to learn about the death of Mélisande. Death was somehow embedded in the pattern of my living self, and in the last scene I surrendered completely to it. But what a beautiful death, Mélisande's! It was in childbirth, you know, and I often think it is a sacrilege to talk about it, it is so tender and pure a death. Never in the world would I take a curtain call after the death of Mélisande. I never did, because, you must understand this, *I really died*. Oh, I wish those of you who never saw me could have seen me at that moment. . . . One night I was very ill, but I sang Mélisande. I had one fearful moment of chills in my dressing-room and remember they put hot-water bottles all over me, and the next minute I was in such a fever I couldn't stand anyone near me. But I sang Mélisande that night. Then I died, and that particular death must have been very convincing, because the next day I can't tell you how many people stopped in carriages to leave their cards and ask about me. I was told there were some who actually thought I was dead. It was Mélisande who died, but *really* died. That is all I know about it.

After we had all studied our parts, we were called into M. Carré's office.

'I assume you have all mastered every note and word of your rôles,' he said.

'We have,' we assured him.

'We are going to modify our procedure this time,' he went on. 'As the next step there will be individual rehearsals with M. Debussy. Each of you will have an afternoon with him. Remember that when you go into that rehearsal room you are expected to know your parts to perfection. Whether you sing them or not will rest entirely with him.'

I suppose I should say something about the structure of the Opéra-Comique building. There are the main stage and the opera house itself, and then up on the fifth floor there is a theatre with another huge stage. When anything was going on downstairs, a rehearsal or a performance, we could still rehearse, all of us, on the fifth floor. It was an enormous hall. When necessary, even the orchestra could come up and rehearse with us.

Besides that big auditorium, there are about ten small rehearsal rooms. It was in one of these smaller chambers that Debussy was to conduct the rehearsals. He took one of us at a time, and the rehearsals lasted from about one-fifteen to six. I remember very clearly going up that first afternoon. I knew, as everyone knew, that this production had to be perfection itself, and I was fully prepared.

Debussy was already in the small rehearsal room when I arrived. Without any preliminary chatter, except a quick exchange of 'How do you do's?' we began. I opened my score, and Debussy sat down at the paino. We did the first act, Debussy singing the rôle of Golaud. His voice was very small and husky . . . I never knew a composer who could sing and few who could play the piano well. Charpentier couldn't play a note. But Debussy was a magnificent pianist. So there he sat, singing the part of Golaud, playing the piano, and never saying a single word. When we came to Pelléas, he sang that too, and all the other rôles as well, except mine.

Then we came to the scene of the Tower. I was singing my lines when, without a word, he got up abruptly and left the room. I stayed there a little while and waited, quite bewildered. I had a feeling I had offended him in some mysterious way and I began to prepare myself for the shock of not singing Mélisande. I put on my hat and was about to leave the rehearsal room when a boy came in and said: 'Miss Garden, M. Carré would like to see you in the office.' When I walked in, there sat Debussy with M. Carré. Rising from his chair, he came right up to me and took both my hands in his.

'Where were you born?' he asked.

'Aberdeen, Scotland.'

'To think that you had to come from the cold far North to create my Mélisande—because that's what you're going to do, Mademoiselle.'

Then he turned to M. Carré, and I remember he put up his hands, and said: '*Je n'ai rien à lui dire*. I have nothing to tell her.'

He paused, as if embarrassed, and, still looking at M. Carré, added: 'What a strange person, this child.'

With that, he fell silent, in that curious detached way of his, took his hat, and, mumbling a 'Good-bye,' walked out of M. Carré's office. Debussy was always doing that—suddenly walking out. He walked out of Lily Debussy's life that way, he walked out of mine, and he even walked out of Mélisande's. When he was finished, he was finished.

'What a strange person, that child!' Carré mimicked.

'But, my God, what a genius, the first one worthy of the name that I have met in Paris!'

'I wonder how long it will take the public to find out.'

'Not long, M. Carré. I'll wager one thing. The public will discover him before the critics!'

'I'm inclined to agree with you, *ma petite* Garden,' M. Carré said with a sigh.

When we had all gone through our rôles in the small rehearsal room, we were taken down to the big stage, and there we went over everything with Debussy, M. Messager, and Maurice Maeterlinck. Then began the real work of putting *Pelléas et Mélisande* on the stage. Rehearsals went on for four solid months, every afternoon, except Sunday, and there were forty orchestral rehearsals—something unheard of! Everything was done to make this opera an unforgettable event in the history of the Opéra-Comique.

There are twelve tableaux in *Pelléas*, and many of these days we worked over just one tableau. In between those tableaux Debussy had composed music that was designed to prepare the listeners for the next scene. Debussy was always making changes in those interludes, and I remember that while they were being rehearsed none of us was permitted to talk or move. Oh, how often we went over those tableaux, always with the greatest concentration on every single detail! I don't remember ever seeing anything so thoroughly worked out to the highest perfection. One day we would have only the piano as accompaniment, and the next we would take it with the orchestra.

Those were four complicated months we went through. No opera I know of, at least of our time, was given such infinite study and attention. You see, it was new in every sense. As far as the harmony was concerned, it was almost another language. And Debussy's orchestra was something miraculous. Its rôle was to speak to the public, letting them know what was happening. It was the orchestra that gave me my Mélisande, not the play. It was Claude Debussy I created, not Maurice Maeterlinck. I never created the librettist, always the composer. I needed the music to start me. Poetry alone has never touched me, except to make me restless and nervous. Debussy's music was always the right music for the word.

'*Je suis si malheureuse.*' The words alone said nothing to me.

But Debussy put music to them, and then they spoke to me and lived. I could not help but be *malheureuse* when I sang it.

Everything was going smoothly till one day Maeterlinck arrived at the Opéra-Comique, walked up to Debussy and M. Carré, and announced very dramatically:

'I don't wish Miss Garden to sing Mélisande!'

Both Debussy and M. Carré were astounded at this effrontery.

'Why not?' they asked.

'Because I want someone else to have the part,' Maeterlinck replied. 'Her name is Georgette Leblanc. It is she who will create my Mélisande.'

There was a terrible upheaval, and Debussy faced Maeterlinck and said, quite firmly: 'You are mistaken, Monsieur. It is Miss Garden who will create Mélisande, *my* Mélisande!'

That ended it for the moment. To spare himself and the company any future mischief, Debussy called together a jury of musicians and had Georgette Leblanc sing an act of *Pelléas* for them. They were to decide whether she could or could not sing Mélisande. Their verdict was quick and emphatic. Debussy had already made up his mind that I was to sing the rôle, and that was all there was to it. I kept the rôle. From that day on we never had the pleasure of seeing Maeterlinck at any rehearsal.

The day of the big dress rehearsal at length arrived. On these occasions, people are admitted by special invitation only. Musicians, writers, society people, government officials —everybody, in short, who is anybody, especially in the arts, is invited. And, of course, the friends of the members of the cast are asked, too. But no critics! One more thing about those dress rehearsals: *no printed programmes are ever handed out.*

Well, the moment we began, something frightful happened. People began to laugh. In moments of the greatest seriousness someone would scream hysterically. We hadn't the faintest idea what was going on, and we were all suddenly paralysed on the stage. Here was a drama of pure poetry and tragedy, and people were giggling and chuckling as if they were at the Folies Bergère. Finally, it was intermission time, and we stood there on the stage, staring at one another, completely unnerved by the experience, wondering and wondering what it all meant. We found out soon enough. During intermission, the members of the orchestra go out into the street for a smoke. One of the musicians was standing there on the curb when a man came up and offered to sell him a programme book. Knowing that programme books were never issued at these dress rehearsals, he purchased one out of curiosity, and opened it. He promptly rushed back and began showing it to the company.

It was a programme book of the *première* of *Pelléas et Mélisande* all right, but what language, and what illustrations! I have never in my life seen such obscenity—clever, perhaps, but in a foul, disgusting way. One of the drawings showed the scene in which Golaud puts his child up to Mélisande's bedroom window to see if Pelléas and Mélisande are together and report to him what they are doing. In France, when you try to find out anything that way, they call it *tirer des vers du nez*. It's an ugly expression, and it went with the illustration in that programme book. And, of course, it explained why the people in the house were in paroxysms of laughter. They had been stealing glimpses at these booklets during the performance, and showing them to one another. M. Carré immediately called the police, who stopped the sale the moment they arrived. A few days later I was alone with M. Carré in his office.

'M. Carré,' I said, 'have you solved the mystery of those programme books?'

'I'm afraid I have,' he said sombrely.

'You are certain who was behind them?'

'Quite certain, Mary. It broke my heart when I found out.'

'Who was it?'

'Maurice Maeterlinck.'

And that wasn't all. The morning of the *première*, *Figaro* came out with a slashing letter by Maeterlinck, predicting that the opera would be a great fiasco and that it would never be heard again. This cry was taken up the following day and for many days after by all the newspapers of Paris. Every critic in Paris denounced *Pelléas* in the most dreadful language. They said the opera had no rhythm, that it was sickly and spineless. In one voice they prophesied that it would die an early death. But the public—ah, there was another story! What I had myself predicted to M. Carré came true. They soon saw what it was that confronted them. For by the time we reached the fifth performance, the Opéra-Comique had become a cathedral. No one dared to speak, even in the faintest whispers; no one came late; no one moved in his seat or made any kind of noise.

The Metropolitan is too large for that opera, and in a big auditorium you lose much. Debussy is so subtle, so fine; tiny things of great importance are happening all the time. Think of all the different emotions of that girl Mélisande. The very look of her eye—you can tell what she's thinking or the lies she's telling. You can't see that in a great big house. The Opéra-Comique was the perfect place for *Pelléas*. Think only of the silences in that opera—they are what make Mélisande—the silences that Debussy put there. In her silences, Mélisande has the orchestra to tell her what to do. On most operatic stages nobody is silent. They all sing, so they can never realize what a silence means. I've had more power over an audience with a silence than I ever had with a note. That's where I would look if I went into an opera house hunting for a genius—I would look into their silences.

From that fifth performance on, *Pelléas* was a triumph, especially with the galleries. That is where the true musical public is, in the galleries. I'm told that many of them came down from the galleries in the middle of the first performance and engaged in violent discussions over the new opera. There were fist fights, too—think of it, over the music of Claude Debussy! But, of course, it's always that way when anything new comes into the world. There is always controversy. Thank God for it! If everyone said 'How beautiful!' at the very start, you could almost be certain something was wrong with it. And *Pelleas* is now in its fifty-first year—an enduring masterpiece. And why? Because it is the work of a genius, and when a genius comes into the world, criticism is soon silenced. The insults and the injuries go, but the genius and his work stand there for ever.

I have said that Louise was the only rôle in which I wore my own hair. For Mélisande I wore the hair of the golden daughters of Brittany. And this is how it came about. I was shown the wigs that the Opéra-Comique had ready for me, and I knew at once they weren't the hair of Mélisande. So I sent my coiffeur to Brittany to buy up real hair, hair of the colour and length that I needed for Mélisande. And he got it from the girls of Brittany, the lovely daughters of the *paysans*. The whole thing cost me six thousand francs. What happened to those two wigs I have no idea, but oh, how I'd like to have them again; I've not worn such beautiful hair since.

It was after the last rehearsal that Debussy did the very characteristic thing of walking out of the life of Mélisande. He never came to a single performance of *Pelléas*. Again and again I asked him to come to watch the complete fulfilment of his dream, and one night he tried to make me understand.

'Mary, I can't ever go,' he said. '*Pelléas* is my child. I had it in my hands for ten years. I gave it to the public, and now it doesn't interest me any longer.'

Debussy was as good as his word. I only remember his being present once again, and that, too, was at a rehearsal. I was creating Mélisande with another company, in Brussels, several years later, and Debussy, who was now married to his second wife, came into the dark house one afternoon. He sat there, silent and detached, and when he had anything to communicate to one of us on the stage, he would write it down on a slip of paper and send it up by a boy. But he never appeared on the stage and he never came over to greet me. Debussy lived in a world of his own, where no one, not even his first wife, Lily, with all her care and adoration, could reach him.

Shortly after the *première* of *Pelléas*, Debussy, his wife Lily, and I became inseparable friends. During question-and-answer period of a talk I gave in December of 1949, someone in the audience sent up a question that was not shown to me till the evening was over. I wish it had been read out, for I would have liked very much to answer it, and answer it truthfully and frankly. The question was, 'Were you ever the mistress of Claude Debussy?'

Debussy and his wife used to come for dinner at my house twice a week, and sometimes three times. Just before the *première* of *Pelléas* I had taken a tiny apartment on the Rue Washington, a modest affair, but quite charming. I was then getting sixteen hundred francs a month, and that was a good deal of money—for me—and it would have been even more for Debussy, who never had any. Debussy loved good eating, and he adored everything that was rich and flavoursome. He also secretly loved sumptuous and luxurious things. In his craving for things, he had the most extravagant brain I have ever known. But he never could do what he wanted and he never could buy what he wanted because he hadn't the money. He had a deep longing for costly things which he could never satisfy, and which in the end destroyed his marriage with Lily, the only woman he ever loved, if, that is, he was at all capable of loving anything but his music. The two of them occupied a small apartment on the Rue

Cardinet, No. 58. I used to go up there later and study all those beautiful songs of his with him.

The day they came to dine with me, I would wait at the window, watching for them. One day I saw a carriage draw up to my house. There sat Debussy in all his glory, alone. When he came into the house, I asked, 'Where's Lily?' and he replied, 'Oh, she's walking.' And Lily arrived soon afterward, on foot. Why they separated that way I don't know, but Debussy must have loved that little show of solitary comfort.

After dinner we used to go into the drawing-room, and Lily and I would go into a corner and talk about things. Then Debussy would sit at the piano, and for an hour or so he would improvise. Those hours stay like jewels in my mind. I have never heard such music in my life, such music as came from the piano at those moments. How beautiful it was, and haunting, and nobody but Lily and I ever heard it! Debussy never put those improvisations down on paper; they went back to the strange place they had come from, never to return. That precious music, lost for ever, was so unlike anything Debussy ever published. There was a quality of its own about it, remote, other-worldly, always saying something on the verge of words.

At those moments Debussy was in that far-off world of his, inspired, as if in a trance. He just sat there and played. He never moved and he never said a word. What it was or what he was trying to say through his music, he never told us and we never knew—he just played. And then, with that suddenness of his, he would get up and come over to speak to us. And that was the end of it.

Later I worked with Debussy on the *première* of his *Damoiselle élue*, which I created at a Concert Colonne. As so often happened when I studied Debussy's music, my emotion got the best of me one day and I burst into tears. Debussy laughed and ridiculed me.

'*Ma petite* Mélisande,' he said, 'you are a sentimental dove.'

Debussy dedicated his *Ariettes* to me, and we studied them, along with *Les Chansons de Bilitis*, in that little room of his on the Rue Cardinet.

Debussy and I made two trips together to London, the first one on the invitation of André Messager, then directing at Covent Garden. Messager, who was Debussy's closest friend, was eager to have him see Forbes Robertson as Hamlet.

I knew Debussy was mad about Shakespeare, but I had no suspicion how far his madness went. I sat next to him at that performance, and he seemed like a child in a trance. So profoundly was he affected that it was some time before he could speak. I have never known anyone to lose himself so completely in the spectacle of great art.

Our second visit to London was less exhilarating. A special matinee was scheduled of Maeterlinck's *Pelléas et Mélisande*, with Sarah Bernhardt as Pelléas and Mrs. Patrick Campbell as Mélisande. That was a combination both Debussy and I would have gone to St. Petersburg to see, out of sheer curiosity.

We left Paris on the night train and arrived in London early the following morning. We went to the home of a friend of mine, ate a delicious lunch, and were soon seated in the theatre, where we arrived long before curtain time. We waited with mounting expectancy.

Then the play began, and it wasn't long before Debussy and I were looking at each other in great wonder. Not one member of the cast had the slightest comprehension of Maeterlinck's drama. Bernhardt, that supreme artist whom no one adored more than I, was utterly miscast.

'She is trying to impersonate Robin Hood,' I whispered to Debussy, who was getting very restless.

With the third act, the thing became painful beyond words. There, Mélisande, leaning from her bedroom window in the tower, lets fall her long, golden locks into the hands of

Pelléas below. Debussy almost screamed when Mrs. Patrick Campbell unloosed an avalanche of jet-black hair!

'When is the next train to Paris?' he asked, his nerves completely shattered.

We left the theatre at once and after a tiresome journey arrived in Paris at midnight.

It was in the third year of our great friendship that I went to live in Versailles. I invited Debussy and his wife to come out to stay with me for two weeks. That was in the month of June of 1904. And the three of us had such fun! We used to go all through Versailles, making such dreadful comments on people and things. What we said about them was the purest vitriol. And Debussy loathed most people—at any rate, people who were not simple and natural. I never met a more baffling man in my life. His friendships were few and his confidences were rare.

One day, in her husband's presence Lily said to me:

'Mary, I want you to scold Claude for me.'

'Why, what has he done, Lily?'

'Well, there's a lady in Paris by the name of Bardac,' she said. 'She has a great salon and she gives wonderful musicales where very important people come. The best pianists go there to play Claude's music, and she has invited Claude again and again, but he won't go.'

'Claude,' I turned to him, 'why don't you go to Mme. Bardac's? It might be a good thing for you and your music.'

All he said was, '*Je ne sais pas*.'

Toward the end of the two weeks, Debussy and I were walking in the park at Versailles. Suddenly he stopped and faced me.

'Mary,' he said, 'I have an obsession, and I must tell you about it.'

'Please do, Claude.'

'Ten years I worked on that opera of mine, and then I was never satisfied,' he began.

'I know, Claude.'

'Ten years I lived with this Mélisande, and I never thought I would ever find anybody who could make her come to life as the woman I lived with. And you did that, Mary.'

'You've made me very happy saying that, Claude.'

Debussy looked as if he were under a strain of some kind, nervous with me for the first time since we had met.

'I am obsessed with love of you, Mary,' he said finally.

'That's a pity, Claude,' I said.

'But I'm very serious,' he went on. 'I can't live without you, and I must know if you have any feeling for me.'

'Not that kind, Claude,' I replied. 'I love and adore your genius, I like you as a friend, but Debussy the man means nothing to me.'

He took it as he took everything, without another word. But it bothered me very much, because, you see, it had never shown itself to me in any way before, and as we walked back to my villa I began to think of why he would say that to me, and suddenly it came to me.

'Claude,' I said, turning to look at him, 'it isn't *me* you love, much as you believe it.'

He made no comment.

'It is Mélisande you love. You've loved her for ten years, and you still do, and it is Mélisande that you love in me, not myself.'

Debussy showed no sign of having heard me. He had made his declaration, and that was the end of it. I am sure I was right. He had always addressed me at '*Ma chère* Mélisande' and his letters to me all opened that way. And I think I got the final proof that I was right later, when he left Lily for Mme. Bardac. He couldn't have been in love with me in June and with Mme. Bardac in September.

Later that afternoon, I saw Lily, and while we were alone I thought it best to tell her what Debussy had said to me in the park.

'Lily,' I said, 'I've got something to tell you. I've always been honest with you, and I think I should be frank now.'

'By all means, Mary,' she said, looking just a little frightened. 'What is it?'

'Claude has just told me he loved me, and I don't like that in our friendship at all. It would ruin it for all three of us.'

'What did you tell Claude?'

'I told him I loved him as a friend and a musician, but that was all, and that I hoped the friendship of all three of us would continue as before.'

Lily now looked at me with that sweet, serene look of hers—she was such a beautiful thing.

'I'm so glad you told me, Mary,' she said. 'I think you're the only woman in the world I would give Claude up for.'

I didn't know what to answer to that. I felt it made matters worse for me in a way, because I now knew she was perfectly willing to have it. But there was no continuation of the drama that might have been. It was finished as far as I was concerned. Just how Debussy went on feeling about me, I had no way of telling, but his leaving Lily for Mme. Bardac convinced me he had been cured of his 'obsession.' Once, many years later, M. Carré did tell me that he had received a letter from Debussy in which he said, in reference to me, 'Her voice is a torment that I can't get out of my mind.' Only the three of us—Claude, Lily, and I—knew about his declaration to me in the *bois* at Versailles. You see, after that day at Versailles everything was finished between Debussy and me. I accompanied them to the station, and there Debussy took me in his arms and for the first and only time kissed me. 'Good-bye, Mary,' he said, and that was the last contact I had with him, except that one time in Brussels when he sent pencil notes to me from his seat in a dark auditorium.

I could never have loved Debussy. Never for a moment

did he affect me that way, and he would have repelled me as a lover. But Lily was a dear, just a sweet, simple girl who didn't care for anything in God's green earth but that man. They had met in Montmartre when Debussy hadn't a sou to his name. Debussy had been living there with his mistress, a woman named Gaby, and he was said to be crazy about her because she had green eyes. It was through Gaby that Debussy met Lily one day, which was ironic, just as it was ironic that it was because of Lily's urging that he went off to Mme. Bardac's musicales. Well, Debussy met Lily, fell in love with her, and she with him, and he left Gaby to marry her.

I honestly don't know if Debussy ever loved anybody really. He loved his music—and perhaps himself. I think he was wrapped up in his genius. People say that he married Mme. Bardac for money, but I don't know. He was a very, very strange man. Perhaps he was unhappy at the end. Messager showed me a letter from him that might bear that out. 'Oh, how I wish I could recapture the happiness of the days of *Pelléas et Mélisande!*' he wrote. 'But it is hopeless. That joy has vanished for ever.' Debussy and I had one thing in common—we neither of us knew what the word jealousy meant.

That little drama had taken place in Versailles in the summer of 1904. When I returned to Paris in September, the first thing I did was to go to the Rue Cardinet, No. 58, and tell Lily and Claude that I was back in town and waiting to have them come to dine with me again. They weren't in, either of them. I left word that they should come to see me, and returned to my apartment rather puzzled. Three hours later, my door opened and in came Lily—alone, and wild with sorrow.

'Lily,' I cried, 'what in heaven's name is wrong?'

'Claude has left me!'

And she burst into a frenzy of tears.

I took her in my arms and tried to comfort her.

'Tell me about it, Lily.'

It seems that Debussy had been in the habit of taking a walk every morning. Well, he went for his walk one morning and never came back. It was a very cruel thing, I suppose, but you can't help admiring people who make a decision like that and keep it—provided they keep it. It needs strength of character. . . . Lily went on crying inconsolably. Finally, she calmed down a little.

'Where is Claude now?' I asked Lily.

'I have no idea, Mary.'

'Have you asked his father?'

'Not yet. He's coming to Paris to-morrow, and I'm going over to see if he can find out where Claude is.'

'Very well, Lily,' I said. 'Let me know the minute you find out, and I'll see if I can help in any way to bring Claude back to you.'

A week went by, and no word from Lily. Then one day a messenger boy brought me a note to come at once to a certain hospital in Paris—nothing more. Fearing the worst, I put on my hat and hurried down to the hospital. When I arrived I got hold of the head man there.

'Who is it?' I asked, breathless with fright.

'Mme. Claude Debussy.'

They took me into a tiny room, and there lay Lily, with a bullet in her breast, wanting to die because her Claude had not come back to her. You must understand that this young girl never knew anything else in life but her love of Debussy. She took care of him like a child. They had worries and debts and disappointments, but nobody ever got into the little apartment of the Rue Cardinet to interrupt Debussy at his music. Lily kept the world away, so her beloved Claude could work—and be hers alone. . . . As Lily lay there, pale and bandaged, she told me the story.

She had seen Debussy's father, and he had told her that his son was in Dieppe, living with Mme. Bardac.

'I knew then, Mary, that he would never come back to me,' she sobbed.

Lily must have known her husband very well to suspect that if ever he made a decision he would stick to it. So she went out and got a revolver, and this beautiful young creature who had never held a gun in her hand, and didn't know how to use it, went into her bedroom and shot it off against the wall to try it.

Then she sat down and wrote Debussy a letter and sent it off by messenger in care of his father. She wanted the letter to be on its way at three o'clock, because at three o'clock she planned to kill herself and she didn't want Claude to get the letter until she had done the fatal thing to herself. Then she turned the gun on herself. . . .

'Oh, Mary,' Lily whimpered, 'I didn't aim right, and I don't know how long I lay on the floor. I never lost consciousness. I heard someone coming into the bedroom. It was Claude. And he came over and stooped down to look at me.

' "Claude," I said, "if you're coming back to me, take me to the hospital, and see if I can live. If you're not coming back to me, leave me here to die." '

Without saying a word, Debussy flew down the stairs and returned with an ambulance. He brought the men up with him and they carried Lily down those five flights of stairs. I found out from the surgeon that when they arrived at the hospital, Debussy asked:

'Can Mme. Debussy's life be saved?'

'I don't know, yet, Monsieur,' the doctor replied. 'But you can wait here in the hospital, and in one or two hours we may be able to let you know.'

Debussy then took a seat in the corner of the waiting-room, and with his hat on waited, like a bad boy in school, for the verdict. After two hours the surgeon came out.

'M. Debussy, we are happy to tell you that your wife will live.'

Debussy looked up at the doctor and in his husky voice muttered just one word: '*Merci.*' And he walked out of the hospital and out of the lives of all of us. It was then that Lily called for me.

'Lily,' I asked, 'what did you put in that letter to Claude?'

'I said, "When you get this, Claude, I shall be dead. Please come to me. I want no hands to touch me but yours." '

When Lily had finished telling me the story, the surgeon came in to dress her wound.

'I'll step outside,' I said.

'You don't have to, if you wish to stay.'

I stayed. The surgeon went to Lily's side and opened her nightdress, and in my life I have never seen anything so beautiful as Lily Debussy from the waist up. It was just like a glorious marble statue, too divine for words! Debussy had always said to me, 'Mary, there's nothing in the world like Lily's body.' Now I knew what he meant.

And lying underneath Lily's left breast was a round dark hole where the bullet had gone in, without touching anything vital—and Lily didn't die. They never got the bullet out. That little token of her love for Claude Debussy stayed with her till she died, and that was in 1932. After the surgeon left, Lily lay there and cried like a wounded animal, with her hands in the air.

'Oh, Claude, Claude!' she kept screaming, 'why did you leave me? Why, oh, why?'

With that girl's grief ringing in my ears, I went out into the corridor, and there waiting was André Messager, the last man in the world I cared to see at that moment.

'May I take you home, Mary?' he asked.

'Very well, André.'

When we arrived at my apartment, I asked him in for tea, and I suppose that emboldened him to make one more attempt to possess me again. When he drew up close to me, I fell back, and I said to him:

'Will you kindly get out and leave me alone.'

And he left without having his tea. I remember that same feeling of nausea rising again in me. What an experience to have had after being with that poor, sweet girl, with the round dark hole under her left breast, calling hopelessly for the man who had left her for another woman! I shall never forget how completely shattered I felt the rest of that day.

I used to go down every day to see Lily at the hospital and take her little things. She hadn't a sou in the world, so I went to many of Debussy's admirers and got together quite a sum of money, to which I added a little of my own. When the doctors thought it time, we took her out of the hospital and put her into a charming little apartment near where I lived. There she lay for several weeks. And for all the outside world knew, that was the end of the relationship between Lily and Claude Debussy.

I said before that Debussy had walked out of the lives of all of us. But there is a secret epilogue to the story of Lily and Claude that only I know, and that I shall now tell for the first time.

Some months after Lily was installed in her new home, she burst into my room, radiant with joy.

'Oh, Mary,' she cried, 'I have seen Claude!'

'I don't understand, Lily.'

She then told me that Debussy had taken a small apartment in Paris and written to her, asking her to come and see him.

'And I've been to see him, Mary!'

I was too bewildered to say anything. I had the feeling that Debussy would do what he had done before, leave her, but this time for ever. I was right, for a few weeks later Lily was back to see me—a tearful, wretched Lily now.

'It's the end this time, Mary!'

'You poor child,' I said, 'tell me about it.'

'I have been visiting Claude,' she said. 'Oh, I hoped and hoped I would regain his love and bring him back to me.'

But Debussy apparently had no such intention, as Lily found out one night when he said to her:

'I won't be seeing you again, Lily.'

And Lily told me she was too stunned to say anything. She just stood there in a stupor and waited for Debussy to speak again.

He paused a few moments and said, 'I demand a divorce.'

When Lily heard that she almost collapsed. Then without saying another word, Debussy led her out of the apartment, and she never saw him again.

Shortly after that I think Lily went back to her family in the north of France, and I didn't see her again for many years. After the divorce, he married Mme. Bardac, and had a daughter by her. Claude and Lily, who had been such dear close friends, were gone to me. That was in 1905. Three years after that I left Paris for America, and in 1918 Debussy died.

Well, in 1925 the new directors of the Opéra-Comique asked me to come back for a revival of *Pelléas et Mélisande*. I was extremely happy to do so, and it proved to be a brilliant production in every way, with many of the original singers—and André Messager to conduct. The day of the revival I was in my room at home when a huge basket of flowers was brought up to me. There was a note with the flowers: 'My mother, Mme. Claude Debussy, is coming to the performance to-night. May I bring her up to your dressing-room after the third act?' This was Mme. Bardac's son by her first husband. I hesitated, and then sent a reply that it would be a privilege to meet Mme. Claude Debussy.

The performance that night was something to treasure for life. Everybody entered into the spirit of the thing, forgetting themselves completely. I was so wholly absorbed in being Mélisande again that I forgot all about Mary Garden and the flowers and the note from Mme. Bardac's son, and there I was standing in my dressing-room after the third act, listening to Prime Minister Briand congratulating me, when the door opened—and in came Lily, as sweet and lovely as ever. We flew into each other's arms.

'Oh, Mary, you're back with *Pelléas!*' she cried. 'It's so marvellous, and, you know, Claude is with me!'

'What do you mean—*Claude is with you?*'

'I bought myself two tickets, one for me and one for him. Claude is with me to-night, Mary, right there in the seat next to mine.'

'Lily, how beautiful!'

'Yes, Mary, his spirit is there in the house. I feel him everywhere. Don't you?'

How divine Lily looked at that moment, her eyes sparkling, her whole face transfigured in pure religious ecstasy! I held her in my arms, sharing her great happiness, and all the memories of our friendship, of the three of us at Versailles, rolled back. Then, suddenly, the door of my dressing-room opened again and in came a man with a lady on his arm. She was dressed in black, walking with a cane, and as she came toward me, her lips trembled, and she couldn't say anything. Then she broke into a fit of sobbing. And this was the second Mme. Debussy. She took up my hand and put it to her face, and still she couldn't utter a single word, for sheer emotion. Lily had moved quietly into a corner, and Briand stood some distance away, a puzzled look on his face. That scene was something to live for. When both Lily and Mme. Bardac finally went, I turned to Briand.

'Monsieur,' I said, 'you've seen something to-night—something you will never forget.'

Briand stared at me questioningly.

'Those two ladies who were standing in this room—they were the two wives of Claude Debussy.'

'Incredible!' he cried. 'But one of them was plunged in grief and the other looked at the very height of her happiness!'

'Which of them do you suppose really loved Debussy for himself?' I asked the great minister of France.

'My dear girl,' he said evasively, 'you must never ask a man to fathom a woman's heart. I suspect they both did—each in her own way.'

Lily had left without saying another word. She had come in like a ray of sunshine and departed quietly to return to her place next to Claude's, and I am sorry that I did not find her again. For one thing, I should have liked to ask her about the manuscript of *Pelléas*, which I believe was in her possession. There were also a great many things that Debussy wrote for her when he was still in love with her, all dedicated '*À ma petite Lily.*'

I don't know what happened to him after he left Lily. He was completely swallowed up in the world of Mme. Bardac. He went out of my life on the station platform of Versailles. Debussy was to have written a *Romeo and Juliet* for me, and perhaps he would have, had he stayed with Lily and remained my friend. But that was not to be. Think of it, *Romeo and Juliet* by the composer of *Pelléas et Mélisande!* I can only dream of what it would have been. It is the most heartbreaking might-have-been of my whole career.

## *À Bientôt,* Paris

IN 1906, M. Carré gave me a three-week holiday, and I decided to go to Rome. I wanted to know another language and another people. When I got off the train and stood in one of those magnificent squares of Rome, I said to myself, 'Good heavens, I've been here before!' I never had, of course. I've been in all the great cities, but I've never felt in any one of them what I felt that day in Rome—that I had been there before. It was very much the same feeling I had when I approached a new rôle—that I had lived that woman's life, somehow, somewhere before. We never once met as strangers, I and my rôles. I was just wild with excitement, living in Rome. Then one day, about a week after I had arrived, I received a telegram from Windsor Castle asking me to come within the next week to sing for the King of Greece, who was Queen Alexandra's brother. Undecided about just what I was to do, I took the telegram to a great friend of mine in Rome, Count Primoli.

'What shall I answer, my dear Count?' I said. 'I'm on holiday and I'm having such a good time in Rome.'

'But, Mary,' he said, 'you have no choice in such matters. That's a command. You've got to go to Windsor Castle. That telegram isn't a request; it's a notification that you are to sing for Alexandra's brother.'

So I had to put on my hat and go back to Paris. I left all my things in Rome, thinking I would just run up to Windsor Castle, sing my few songs, and come straight back. I got myself a beautiful new gown in Paris while going through, and arrived in London very late on a cold November night.

I learned that Nellie Melba was to be on the same programme with me. We didn't know each other then. Well, we arrived at Windsor Castle at the same time and were put in a large, cold room to dress. Then we were told to come upstairs where the concert was to be held. As I entered I beheld a sight of sheer grandeur that I shall never forget as long as I live. We were put into a small, round room with no door, and in front of that round room was the enormous salon, with all the chairs ready for the guests to be seated. Adjoining that room was the state dining-room, and they were all drinking the health of somebody, because they were standing with their glasses in the air, and the crowns and diamonds, the glittering uniforms of the men, the chandeliers of crystal, all was a mass of dazzling splendour such as I had never seen before and never saw again.

And little Mary Garden looked into that room and all she could say to herself was, 'My, I'm glad I came from Rome to see this!' Then they all came in and took their seats in the enormous salon, and Melba and I sang. There was also a violinist, a young boy, who was a protégé of the Queen's. I sang '*Depuis le jour*' from *Louise* and '*Vissi d'arte*' from *Tosca*, and Melba sang '*Mi chiamano Mimi*' from *La Bohème* and '*Caro nome*' from *Rigoletto*. When we were finished the kings and queens and princes and princesses all came up to congratulate us, and then they all left the room.

We were taken down to supper, and Lord Farquhar introduced everyone around, there being twenty of us at the table. While he was presenting us, Melba suddenly chirped up:

'What a dreadful concert this would have been if I hadn't come!'

Twenty pairs of eyes were fixed on me. I sat only two chairs away from Melba, and Lord Farquhar, who was very embarrassed, began to pay me a compliment to cover up Melba's remark, but I raised my hand.

'Please don't bother about me, Lord Farquhar,' I said. 'I love Melba's rudeness. It amuses me.'

Then they asked us if we wanted to go back to London in the private train or remain overnight at the castle, and Melba and I both said we preferred to go home. So we got into the carriage of the train, and before we reached London Melba and I were fast friends. During the journey she turned to me and said:

'Mary, I want you to tell me how to act Tosca. I've been studying it, and there are a lot of things about it that puzzle me. And what sort of wig should I wear?'

Well, I told Nellie Melba everything I could about Tosca, about costuming her and so forth, but I knew it was perfectly useless because she never could sing Tosca—and never did. She just wasn't made for Tosca.

I found Melba a cold person, but she could be charming when you knew her. You see, she grew to like me because I wasn't a coloratura singer. Our friendship would never have come to anything if I had been a coloratura like herself. Later she came to visit me at my villa in Monte Carlo, and we had lots of fun together, especially at the gaming tables. Both of us were incurable gamblers. Melba would win a few francs, and you'd have thought it was a million pounds.

She could be quite funny, Melba, and wherever she went she always had people laughing. In the evening she would often sit at the piano and play and sing for me—just small English songs, but she turned them all into little things of heavenly beauty. Once she asked me to go to Australia with her company, but I thought it too far away, and the repertory didn't interest me. I didn't see very much of Melba in the last part of her life. We used to write to each other at Christmas, and then she died. When you knew her, you couldn't help liking her. When you didn't know her, you thought her frightfully rude. Now I want to say something about Melba's voice.

I have no hesitation in declaring that Melba had the most phenomenal effect on me of any singer I have ever heard. I once went to Covent Garden to hear her do Mimì in *La Bohème*. Of course, Melba didn't look any more like Mimì than Schumann-Heink did. I never saw such a fat Mimì in my life. Melba didn't impersonate the rôle at all—she never did that—but, my God, how she sang it!

You know, the last note of the first act of *La Bohème* is the last note that comes out of Mimì's throat. It is a high C, and Mimì sings it when she walks out of the door with Rodolfo. She closes the door and then takes that note. The way Melba sang that high C was the strangest and weirdest thing I have ever experienced in my life. The note came floating over the auditorium of Covent Garden: it left Melba's throat, it left Melba's body, it left everything, and came over like a star and passed us in our box, and went out into the infinite. I have never heard anything like it in my life, not from any other singer, ever. It just rolled over the hall of Covent Garden. My God, how beautiful it was!

Since then I always wait for that note when I hear the first act of *Bohème*, and they reach and reach for it, and then they scream it, and it's underneath and it's false, and it rolls down the stairs, and it never comes out from behind that door, never. That note of Melba's was just like a ball of light. It wasn't attached to anything at all—it was *out* of everything.

I adore *Bohème*. But then I adore everything Puccini ever wrote, everything except *Manon Lescaut*; his Manon just isn't French, and Manon is pure Louis XV. She should be left to the tender mercies of a Frenchman. *Madame Butterfly* always thrills me, no matter how often I hear it; but I never had any desire to sing Cio-Cio-San. The reason: I suppose she didn't attract me as a personage or challenge me as a rôle.

But *Bohème!* How I should have liked to have done it! You see, I almost did, and it was this way.

While in Paris, I received word from Covent Garden that they wanted me to come up to do Mimì the following season. Of course, Mimì was Melba's property in London. But that year Melba had announced that she wouldn't sing. The invitation pleased me enormously, and I got to work. Besides *The Love of Three Kings*, *Bohème* was the only opera I ever studied in Italian. And how I enjoyed every moment of it! Then, when I was ready to go to sign my contract, Melba changed her mind. I suppose the news that somebody was going to appropriate her beloved Mimì was too much for her. She came back to London, and I was soon informed that I would not be needed. That was the end of Mimì for me. Later they asked me to sing *Bohème* at the Opéra-Comique, but I refused. I then had so many other things to do. But what an experience it was studying that rôle in Italian!

If anybody is going to study voice, I say take the Italian method. When you sing correctly in that method you can sing any language and any repertory. Your voice is then placed: gloriously open and free. If you then go into the French repertory, you will sing like a real Italian, with a beautiful hot quality of tone, something you don't always get in French. French singers are inclined to be a little nasal because of the language.

It is the vowels that account for the open throat in the Italian method of singing. Compare *amore* in Italian with *amour* in French, *vita* with *vie*. What a language! When people study the French method from the beginning they are apt to get their voices in their noses instead of in their throats. Nobody in the world can sing like the Italians.

When I sang the Italian language my voice was as different as night and day and twice as big, and that was all due to the vowels. That language is as open as the sky and the very soul of resonance.

Italy is a haven for singing. And the climate: that has a lot to do with it, too. Maybe that's why so many good voices may be heard in California and Texas these days. But Italy has the best climate of all for voices. Oh, the voices of the gondoliers singing on the lagoons at night! I used to hear them ripple over the water. I would sit at my open window of the Grand Hotel in Venice and listen to them for hours. The lanterns would glisten all along the water, as the boats came up the canal. and the men would stop and sing. They were not artists of any opera house, these men; they sang for the love of it, and because they were Italians.

The most beautiful opera house I ever saw in my life was the Fenice of Venice. I used to go there whenever I went to Venice. I shall never forget the first night I attended an opera there. I was stepping out of the gondola, trembling with excitement because I was going to hear *Bohème* in the opera house I had dreamed about for so many years. And, of course, I missed the step and fell up to my chin in the water. The gondoliers pulled me out, and everybody wanted to send me home.

'Home?' I echoed. 'Why, that's nonsense! I'm going to the Fenice to-night and nobody is going to stop me!'

'But you're drenched to the skin! You'll get rheumatism or pneumonia!'

'I don't care what I get!' I cried. 'I'm going to hear *Bohème* to-night!'

So they all went into the Fenice and came out with armfuls of towels, which they wrapped all around me from neck to toe. They put them around my waist and around my legs and wherever else I was wet, which was everywhere.

And that was how I attended my first opera at the Fenice of Venice: smothered in towels and wet through and through. What a glorious performance of *Bohème* that was! I never once thought of the towels around my body. There I sat in a box with my friends, looking like something that had crept out of an Egyptian tomb. And I didn't take those towels off me till I got home. Did those gondoliers think that I'd let a little thing like a drenching keep me from *La Bohème?* I'm sure that, with their love of music, they knew better.

•

Well, to return to my cold November visit to a cold room at Windsor Castle. Down I went to London from all those kings and queens, and I stopped at the Savoy Hotel and lay in bed for three whole weeks with the most wretched laryngitis and tonsillitis I have ever had. I was alone in London —alone, sick, and miserable. And on my first real holiday. When I was finally on my feet again, I went on to Paris and never returned to Rome. Arriving in Paris, I sent to Rome for my things and went to see M. Carré. With him in his office was a man named Camille Erlanger. The two of them were discussing a new opera when I entered the office. It was called *Aphrodite*, and the book was by Pierre Louÿs.

'I'm afraid of the book,' M. Carré said, after introducing me.

'What's wrong with it, M. Carré?' I asked.

'For one thing, it's very Lesbian.'

Erlanger, looking hurt and disconsolate, appealed to me.

'May I play it for you, Mlle. Garden?' he asked. 'You might persuade M. Carré to change his mind.'

'Come up to my house to-morrow,' I said. 'I'd love to hear it. I had no idea you were such a prude, M. Carré.'

So Erlanger came to my apartment the next day and played the whole opera for me.

'It's got to be mine!' I shouted when he had finished, and I rushed back to the Opéra-Comique to see M. Carré.

'M. Carré, you can't let an opera like that go by,' I said. 'What are you worried about?'

'The public, for one thing—and the authorities.'

'Nonsense,' I said. 'There can be nothing offensive in any work of true beauty. I'd love to do it.'

'You win, Mary,' he said with a shrug. 'If you'll do it, I'll put it on.'

Erlanger was called back to M. Carré's office to sign a contract for the production of *Aphrodite* at the Opéra-Comique. What a brilliant opera that was—like a diamond, hard and dazzling! And the rôle of Chrysis was one of the most challenging I have ever created, beautiful, though by no means the greatest. The interest of the public in the opera was something you wouldn't believe if you hadn't been there. The minute it was announced that we were going to give it, the house was completely sold out. It proved to be one of the most spectacular successes the Opéra-Comique had ever enjoyed. Of course, everybody wanted to see it for reasons other than art.

*Aphrodite* wasn't like *Pelléas*, which we had to build up step by step till it sank into the minds of the people and the critics. Its success was instantaneous. And I had such an exciting time costuming that lady. Pierre Louÿs came along to every date I had with my costumers, to see that each single pleat and line of my dresses was Greek.

I remember the third act of the opera so vividly. I had come to the studio of Demetrius to get the three things he had promised me if I let him possess me—the comb, the mirror, and the seven rows of pearls—those sacred, untouchable pearls he had stolen for me from the neck of the great statue of Venus in the temple.

I, Chrysis, was supposed to come into his studio almost naked, and M. Carré tried every light that he had in his possession to get me through a veil. I wore just that veil over my body, and he wanted the people to think that I was naked. But we never could arrive at that illusion. I can still see him taking all the lights and throwing them on me, but none of them was strong enough to get through that veil to show the nudity of the woman. Finally we gave up trying.

What a triumph that opera was, and what needless worry

on the part of Albert Carré! Neither the public nor the authorities felt it was a blight on the moral fibre of Paris.

One night, while I was singing *Aphrodite*, a card was brought to me at intermission time. I didn't as a rule receive people in my dressing-room—at any rate, not people I didn't know, and I had never heard or seen this man's name before. I sent back word that he should call me the following day at my home. He evidently was very angry with me, for he never came to see me and took a boat back to the country he had come from—America. As I said, I didn't know who he was, so I didn't care, and forgot all about it. The name on that card was Oscar Hammerstein.

The following year, which was 1907, I was returning home from the Opéra-Comique one beautiful spring day, when I opened my door, and there was Oscar Hammerstein, waiting for me in my drawing-room. Without preliminary formalities of any kind, he looked at me steadily and said:

'Turn around, Mary, and let me see your figure.'

I liked him at once, that breezy and hearty American, so unlike all the other impresarios I have ever known, with their usual questions about what operas you've sung and how much money you want, and with whom you studied. Not Oscar! Oh, no, he wanted to know what I looked like from behind. Well, after I showed him, we sat down and talked about a contract, and he told me he had already bought *Thaïs* and *Louise*. Mr. Hammerstein's Manhattan Opera House was then about a year old, but I knew nothing about it, and I don't think I had heard or read anything about it in Paris, or perhaps I had and had forgotten.

'Say, Mary, there's another opera I want to ask you about,' Mr. Hammerstein said.

'Which one is that?' I asked, hoping we had the same one in mind.

'It's called *Pelzees and Maylisander*, and it's by a man named Deboozy.'

I laughed.

'Don't you think you'd better go and hear *Pelzees and Maylisander* yourself, Mr. Hammerstein, and then make up your own mind?'

I had a feeling I was standing before a man of instinctive good taste and judgment in music, and that I had no reason to fear his response to opera of such sensitive beauty as *Pelléas*.

I asked my sister to go along with Mr. Hammerstein.

'I want him to see for himself what this *Pelzees and Maylisander* is about,' I said to Aggie.

Aggie reported back to me that night that Mr. Hammerstein sat perfectly still during the first act, and then turned suddenly to her and said:

'Come on backstage and tell Mary it's bought.'

The moment he entered my dressing-room, he blurted out one word: 'Sold!'

'That doesn't interest me in the slightest, Mr. Hammerstein,' I said.

'What do you mean?' he bellowed.

'Merely that you can buy something you want. But what does interest me is who is going to sing this opera in America.'

'Why should that worry you?'

'It worries me a good deal, and I have every right to know. Have you got anybody in your company who can do an opera of this kind with me?'

He ran off a list of names, very impressive names, I'm certain.

'I don't know any of them,' I said.

'You can count on every one of them doing a good job.'

'I won't sing *Pelléas*,' I said finally, 'with anybody who isn't French, or, at least, in the French tradition.'

I knew he didn't have French artists in his company, and, being a very clever man, he probably began to suspect what I was driving at.

'What do you want me to do, Mary?'

'Oh, just think it over, Mr. Hammerstein. I'm sure something will occur to you.'

Something did. The next day he came to me in a state of great excitement.

'Mary,' he cried, 'I've satisfied you!'

'Please tell me how, Mr. Hammerstein.'

'I've engaged the whole Opéra-Comique to go along with you!'

What a man! He had signed up the five people who had created *Pelléas* with me in Paris. Then he had all the scenery painted in Paris by the same man who had done it for the Opéra-Comique, and when we finally gave it in New York it was perfection. That's what I liked about Oscar Hammerstein—the finest, or nothing at all. Money never meant a damn to him.

We were about to sign our contract, when Mr. Hammerstein had another flash of inspiration.

'Mary,' he said, with the boyish suddenness of his, 'let's sign the contract in the palace at Fontainebleau! I've never been there, and I'm very anxious to give it the once-over before I go back to New York.'

'Good, Mr. Hammerstein,' I replied. 'We'll sign the contract on the very same desk that Napoleon signed his abdication on.'

'That's my girl!' he shouted, turning to my sister Aggie, who was present.

So we hired an automobile and chauffeur, and the three of us, Oscar Hammerstein, my sister Aggie, and I, started out for Fontainebleau. We were riding along smoothly, all of us in a gay, springtime mood, when suddenly a wheel flew off the car, and we were all thrown into a field of poppies.

We had a moment of panic, but, miraculously, nobody was hurt, and while the chauffeur was wondering what in God's name he would do, I picked myself up and walked through the poppies, which are so beautiful in the spring in France. Then I sat myself down in the middle of them, and called out:

'Mr. Hammerstein, come on over here and keep me company!'

And that great and lovable impresario, immaculately dressed, with his silk hat, and that everlasting cigar in his mouth, came over and sat down beside me among the poppies on that beautiful spring day in France.

'Mary,' he said, 'I've a better idea than yours. Let's sign that contract right here.'

And there, propped up on a mass of lovely poppies, we signed a four-year contract, and I'm certain that there was never another contract signed that way at any time anywhere else in the world. Oh, we loved it, and we sat there laughing and waited till we got another automobile and went back to Paris, and poor Oscar Hammerstein never got to see Fontainebleau. I didn't see him again till I arrived in America. What a sweet and gentle soul he was really, under that gruff manner of his! We became very fond of one another. He had a fearful temper and so had I, but we always came together again, with no bad feeling on either side.

I should like to pause at this point to speak of another great friend who entered my life at the time of *Aphrodite*—Jean de Reszke. When Jean and I became friends in Paris he had finished his career in opera and begun teaching. It is a pity that he ended just as I was beginning, because I would have loved singing with him. I was about to create *Aphrodite* when I first met Jean, and I remember he had a strong desire to appear in it with me, but was hesitant about accepting.

M. Carré and I used all our powers of persuasion to make him decide. In the end, Jean refused.

'My career as tenor is over,' he said. 'I am not sure enough of myself to start all over again.'

That was sad news to M. Carré and me, but perhaps Jean

was wise. No one knows better than the artist himself when it is time to stop. Like myself when the time came, Jean had made his decision and he stuck to it.

During the First World War, Jean became my neighbour by opening a large school of singing in Nice. I had tired of Monte Carlo, especially when the cocktail parties came, and had bought myself a villa right on the sea at Beaulieu, which is not far from Nice. So we saw a great deal of one another, Jean and I, during the summer months.

He was the greatest host I have ever known. There was a genuine welcome for everyone who came to visit him, and his friends found an unfailing devotion in him. His sense of humour was unforgettable, and he was a constant delight at table. One of his greatest passions was a beautiful green parrot that remained for ever perched on his shoulder. Those who so much as touched that bird regretted it. I have rarely seen such a strange and close bond between master and pet.

I never knew a man to be as interested in so many things as Jean de Reszke. One of his great joys, I remember, was the yearly French bicycle race. Since I was just as wild about it, he and I always stood together on the Promenade des Anglais to watch the racers pass through Nice. Sometimes it took an hour, and Mme. de Reszke thought us both quite mad.

I said I never sang with de Reszke, but I did, once, and in the same opera in which I had first heard him, Gounod's *Roméo et Juliette*. It was at Jean's villa in Nice, and it was the last time I saw him. We had all had dinner, and among the guests were a great many people of the arts.

Jean suddenly rose from his seat and cried out:

'Mary, let's sing the Balcony Scene!'

And of course I wasn't going to let that opportunity slip by.

'Lead the way, Jean!' I exclaimed.

There was great excitement in the room as Jean flung open the huge terrace windows. Then we began that glorious scene together. I would never have suspected what artistry and beauty were still at his command if it hadn't been for a sudden fancy that seized him on that June day in Nice.

'I haven't heard him sing that way in ten years,' Mme. de Reszke said to me later.

But then we were in a room, among friends, and not in an opera house.

Mme. de Reszke was a sad, fragile woman of a haunting beauty. She had a magnificent contralto voice and sang German lieder like no one else I have ever heard, but she never sang out of her own home, and she sang not at all when tragedy finally struck.

Their son, an only child, had enlisted in the French army. A few hours after the Armistice was signed, he and two companions were marching jubilantly over an open field when a shell exploded at their feet, blowing young de Reszke's head off. Jean took it bravely, though the few who were close to him knew what he went through in the years that remained to him. When the news reached her, Mme. de Reszke plunged into a prolonged frenzy of screaming. She walked for the rest of her life with tragedy all over her frail being.

Then Jean died and the singing school in Nice was closed. Mme. de Reszke returned to Paris, a ghost of her beautiful self, held together only by drugs, and then she too died, and a total silence closed over that devoted little family.

Before I went on to America I had two or three months more of work at the Opéra-Comique. My season at the Manhattan Opera House was to begin in November, 1907. As my season at the Comique drew near, I decided I wanted to finish my eight years there with the opera I had begun with. So I said 'Good-bye' to my friends and colleagues in Charpentier's *Louise*. My contract was now fulfilled at the Comique. I would have had to sign another. Instead, I had signed with Mr. Hammerstein. I was then receiving the maximum salary at the Comique, which was 7,500 francs a month, having worked up to that from 250 a month.

What a thrilling experience that last *Louise* was! Oh, the galleries, the galleries, that was where my real public in Paris was. Well, that night they came with baskets of rose leaves. When I took my last curtain, they shouted down to me:

'*Ne partez pas, ne partez pas!*'

And I looked up to them and just gave them a motion with my hand—I was never fond of throwing kisses around—and they picked up their baskets and emptied them on the house below, and the whole Opéra-Comique was filled with rose leaves.

So I looked up again and said, '*À bientôt!*'

And that ended my eight years at the Opéra-Comique of Paris.

# I Return to America

I LEFT for America with thirty trunks and a dog. Why I took the dog along I don't know, but that was the last and only time I ever travelled with one. I shall never forget my third day out at sea. I was lying in my cabin reading, my little dog close beside me. In one of my hands I held a long thin nail file to cut the pages of the book I was reading. I must have been holding it close to my ear, for a knock at the cabin door made the dog jump up, and as he jumped he drove the nail file into my ear. A small trickle of blood appeared, and I suddenly found myself deaf. I became quite hysterical, and my first impulse was to leap into the sea. I ran toward the porthole to see if it was big enough for me to jump through. Of course, I was quite mad. Finally I called the ship's doctor.

'I'm almost totally deaf, Doctor!' I cried to him as he examined me. 'Think of Oscar Hammerstein meeting a deaf Thaïs when we arrive in New York!'

'Miss Garden,' the doctor said coolly, 'I assure you your hearing will be completely normal by then. Will you please calm down?'

I wasn't at all convinced, but, fortunately for me, on my arrival I was able to smile and answer all the questions Mr. Hammerstein put to me.

We docked in New York early in November, and there on the pier to greet me, besides Mr. Hammerstein, were Father and Mother. We all went in a car to an apartment at 85 East

Fifty-sixth Street, which then became my first home in America after my long absence. My sister had preceded me to America, and this was her home, a lovely and spacious place, which she turned over to me for the season, being on the point of returning to Europe herself.

As I had hoped and suggested, Mr. Hammerstein informed me that I would make my debut in Massenet's *Thaïs*, in two weeks. So we went on down to the Manhattan Opera House, and I was introduced to all the wonderful people in Mr. Hammerstein's company. There for the first time I met the magnificent conductor, Cleofonte Campanini, one of the greatest to conduct for me, and soon we began rehearsing *Thaïs*. Then, just one day before my debut, I ran into trouble. I suddenly found myself up against the climate of New York. I came down with a most dreadful cold—a foretaste of the havoc the weather was to play with me during my entire first season in New York. I had lived my life in France, where the climate is generally mild, no great cold and winds and snow. I sent word to Mr. Hammerstein, who immediately came to see me.

'You've got to put off my début, Mr. Hammerstein,' I said.

'But that's impossible, Mary!'

'Impossible? Why, listen to me—I'm talking like crow. I have no voice at all. How do you expect me to sing to-morrow night?'

'You can't do this to me, Mary. Don't you see that string of carriages moving down to Thirty-fourth Street to-morrow? You can't let those people down!'

'I'm sorry, Mr. Hammerstein, I'm not going to sing without a voice, and at the moment I can barely talk.'

'Maybe by to-morrow night. . . .'

'It's out of the question. I can't do it, and that's that.'

When he saw there was no use prolonging the discussion, he threw out his arms and gave a deep sigh.

'All right, Mary, I suppose you know best. But you're not going to get over that bronchitis and whatever else it is you have here in New York. I'm sending you to Atlantic City.'

The week after I returned—without my bronchitis—from Atlantic City I made my debut at the Manhattan Opera House in the title rôle of Massenet's *Thaïs*. That was the night of November 25th, 1907. And did the critics let me have it! Now, the Metropolitan Opera House, which still remains the only opera house in America, had been playing Verdi, Meyerbeer, Wagner, for years and years and years, but no modern French music dramas. So, when I appeared as this great courtesan in the glorious music of Massenet, they didn't understand what we were doing. We were condemned me, Thais, and everything.

The papers just pulled me to pieces, all except one, the New York *World*. There a man named Reginald de Koven reported that the night before 'something new'—meaning me—had come into grand opera in America. That gave me a little courage, though I'm perfectly calm as a rule about critics, and I personally don't believe in criticism.

I remember one of the critics wrote that my high notes were 'like the snakes of Ireland,' This puzzled me, so I went to Father and said, 'Papa, what kinds of snakes are there in Ireland?'

And he replied, 'Mary, there aren't any snakes in Ireland.' Then I understood that I wasn't supposed to have any high notes. But, good gracious, I had been singing high notes in France for eight years, and the French had never complained that they were bad or that they weren't there at all! I have no idea why they didn't like my high notes in this country. In France I was a singer; in America I now became a 'singing actress.' That was the title they gave me. It stuck, and I must confess I liked it.

The critics also found fault with the way I clothed, or didn't clothe, Thaïs. They said that I had very little on. I had loads on. Compared to what women wear to-day, that night of my début at the Manhattan Opera House I had red flannels on.

The avalanche of abusive criticism that followed my New York debut in *Thaïs* would have made any other singer pack her trunk and go back to where she had come from. Not me. I gloated over it.

I had a great admirer in one of the owners of the *New York Herald*. He asked me if I wished, through his paper, to answer the critics. I accepted the offer, and possibly many things I said made the gentlemen angry. I remember one of them, the dean of them all, I believe, 'phoned me.

'Do you realize, Miss Garden,' he said in a voice of great pompousness, 'that you have fallen into a hornet's nest?'

'Who are the hornets?' I asked.

'The New York critics,' he replied.

'Well,' I answered, 'that's just where I want to be.'

And without saying another word, he hung up. The war was on.

Then one Sunday James Huneker gave over a whole page of *The New York Times* to my work. Across the article, in huge letters, ran the headline, MARY GARDEN, SUPERWOMAN.

My friends, his colleagues of the New York press, were evidently not of his opinion. A few days after that article appeared, Mr. Huneker received as a token of their esteem a baby's milk bottle. Naturally, he was furious, but I thought it quite funny and rather clever of the old boys.

Is criticism necessary? I can hear many of you utterly disagreeing with me, saying 'Miss Garden, you're wrong; criticism creates discussion.'

Yes, that is true. Criticism creates fiery discussion, and then what?

After all the discussions have died down, what do they amount to? What has been their value? Nothing. Just like smoke from a cigarette, you blow it from your mouth and it evaporates. The only value I can see in criticism is that it gives a fine topic of conversation to those who are unable to think for themselves. I have seen cruel criticism destroy a sensitive spirit. I have also known it to break a strong nature.

A very old friend of mine, Magdeleine Godard, the sister of the French musician, Benjamin Godard, told me that after the first performance of *Carmen* her brother went to congratulate Bizet. He found him all alone in his room, sitting in front of a table with his head in his hands, crying bitter tears. Godard said it was a cruel sight to see so great a musician in the depths of despair. There are those who say that the brutal and rancorous criticism of his opera did much to bring about his untimely death at the age of thirty-seven.

Did the music critics banish *Carmen* from the stage? Could all the violent criticism in the world do that? Never. The final decision, as with all great works of art, rested with the public, and the public took *Carmen* to its ample bosom.

Criticism should be profound and instructive teaching. A critic must possess knowledge, broad sympathy, and good taste. Some of the music criticism of my day approached ridicule and rudeness. However, it has never frightened, exhilarated, or affected me in any way. And the bottles of ink that have been used up trying to decide whether I could sing or not.

It is so ridiculous to let any criticism down you. I don't care what it is, it is the public that matters.

Mme. Delna, one of the greatest singer of France—there was never anybody who sang Gluck's *Orpheus* like her—well, she sang *Orpheus* here, and the critics denounced her, so she gathered up her things and went away.

Then there was Feodor Chaliapin. When he first appeared here in *Mefistofele*, they raised merry hell, the critics, and Chaliapin went back to Europe. When the First World War was done, he came back. And Chaliapin was the greatest thing that ever lived.

I never got a single flash of inspiration from the millions of words, good and bad, written about me by the critics. It was the public that paid to hear and see me, and my only concern was to please them.

After the seond performance of *Thaïs*, Mr. Hammerstein came into the dressing-room, looking as if the roof over our heads had just collapsed.

'Mary, there's not enough money in the house to pay the gas bill,' he moaned.

Now, that wasn't the sort of thing anybody could say to me. I resolved to campaign personally for this great modern French opera. In every interview I had with the Press—and there were many—I spoke endlessly about *Thaïs*, its composer, its significance. Everywhere I went I sang its praises. After I had my portrait, as *Thaïs*, painted by Ben Ali Haggin, I let them put it in Knoedler's window, and by God, it stopped the buses! I don't know what else ever stopped New York's buses—perhaps a good snowstorm—but I know I did.

It wasn't long before every performance of *Thaïs* was sold out. From then to the very end of my career *Thaïs* was the war horse that brought in all the money. Whenever anything went wrong in the theatre, and they wanted to make up their losses, they brought out *Thaïs*.

How did I study Thaïs? Out of my own brain, mostly. I had all the clothes made after my own ideas, and I never altered them in any way. Thaïs was the great dancer of Alexandria, a sinister power there, and I didn't dress her like Cleopatra, who belonged to an earlier epoch. I put her in gorgeous colours, with lots of veils and a great many jewels, especially pearls, because pearls were the great jewels of Alexandria. I read up a bit in the books and asked advice of anybody who knew more than I did about that sort of thing. I kept strictly to the epoch, as I did in all my rôles.

My dress was made of *crêpe de Chine*, and there was nothing to it. The dress stuck to my flesh, and because it was of the palest pink it made me look as if I were naked. I understood perfectly well why everybody in the Manhattan Opera House gasped for breath that night when I threw off my mantle and stood before them in that clinging, pale-pink *crêpe de Chine*. There were no buttons on the mantle, and I had just draped myself around. When it came off, they were all ready to swear I had nothing on.

I have nothing to say about my body except that it is the way God made it and the way I kept it. You see, I never allowed fat to get on it. I was very fussy about weighing myself every Sunday morning of my life, and I even do it now. I get on the scales once a week, and if I see a fraction of weight more, that fraction is gone the following Sunday. So many women come to me and say, 'Miss Garden, how do you keep your figure?' I don't think they know what a scale is. I never walked or did exercise of any kind while I was singing. I never took a step I didn't have to take. I just looked at my scales. But when I went for my holidays, in Monte Carlo and Corsica, I never did anything but exercise—swimming, golf, tennis—never walking; I hate it.

My body didn't begin to develop till seven years after my début, and the change became noticeable in the opera *Aphrodite*. I had never had any breasts, and suddenly I began to grow there, and then I had a bosom, with a tiny waist, but no thighs, and no hips. My chest developed with singing.

After that bad beginning at the Manhattan, *Thaïs* grew like a plant. It was just heavenly. Singing it with me, in the role of Athanaël, was Maurice Renaud, one of the greatest artists in the world. We put our hearts into it, and it took its place where it should.

Well, we produced everything at the Manhattan that the Metropolitan didn't and a few things that they did. We had Luisa Tetrazzini, and that of course meant Italian opera.

We had no Wagner at all, but we had all the French works. Where he acquired his passion for them I don't know, but Mr. Hammerstein simply adored the French operas, and he brought them into his Manhattan Opera House. And we had influential people, millionaire boxholders, come over from the Metropolitan—and stay with us. Two of our greatest patrons were Clarence Mackay and his wife. Mr. Mackay was later to become the dearest friend I ever had on earth. As for Mrs. Mackay, she was mad about our French repertory. The two of them occupied their box every night, and I know that Mrs. Mackay personally brought over a great number of subscribers from the Metropolitan. That was a brilliant audience we had at the Manhattan! And thanks to Mr. Hammerstein, they all began to understand French opera, and they came to know what a 'singing actress' was when I sang *Louise* on January 3rd, 1908.

That was my second opera at the Manhattan. Everybody—even the critics—was wild about it. We had all the houses we needed for *Louise*, and there were no gas bills to pay. What a triumph! The odd thing about it is that we didn't have to work to make *Louise* a triumph. We all knew it so well and loved it like someone very dear to us.

And then, in February, came *Pelléas et Mélisande*. That was something the like of which they had never seen in this country. It was something out of heaven. Oh, how they accepted it! And why not? Everyone was from Paris, and we gave it here just as if we were back at the Opéra-Comique, all of us who had created it there a few years earlier. It just had to be a success. And later, when we were repeating *Pelléas*, I had the greatest personal triumph of all. There in a box sat Maurice Maeterlinck. The man who had vowed never to attend a performance of Debussy's opera had at last relented. After the last curtain, he came backstage and was perfectly charming as he introduced me to his beautiful young wife.

'*En fin*, Maeterlinck,' I said, 'you have come to hear your work, and in America, not France.'

He bowed very graciously.

'Had I known,' he said, 'I should have come a long time ago. *Je suis très heureux, très heureux!*'

Then the photographers came in and took a picture of the three of us sitting there in my dressing-room. Two days later I received a letter, my final token of victory in what had been a very unsavoury business:

> *I had sworn to myself never to see the lyric drama,* Pelléas et Mélisande [*it read*]. *Yesterday I violated my vow and I am a happy man. For the first time I have entirely understood my own play, and because of you.*
>
> *I saw there many things which I had never perceived or which I had forgotten. Like every great artist, more than any other perhaps, you have the genius to add to a work or to vivify in it those things which I omitted or had left in a state of sleep.*
>
> *With all my heart's thanks for the beautiful revelation of last night's performance, in the most cordial homage of your devoted admirer.*
>
> *Maurice Maeterlinck*

I never saw Marterlinck again until I had lunch with him and his wife many years later in the villa of Henry Russell in the mountains behind Monte Carlo. That must have been in 1921, because I acquired my own villa at Beaulieu in 1922. We were all sitting in Mr. Russell's garden after lunch, when Maeterlinck turned to me.

'Mlle. Garden,' he asked, 'will you let me photograph something of you that has never been photographed before?'

We all knew that Maeterlinck had become quite a camera fan.

'But, M. Maeterlinck,' I replied, 'there isn't a part of me that hasn't been photographed.'

'But there is,' he persisted.

'What is it?'

'Your soul!'

'My soul, M. Maeterlinck!' I cried. 'But I should like to keep that to myself.'

'Then I shall not insist on invading your privacy,' he said, bowing courteously.

'But do you really photograph souls?' I asked.

'It's his hobby,' Mme. Maeterlinck said.

'Well,' I said, 'have you snapped any souls to-day, M. Maeterlinck?'

'I have.'

'Will you show me a photograph of a soul?'

Maeterlinck got up, went into the house, and was soon back with a large portfolio under his arm. From it he pulled out a sheet of jet-black paper, and it looked as if someone had just thrown a little milk over it.

'Is that a soul, M. Maeterlinck?' I asked.

'That is a soul.'

'Well,' I said, 'you'll never get mine on a piece of black paper.'

That finished the episode. Maeterlinck never asked me again for a picture of my soul, and I never saw him or his lovely young wife again.

Then there was my strange encounter with Sir Oliver Lodge shortly after Debussy's death. It happened one day in New York, while I was singing at a morning concert given in the ballroom of the Biltmore Hotel.

The last song on my programme was the *Beau Soir* of Debussy. As I was singing the last three words of the song, out of nowhere and for no reason whatsoever, Sir Oliver Lodge came into my mind.

Now the name of this great man was known to me, but I had never seen him in my life. I had never read any of his writings and I couldn't recall ever having talked to anybody about him. Sir Oliver was an utter stranger to me, nothing more than a name.

Well, at the end of the concert, I went up to the room that the hotel had put at my disposal. I dressed and was just about to leave, when there was a knock on the door. I answered, and a very tall, fine-looking, elderly man entered.

'Yes?' I asked, puzzled.

'I am Sir Oliver Lodge,' he said quietly.

I stood a moment, bewildered, and I remember I felt a slight shiver come over me. For a few moments I scarcely knew what to say; then I asked him:

'Have you been listening to my concert?'

'No,' he replied solemnly.

'This is all very odd,' I said.

'Not really,' he replied. 'It's all quite simple.'

'But the thought of you crossed my mind during my last song,' I said, 'and here you are.'

'I am here,' he said, 'because you called me.'

I cannot explain the queer, dizzy feeling that seized me as he said that. Then he took both my hands in his, very gently.

'I want to see you again and often,' he said softly, 'and we shall talk to Debussy.'

He told me he was leaving New York for a month and gave me an address where I could write to him on his return.

I never saw Sir Oliver again. I didn't write. Perhaps I forgot, or perhaps I just didn't want to.

Was it all just a coincidence?

I repeat. Both the critics and the public stood up to *Pelléas* at the Manhattan Opera House. There was some absurd criticism, as there had been in Paris, but most of it was with us. It was again the public that led the way, and the opera stayed in my repertory the twenty years that I was in America. And when I made my début in Chicago, it was accepted with even greater enthusiasm.

Shortly after the first performance of *Pelléas* at the Manhattan Opera House, I had my first serious clash with Mr. Hammerstein. One day, just before going into a rehearsal, I stopped to look at the billboard outside. There, staring at me in large letters, were the words:

FRIDAY NIGHT, THAÏS, WITH LINA CAVALIERI

So I went right in and got hold of Mr. Hammerstein.

'Look here, Mr. Hammerstein,' I said, 'what's this I've just read on the billboard?'

'What about it?' he said defiantly.

'You can't mean it!'

'Who's boss here, anyway?' he snapped.

'I won't permit it!' I shouted at him.

Then he exploded—he just opened up and told me where to get off.

'You've got nothing to do with my theatre,' he blazed away. 'I'll do what I goddamn please, and nobody, not you or anybody else, is going to stop me!'

'Mr. Hammerstein,' I said, 'you can do what *you* please, and I can do what *I* please! If Mme. Cavalieri sings *Thaïs* on Friday night, I'm through!'

He evidently didn't take me seriously, for he brushed my threat aside and went right on.

'Mary, I'll do what I like, and no singer is going to tell me how to run my business. Now be a good girl and go into the house. They're waiting for you.'

After rehearsal that afternoon, I went down to see Sam Untermeyer, who was a good friend of mine. When I told him the story, he was highly amused.

'What do you want me to do?' he asked.

'Write me a letter of resignation.'

'You're sure you know what you're doing?'

'Mr. Untermeyer, I think we both understand Hammerstein perfectly.'

Well, he dictated my letter of resignation, I signed it, and off it went to Mr. Hammerstein. Then I went ahead and got my ticket to sail on Saturday. I was home on East Fifty-sixth Street Thursday morning when Mr. Hammerstein burst into my room.

'You win, Mary,' he shouted; 'you'll sing *Thaïs* to-morrow night.'

In my life I have never seen anybody so completely defeated, and was he furious!

So, when I arrived on the stage of the Manhattan Opera House Friday and began throwing roses in the air, the whole audience stood up. Mr. Campanini had to stop the orchestra because they went right on applauding me for I don't know how many minutes, I suppose to show that they were with me in this. It must have been that, because I never heard so much screaming and yelling and 'Bravas!' in all my life. I sang *Thaïs* that Friday night—and ever afterward.

I wasn't going to bring the great works from Paris and have an Italian woman take them from me. Cavalieri could have brought her own operas from Italy, and they would have been hers, and nobody need have touched them. She had been at the Metropolitan, where they hadn't liked her very much, and she left them to come over to us.

It took Mr. Hammerstein a little time to get over that unpleasantness—it was our first real fight. For a while he wasn't very polite to me, but the strain continued only for a week at the most. I knew he was very fond of me, really, and he knew perfectly well that he was in the wrong. From not being able to pay the gas bill, he had been doing very well indeed with the box office. No one had to tell him that Renaud and I were doing that for him.

Cavalieri finally made her debut with us in *Carmen*. I was in the front box, and my, was it awful! She wasn't Carmen at all. Hammerstein never gave her the rôle again. Then she was given *Tales of Hoffmann* to do, and in that she was radiant, full of diamonds and beauty. After that season she never sang for Hammerstein again.

I was to have sung *Thaïs* one afternoon in Philadelphia but was taken ill and could not appear. So they put another singer in my place. My sister, who was with me, went over to hear the performance.

Before the opera began, an announcement was made from the stage that I was ill and would not sing that afternoon. A man sitting next to my sister threw his hands in the air and cried out:

'My God, drunk again!'

Of course, my sister couldn't let that pass.

'I am Miss Garden's sister,' she said coldly, 'and I cannot permit you to talk like that. My sister happens to be quite ill at this moment.'

But before she could say another word, he was out of his seat and away like a stroke of lightning, and he never came back.

What bothered me, when my sister reported the episode, was the word 'again.' You see, I was 'drunk' only once in my life.

It happened in Deauville on the hottest day I can remember. My mother and I were invited out to lunch, and I can still see the butler coming in with glasses filled with something white like water. There was snow all around the glasses.

'My, that looks good!' I said to Mother.

So they offered me one, and I took it and drank it down. Then they came around with another, and I drank that down, too. Oh, it was good, that drink, so cold and refreshing. Then I went into the dining-room, and the first thing I knew I was lying in bed in the hotel, with my mother standing beside me in mortal fear of my life. Nobody knew what was the matter with me, and I could hear them saying, 'She's dying! Get an ambulance!'

And they got an ambulance and took me to Paris, and when we arrived in Paris they picked me up and got me to bed. But there were no doctors in Paris, because everybody was on holiday, it was so frightfully hot. So Mother called a Professor Robin, whom I knew very well. Luckily he was home, and he came immediately. There I lay in bed like a dead fish.

'My God!' exclaimed Professor Robin, 'the woman is poisoned!'

And for five solid weeks I lay in bed just as ill as anybody could be. The professor gave me medicines that made me sweat, and I remember how that perspiration went through all my clothes and bedsheets and blankets. The whole bed and all my clothes had to be changed every two hours. When the five weeks were up Professor Robin spoke to me.

'Don't you ever drink any alcohol in your life,' he said, 'because it is instantaneous poison to you.'

Never again did I touch a thing, with one exception. Whenever I was very tired I drank a glass of champagne; that never hurt me. But I never touched whisky or gin or beer, and the cocktail and I have been complete strangers since that hot afternoon in Deauville.

One day toward the end of my first season at the Manhattan Opera House, Mr. Hammerstein called me into his office.

'Mary,' he said, 'I'm going to put on *Salomé* next season.'

'Good for you, Mr. Hammerstein!' I exclaimed, and, then, recalling the Metropolitan scandal with Strauss' opera the year before, I added: 'But isn't it risky?'

I hadn't been in New York at the time, but everyone had told me of the furore in the press over Conried's production; how there had been a semi-public dress rehearsal one Sunday morning, then a performance the following Tuesday; how the board of directors began threatening Conried.

'I'm not worried in the least,' said Mr. Hammerstein. 'I'm free to do what I like. I don't have a board of directors.'

'The police . . .'

'They never padlocked *Salomé*,' he replied. 'Conried faced a cancellation of his lease. That's why he withdrew the opera after that one performance.'

'I think it's just too thrilling for words, your deciding to do it.'

'I'm planning to give it to you,' he said. 'How about it?'

'On one condition, Mr. Hammerstein.'

He frowned and stared at me in silence for a few moments.

'Name it,' he said cautiously.

'If I can dance it myself.'

'Why do you insist? You're not a dancer, Mary.'

'I'm not going to have another dancer pirouetting around on her toes in such a drama.'

'I agree—the dance is yours, but make it good!'

So I went to Paris and got the head teacher of dancing at the Opéra and explained to her the sort of dance I wanted to do between the throne of Herod and the cistern in which John the Baptist was being held prisoner.

'I want the Dance of the Seven Veils to be *drama*,' I emphasized, 'not Folies Bergère.'

She thought it over and began teaching me. And when I came back, I danced it, and what a beautiful dance it was! I had on enormous veils, which I took off one by one and threw in Herod's face. With the very last veil I enveloped myself entirely. There I stood at the cistern, and under that last veil was just the thinnest, thinnest muslin. As I ran from the cistern over to Herod, I thrust the last veil at him and knelt and said, 'I want the head of Jokanaan.'

It was an enchanting dance, lovely, and classical in feeling. It wasn't a hoochi-koochi dance at all—that sort of exhibition has nothing to do with the epoch of Herod. Everything was glorious and nude and suggestive, but not coarse. Herod wasn't looking for anything coarse in Salomé's dance; he was looking for beauty. I saw them dance the hoochi-koochi once in Algiers, stomachs all bare and rolling. My stomach wasn't bare in *Salomé* and I never rolled it.

And those veils; they were of the palest pink, and I used to run with them high in the air, and they stayed up there and followed me everywhere. Then when I finished my dance, I put on my dress, a very short dress that went just under my knees, and made of a thick gold mesh covered with jewels, and, oh, those emeralds and diamonds and rubies, how they sparkled and laughed in the light!

We gave the opera in the French of Oscar Wilde, word for word. I would like to see it done that way always. I don't like it in German, and I remember Wilde himself once remarked to someone, 'I could never have written this thing in English. I could think and feel it only in French.' It just had to be in that language.

I worked on Salomé with my accompanist, Bartholemy, the same man who was with Enrico Caruso for years, and with no one else except the dancing teacher at the Opéra. I knew the drama by heart, every line of it. And it was the same with Salomé as with my other rôles: all my creations went into me and out. They were there inside of me, and I threw them out to the public. I never really worked over them, not in the usual sense—I just *knew* them. I *knew* everything about Salomé. I didn't go to books and I didn't go to museums, as many people say they do, and I didn't go to see what death was like. Why don't these singers have the imagination to see it themselves? I just had it *in* me, all of it. I *was* Thaïs, I *was* Mélisande, I *was* Salomé. That was all there was to it. I put on the clothes and the wigs and I became Salomé.

But, oh, what difficult music that was, *Salomé*—getting all the rhythms and all the correct accents! And those fearful intervals! I worked and worked on the first part till I had it, and then I took the second part, which is very much easier. Bartholemy used to come to my house in Paris, where I worked on Salomé, and see to it that I sang the whole thing correctly in measure. He remained my accompanist for about ten years.

We had no dress rehearsals at the Manhattan Opera House. I suppose Mr. Hammerstein just didn't believe in them, and I agreed with him. The first night is quite sufficient, and the dress rehearsal is merely a substitute for it; there's no real need for it that I can see, and no criticism following it. At the Opéra-Comique it was just something for society and the writers and the painters and all the friends of the cast. I suppose where they still have the dress rehearsal it's just a habit that no director has had the daring to break.

We sang *Salomé* at the Manhattan for the first time on January 28th, 1909. Dalmorès was the Herod, and what a superb musician, singer, and actor that man was! There was great expectancy that night because of what had happened at the Metropolitan two years earlier. What was the audience like that night? I haven't the slightest idea. I never knew what audiences were like because I was no longer Mary Garden. That night I was living as Salomé on the stage. I can't repeat this often enough—*all I ever thought about was the rôle*. The audience never existed for me till the curtain was down and the spell was off.

That's what many people can't understand. I was a peculiar operatic being. As long as I was singing I had nothing whatever to do with anything or anybody else in the world. I never thought of the audience; I never looked at them, except for that one time in my début as Louise, when the men in their evening clothes looked like penguins. I never knew they were there till I took my bows. I honestly don't think I could have done what I did if I had begun wondering whether those people out there liked it or not. While I was on the stage, nothing interested me but the part I was playing, and the part I was playing had become *me*. There was my life. Well, Mr. Hammerstein's *Salomé* was a great triumph that night, and no attempt that I know of was made to crush it on moral or any other grounds.

Then we sang *Salomé* in Philadelphia, and there was just as much enthusiasm for it there. The house was jammed, and hundreds of people went about in the streets trying to buy tickets. Policemen on horses had to hold them back and tell them there just weren't any more tickets to buy. No, *Salomé* had stopped being a scandal. There was no fuss over our performances in either New York or Philadelphia. No scandal, no wild talk, no anything; just a brilliant success. There was never any question of padlocking the opera. I suppose Salomé had now become a perfect lady. In Chicago we did run into trouble, but that's another, and later, story.

I remember Mr. Hammerstein used to sit right off the stage in the wings during every single performance of *Salomé*, the same immaculately dressed Hammerstein, with the high silk hat on his head. And he used to keep asking:

'Has Mary got the head yet?'

'No, Mr. Hammerstein,' someone would say.

He would give a deep sigh, puff away at the cigar that was always in his mouth, and after a while ask again:

'Has Mary got the head now?'

And someone would reply, 'Yes, Mr. Hammerstein.'

Then he would get up from his chair, straighten out his shoulders, and announce:

'Well, I guess I can go home to bed.'

I experienced the only great surprise I ever had in America while I was singing *Tosca* one evening in Boston with Vanni Marcoux. The trouble came, of course, with the seduction scene. Apparently the way we acted it was too realistic for the Boston ladies in the boxes. I was told that when Marcoux and I went through that scene, those very proper ladies, as if at a signal from some leader, all turned their backs to the stage. Then we were in trouble—with the papers the following morning, with the censors, with everybody. And we never could sing *Tosca* in Boston again.

You see, I was dressed in a gown of silver cloth and Marcoux was dressed in black satin, and I suppose that when we came to that marvellous scene of the assault, the picture must have been highly convincing. There I lay on the lounge to get away from him, and Marcoux came forward with all his force, throwing himself on me. It was the contrast of the black on the white that must have made it so scandalous a sight for those sensitive souls in the boxes.

And while we are on the subject of the seduction scene, I should like to mention a detail of my impersonation of Tosca that came to me in a flash of improvization one night at the Opéra-Comique. It concerns the candles in the second act. You see, most singers are hypnotized from the start by the idea of putting the candles beside the body of Scarpia. At that particular performance it suddenly dawned on me that there was a better way of doing it.

I, Tosca, never had that in mind, the thought of putting the candles down beside him. I blew them out on the table and went over to blow out the other two, the two that, without my knowing it then, were destined to be put down on the floor beside the body of the man whom I had just stabbed. I began to blow them out too, when all of a sudden, I, Tosca, seemed to say to herself, 'Why not place them beside him? That will be better.'

And you saw by my actions what I meant. I took one candle up and then the other and I went over and placed them there. It was a sudden impulse to do it; it wasn't at all in the *mise en scène* of the opera, and when I did it first for the

Paris public, which is so quick to see anything natural on the stage, I could hear them whispering, all of them. 'Brava! Brava!'

How I enjoyed adding that unexpected little touch! I just said to myself as the moment came, 'To-night this is what you must do!' I had not planned it at all. I knew, or Tosca knew, that was the way it had to be—that night, anyway.

It was while I was scandalizing the Bostonians with my candid version of Tosca that the name of Peter Parker came up again. I was asked by reporters if I had had anything in the way of a romance before I left for Paris. Quite innocently, I told them about this charming naval officer whom I had known ten years before in Hartford. I don't believe I gave his name to the reporters. Well, the following day the newspapers made a great story of this girlhood 'romance' of mine, and then a few days later I received a letter from a man named Parker, asking me whether he could come to see me. I wrote back that he could, never for a moment suspecting who he might be.

'I'm Pete's brother, Miss Garden,' he said, after being admitted to my room at the hotel.

'Oh, Mr. Parker, I do hope those stories about Peter didn't do any harm,' I said. 'They kept pestering me for a romance.'

'On the contrary,' he interrupted, 'I'm so glad you said what you did. Because, you see, my brother adored you so much he never could marry anybody else.'

'Where is Pete now?' I asked.

'Dead. He went out hunting one day and fell from his horse.'

His brother grew very sad as he related the tragedy to me, and then he assured me again how happy it had made him to read the nice things I had said about Peter in the newspapers.

I was naturally sorry to hear of his death, but I must confess that as his brother spoke to me I couldn't even remember Pete's face. So many things had happened in ten years to crowd out the memory of those sweet winter days in Hartford with the first man who had asked me to be his wife. I had stuck to my decision—I had my career and I had not married.

## The Story of *The Juggler* and the Story of a Bear

❁

IT was Maurice Renaud who put the idea into Mr. Hammerstein's head to bring Massenet's *Le Jongleur de Notre-Dame* to New York.

'We'll have it, Maurice,' agreed Mr. Hammerstein. 'Who do you have in mind for the part of the Jongleur?'

'Mary Garden,' replied Renaud.

'But isn't the rôle written for tenor?' Mr. Hammerstein protested.

'True, that is how the French have always done it,' Renaud said. 'But it is a mistake. Only a woman, and a woman built like Garden, should sing it.'

Mr. Hammerstein assigned me the part during my first season at the Manhattan, and I studied it the following summer in Paris together with *Salomé*. I was to be the first woman ever to sing the rôle of the boy juggler who did homage to the Madonna in a humble way of his own.

Now, this was one of my strangest and most problematic creations. Here was a little boy of fifteen, a sexless child, with a voice that wasn't yet broken, and there was Salomé, with a voice of passion and colour, and I had to take my voice and make it that other thing. I couldn't put into that boy passion of any kind. The voice had to be pure and high, like a choir boy's before it changes, and how it tired me! It wasn't easy, but what a part, the Jongleur! The critics and the public all loved it. They never even thought about the fact that it was a woman doing it. When I sang it in Paris, they, too, accepted me.

It should always be a woman who sings the Jongleur. The part is so spiritual and so simple, and when a man sings it, it becomes too *terre à terre*. The rôle had been created in Monte Carlo in 1902 by a tenor named Maréchal, a charming man, but a man, not a boy. You needed to get the naïve spiritual beauty of an unspoiled child into that rôle, and you didn't get it in a man.

And I had just the body for it. I was built like a boy, and that's why I could sing a boy's rôle like the Jongleur. You see, I had no thighs, and I never had, and I don't have, any hips. Which makes it easy to understand why I could sing the Jongleur. Only a woman with a body like mine could give any semblance of realism to that rôle.

How did I do the *Jongleur?*

I danced my country dances. I played my fiddle. I juggled the three balls, and sometimes I used to let one go and make the people of the village laugh. It made them happier to think I was such a bad juggler. But I was always the boy, excited and awkward and adoring. And spiritual. Even now I meet people who remember me in that rôle and adored it above all my creations. And it is strange how it is generally the men who come to me, and the men of the Church, too, to tell me about it.

I sometimes think that I am really a very spiritual person. My greatest creations were spiritual—Thaïs, Jongleur, Marie Magdalène—even Mélisande—they touched the religious core. Most people don't think Mélisande was spiritual, but she was. And it was because of this deep spiritual side of me that I almost joined the Catholic Church. I think it began with *La Jongleur de Notre-Dame*, but I'm not sure.

I do know it was shortly after I had created the Jongleur at the Manhattan Opera House. I was back in Paris, and this religious thing was upon me. I went so far as to have a priest come to my apartment with his books to instruct me how to accept the faith. And I know to-day that I would have entered the Church if it hadn't found its way into the papers. Somehow it got out that Mary Garden was becoming a Catholic. It went all over Europe, and they even posted it up on bulletin boards in the theatres of Paris.

Of course, it reached Aberdeen in no time at all, and that was quite a scandal. One of my mother's sisters wrote to her, 'If Mary ever comes back to Aberdeen, she must not ring our doorbell!' This made no impression on me at all. I had made up my mind, and that was that; all my aunts and uncles in Aberdeen couldn't shake me. Then my mother wrote to me, and that was different.

'Mary,' she pleaded, 'will you keep your own religion as long as I live? After I'm dead you can do as you wish.'

And I stopped.

There was no crisis in my life when I made up my mind to become a Catholic. I just wanted it, and I was even thinking seriously of taking the veil. I remember going to a convent in France and finding out everything about it. Some years ago, a great friend of mine, Claire Sheridan, became a nun, and that made me think about it again. I'm not tempted any more, but it still interests me.

In my religion I have remained an Episcopalian. I take holy communion once a year on Easter Day. Throughout my life I have kept the simple religion Mother gave me when I was young. I never discuss life beyond death, as I have never found anyone in the world who knows any more about it than I do myself—which is nothing. . . .

I have often been asked to name my favourite rôle. They were all my favourites—Louise, Salomé, Mélisande, Thaïs, Jongleur; they were bound to me and I to them, and I lived with them and loved them equally. But perhaps I do cherish most the memory of that little boy who juggled and danced to show Our Lady that he, too, had a great love in his heart.

Many years after I created *Jongleur* in America, I was in Monte Carlo for my summer holiday. I went up to the golf links one afternoon, and there on the course a circular of some kind caught my eye. It asked for money for a tiny village in the mountains that wanted to build a statue as a memorial for their dead in the First World War. The idea interested me very much, and I took a spin up to that village, which was called Peille, and went to see the Mayor.

'I should like very much to help you build your monument,' I said. 'I'm going to America very soon, and when I come back, if you haven't found the money you need for the statue, I'll give it to you.'

On the way back to America I kept thinking of this promise of mine, and the more I thought the more Our Lady's little juggler came creeping into my mind. I decided that perhaps he was offering to help too, and this is how we did it together. After every performance of *Le Jongleur* that I gave in America, I put the cheque aside, and then at the end of the season I gathered all that money together and took it the following summer to the Mayor of Peille.

'If this isn't enough,' I said, 'please let me know.'

'Oh, I'm sure this will be more than enough, Mlle. Garden,' he said. 'How shall we ever thank you?'

'Have you got any idea yet what the statue is going to look like?' I asked.

'Why, yes,' he replied. 'A man in Nice has made us a small model of what we had in mind. I wish you would go to look at it.'

So I had the man bring the model to my villa at Monte Carlo, and it was perfectly beautiful. It showed a soldier standing just as he received death—he must have been shot, for he had his hand on his breast, and he was just going to fall over. It was very moving in its simplicity.

The memorial to the dead of the first World War
that Miss Garden gave to the village of Peille

FRANCO ALFANO

ITALO MONTEMEZZI

RICHARD STRAUSS

OSCAR HAMMERSTEIN

Four of the men who worked with Mary Garden

'Now you go ahead,' I said, 'and make that statue life-size, and then we're going to put it up on the side of the mountain at Peille.'

When I went back to Peille we began wondering where we were going to put that statue, because this little hamlet was built house upon house upon house all the way up the mountainside. There wasn't a flat spot anywhere. Well, in front of Peille another big string of mountains rose up, and between that and the village there was a valley, and in the valley, facing Peille, a great peak came right up out of nothing.

'We will put the statue on the top of that peak,' I said to the Mayor of Peille, pointing across the valley.

'But, Mlle., there are no roads, no anything around here,' he objected. 'We could never do it.'

'We shall make the roads,' I said.

So all the men of the village got to work, and in little time they built a road up the side of the mountain to this peak. Then they blasted the top of it off and made a great big platform, and when I again came back from America it was all ready, the platform, the statue, and everything.

The Mayor of Peille asked me to do the unveiling, which was to be on the fifteenth of June. Everybody for miles and miles around came up that afternoon and even the great French statesman, Painlevé, left Paris to be there. When the last call was given, all the women, wives, sisters, and sweethearts, of those men who had died began to cry and sob, and it was one of the most tragic scenes I ever went through.

There were fifty-eight names on the statue erected by this tiny mountain village. You would have thought that those fifty-eight men belonged to me, I was in such a paroxysm of crying. I stood there and could hardly pull the cord to bring the flag off. Finally, I got it down, and there was that beautiful statue—the most impressive moment in all my life. And I did it for the Jongleur, because he was a little boy who went from village to village, doing all his tricks of dancing and juggling for a few sous. I wanted his spirit to be there, and that's why I juggled and danced and sang the *Jongleur* for an entire season.

When they had done all their digging and building, they found, in that little town of Peille, that they had some money left over. After the unveiling, the Mayor came to me and said:

'This money belongs to you, Mlle. You gave us more than we needed.'

'I don't want it,' I said. 'I'm sure you can use it somehow.'

'To be honest with you, we can,' he said. 'We would like to build a public square for our festivals and dances.'

'Build your square, then,' I said. 'I'd be delighted. But where will you put it—on the mountainside?'

'We'll find a place,' the Mayor assured me, 'but we didn't want to do it before we unveiled the statue.'

They did find a place somewhere on the side of the mountain, dug it out, and made a beautiful square for all their wonderful summer entertainments. They called it Mary Garden Square, and the road they built up to the peak on which the statue was perched they called Mary Garden Road.

A few months later I read a letter in the Paris edition of the *New York Herald*, from a man who had just come back to Paris from Peille. This gentleman had seen the square and the road, and what puzzled him was 'why Mary Garden had put all that money and love into that little village.' I didn't bother to answer the letter, because any man asking that kind of question would never understand the feeling I had put into the statue. My little Jongleur would never have asked. . . .

And this reminds me that I once created another boy, a very different kind of boy, also in an opera of Jules Massenet. This was *Chérubin*. We presented it for the first time in Monte

Carlo, and later Albert Carré brought it to the Opéra-Comique, where I sang it again. He was no Jongleur, this little rascal of the time of Louis XV, beautifully dressed and running after the ladies and fighting duels over them.

*Chérubin* brought me into contact with Massenet, who used to have an office in the publishing house of Heugel. That was where I went twice a week to discuss the part with him. I'm afraid I never cared for Massenet. I know how much the French adore him, and the French know how much I adore them. Massenet was the yes-man *par excellence*. Everything was 'all right, fine, perfect.' He was always gushing. He could say the most marvellous things to someone, pay the greatest compliments in the world. And the moment the door closed behind that someone he would turn to the others in the room and say something quite the contrary.

Then he would write endless letters dripping with the most sickening kind of sentiment, everything underlined, not once, but two, three, and four times. He hadn't the character I liked in a man, and he hadn't the genius of Debussy, not by a long shot.

But I enjoyed doing that little Chérubin of his, with his pranks and peccadilloes. It wasn't *Jongleur*, but there was a certain dash and exuberance to the rôle, and again, thanks to that body of mine, I was the perfect boy. . . .

One day at Monte Carlo I had the strangest compliment paid to me after a performance of *Chérubin*. I was in my dressing-room, still in my Louis XV costume and wig, when there was a knock on the door. I opened it, and there on his knees, with a bouquet of flowers in his right hand, was one of the greatest writers of France. Still on his knees, he crept into the room, and with his head and hands shaking, he offered me the flowers—a very strange tribute indeed—because this man was bringing the bouquet of flowers not to Mary Garden, but to the boy Chérubin.

To return to Maurice Renaud. I worshipped him as an artist, but I never cared for him personally. He wasn't too nice on the stage, at least not to me. I always had to look out for him.

There was our performance of the *Jongleur*, for instance. I was this little boy of fifteen, with that sweet, pure piety of his. I was so excited by my faith. I remember how in that ecstasy of devotion I would get close to Renaud, and he would push my foot away with his, not to let me get any further and crowd his part of the stage.

Renaud could be charming and stimulating, and no one knew better than I did what a magnificent artist he was, and I was grateful for his having suggested *Jongleur* for me. But I always had a funny little feeling about him—as if he were always saying, 'It's me.'

On my left hand, whenever I go out, I wear two rings made of very thick platinum. One of them is set with a ruby and an emerald, and the other is set with an emerald and a sapphire. They are heavy, handsome rings, and I'm never dressed if I don't have them on my hand. I don't remember ever leaving my rings behind—not since they were given to me by Mr. Andersen, the fascinating—and tragic—Dane in my life. He brought them back with him from one of his trips to St. Petersburg, where he had purchased them from the famous jewellery house of Fabergé.

My story of Mr. Andersen begins in 1907, while I was creating my last rôle at the Opéra-Comique—*Aphrodite*. I met him in Paris at a tea given by one of my friends, and I liked him at once. Perhaps of all the men I have ever known he was the most fascinating—not so much in a physical way, though he was extremely good-looking. What enchanted me about him was the way he adored all the arts and talked about them. I believe I learned more from him about such things as paintings and tapestries than from anyone else I have ever known. We would tour the museums together, and there wasn't an *objet d'art* about which he couldn't tell an exciting and revealing story. I used to have him up to my apartment, and I still remember the endless hours of talk we spent together. We were never lovers—oh, no! You see, he fascinated me and troubled me at the same time.

Being such a great authority on the arts, Mr. Andersen was engaged by the best art dealers of Paris to visit people in various countries who possessed beautiful things and because of some shift in their fortunes were eager to dispose of them at a good price. He would bring these things back to Paris and receive his commission. I knew about these trips to distant places, but I soon began to notice something odd about Mr. Andersen.

He would come to my house, and then, after several hours of wonderful conversation, abruptly jump to his feet as if something had stung him and announce that he had to be somewhere else. Once, in the middle of a talk about Leonardo da Vinci, he suddenly said, 'Good-bye, Mary, I've got to go to Berlin. The Kaiser has sent for me.' Another time, we were sitting at tea and he leaped to his feet, seized his hat, and declared that the Czar was awaiting him in St. Petersburg. I thought it very queer, but for some reason I never doubted him.

Then one day my young Dane came to me, grave and frowning.

'Mary,' he said in a solemn tone, 'something extraordinary happened this morning while I was taking my bath. I turned on the cold water and a rat as big as my arm came out of the tap.'

'But how in God's name could a rat that size come out of a tiny tap?' I asked.

'I don't know, but it did,' he answered gloomily.

I was now beginning to be mystified—and a bit frightened—by my Mr. Andersen. The conversation about the odd occurrence in his bathroom took place just about the time I had signed up for Mr. Hammerstein's Manhattan Opera House. When I told Mr. Andersen about my new contract, he was frantic.

'Mary,' he said, 'before you go to America, let's get married.'

'No,' I said.

'Why not?'

'I'm sorry,' I said wearily, 'I don't want to marry you or anybody, now or ever.'

'Maybe you'll marry me if I come to America.'

'Not even there.'

'Whether you like it or not, I'm coming to America.'

'It will be quite useless, I assure you.'

'I'm going to ask your father for your hand.'

I laughed in his face.

'I'm quite capable of giving my own hand, thank you. You don't have to go to Papa, my big, handsome Dane. Stop acting like a child. I'm never going to marry—never! Do you understand?'

'Mary,' he went on, 'I've had no peace since I met you.'

'But we've had beautiful times and talks together.'

'If I could only get you out of here,' he said, touching his head, 'and put you somewhere else, I'd be at peace, Mary.'

'I shall never marry you,' I repeated firmly, 'no matter where you put me.'

That didn't stop my Dane, however. Shortly after I arrived in America, I received a cable from him that he was leaving for New York. So I went up to Father and said, 'Papa, there's a Danish gentleman coming from Europe to ask you for my hand.'

'That should be fun,' Father said. 'Let's have him over to dinner when he arrives. Your mother and I will subject him to the closest examination.'

Well, we had Mr. Andersen for dinner, and he hadn't been there more than a half hour when Mother and Father took me aside. Father said, 'He's a queer fish,' and Mother chimed in, 'But so charming!' So, after dinner, while we were sitting around talking, Mr. Andersen clasped his hands together and looked at Father:

'Mr. Garden, I'd like to marry your daughter.'

Father put on a very stern face.

'What does my daughter say to that, Mr. Andersen?'

'Papa, I don't want to marry anyone,' I burst out before Mr. Andersen could answer.

And then I began to notice something strange about Mr. Andersen. He was growing fidgety, constantly looking at the clock, and making strange, nervous gestures with his hands and face.

'Have you another engagement?' I asked him ever so sweetly.

'No,' he answered, embarrassed. 'I'm waiting for my valet to come and get me.'

At about ten o'clock, Mr. Andersen's valet arrived, and the two departed.

Two days after that, we were sitting at dinner, Father, Mother, my sister Amy, and I, still discussing Mr. Andersen's odd behaviour, when the telephone rang. I went to answer it. It was the manager of a nearby hotel.

'Miss Garden,' he said, 'we have a gentleman in one of our rooms who says he is dying and he is calling for you. Would you kindly come over to the hotel? His name is Andersen.'

So I went back to my dinner and communicated the news to Father and Mother.

'Papa dear,' I said, 'will you go over to the hotel and see if Mr. Andersen is really dying?'

'I will not,' said Father emphatically.

'I'll go,' volunteered Amy.

'You angel!' I cried. 'Amy, if he's dying, you'll 'phone me and I'll hurry over.'

So Amy went over to the hotel and asked for Mr. Andersen's room number, and when she opened the door there he was, propped up in bed, with two photographs pinned to his pyjamas, the one at his breast being a picture of me and the one below it a picture of his father.

Not knowing what to think, Amy stood there mystified, and then she saw something else—on a table at the side of his bed were what must have been hundreds and hundreds of dollars in gold coin. Before Amy could mutter a word of greeting, Mr. Anderson raised an arm and pointed to the table.

'Miss Garden,' he said, 'all that gold is yours if you will do me a favour.'

'What is it you want me to do, Mr. Andersen?'

'Get me some cocaine!'

Amy saw at once what the man was, and when she spoke to the doctor, it all became clear what had happened the night Mr. Andersen dined with us. He got fidgety waiting for his valet, because the man had been down to the docks to get cocaine from the ships that were coming in, and there was no cocaine to be had, then or later. Poor Mr. Andersen then became like a madman. He wasn't dying—it was just that craving driving him insane.

So, my big handsome Dane left America without seeing me again. When I went back to Paris I never laid eyes on him again till the first year of the First World War. My sister and I were seated in the front row of the balcony of a movie in Paris, looking down at the people coming in, when we saw two nurses enter, holding the arms of what appeared to be a paralyzed old man, shrivelled up like a dried alligator. They were taking him to the front row. 'Look!' I gasped to Amy, 'that's Mr. Andersen!'

What an absolute skeleton he had become, rotted through

and through with drugs! Very soon after that I heard that he died, an old wreck of a man at thirty-seven. So all those hurried farewells, those calls from the Czar and the Kaiser, the rat coming out of the water tap—it was the talk of a fearfully drugged mind, and I never saw the truth till I came to America. What a connoisseur of the arts that man was, and what a brain he let crumble from vice! Yet shouldn't a woman with the intelligence I pride myself on possessing have said to herself, 'Look here, this man isn't normal'?

I was never in love with Mr. Andersen and I never for a moment thought of marrying him—or anybody else. When I sit and think that I can be alone in this world, that I can go into my bedroom and sleep alone, it gives me a shiver of freedom. That is my ecstasy, that knowledge of freedom. I've seen others throw their lives away on vices of one kind or another, the men and the women, but none of those vices ever touched me. Sometimes I wonder why I've never been crazy about men like so many other women. Maybe the men have been too enthusiastic about me, and then, I like to do my own thinking, not their thinking—*mine*.

Besides the great intellectual stimulation he gave me, I owe Mr. Andersen several mementos of his feeling for me. The rings on my left hand were the first. Another was a small maquette of Houdon's bust of Voltaire. The last, which I shall mention in a moment, was a little more characteristic of my incredible Dane.

During one of his visits to St. Petersburg, Mr. Andersen was dining with some rich friends when he saw a beautiful replica of Houdon's *Voltaire*. Of course, he immediately thought of possessing it. When he was told by his hostess that it had originally been made for Catherine the Great, there was no stopping him.

'I don't leave this house until I get that bust,' he announced.

So he used all his charm on this lady, sending her flowers

and sweets. I don't know what else he did, but she was enchanted with him, and one day he asked, 'Do I buy the bust?' Of course she gave in. On his return to Paris, he gave it to me. I've still got it, and I've carried that magnificent old sinner everywhere with me.

Toward the end of the First World War, as the Germans were drawing near Paris again, the British Embassy instructed us to move on to the South. So, with my sister Aggie hugging my jewels, I took my *Voltaire* and we departed for Monte Carlo. I shall never forget that excursion. We were fifty-eight hours on the train, and all the way to Monte Carlo I held on to *Voltaire*, and when I wasn't holding him I laid him very tenderly to sleep in a hammock.

During my last season at the Opéra-Comique, I received word from Mr. Andersen that he was sending me another little souvenir from Russia. I gave it no further thought. Well, I returned home one afternoon and there on the floor of my kitchen, in an enormous crate, with its soft sweet eyes peeping through, was a tiny brown bear.

'What in God's name shall I do with this animal in my apartment?' I said to my maid.

But we fell in love with the little creature at once; it was so tender you wanted to take it right up in your arms. We fed it a bunch of grapes, and then sat back and looked at him, wondering where we could find him a home.

'There are the guards of the Bois, Madame,' suggested my maid; 'they might take him.'

'Why, of course,' I cried, 'that would be just the place for the little fellow.'

In the Bois outside Paris there is a spot where these workmen have their beautiful little homes, every one of them with a large, well-kept garden. Often the families of these guards keep dogs for ladies who leave the city in the summer. I went to one of these men and asked him if he would take care of my little Russian bear, for a fee, of course. He said he would. My maid and I then brought him the bear, and he was set up in a pen in the garden of a little house in the Bois. I used to go to see him every day and feed him grapes and meal, which he loved. My little bear grew a bit that summer —it didn't seem to be very much—and then I left for America.

On my return to Paris two years later, I was immediately called upon by the prefect of police.

'Madame has a bear in the Bois?' he asked very gravely.

'Why, yes,' I said, relieved it was nothing more than that.

'That bear must be removed at once,' he said.

'But the little creature is harming no one,' I protested.

'*Little!*' he echoed. 'Madame, your little creature has grown into a dangerous and ferocious animal. He is much too large for that garden, and his growls have been keeping half of Paris awake.'

'What am I to do?'

'He must be removed from the Bois—or destroyed.'

I was aghast.

'Oh, Monsieur, you couldn't think of doing that?'

'I'm sorry, Mademoiselle, I must think of the sleep and safety of the people of Paris.'

'What do you suggest, Monsieur?'

'The zoo. But you must handle the whole matter yourself.'

So I went to the zoo, which is just out of the Bois, and I asked them if they would accept a Russian bear.

'With the greatest pleasure,' they answered. 'But you must bring him yourself. We cannot provide the transportation.'

'But have you a cage large enough?'

'You bring us the bear, Mademoiselle, and we will worry about the cage.'

Bringing the bear was quite another story. While I was pondering my next step, I suddenly remembered that a friend of mine in Paris had a huge dogcart. I went to him with my problem, and he was perfectly sweet about wanting to help. So, one beautiful moonlight night we went out to the Bois and saw this great big monster tearing at his chains in the middle of the garden behind the guard's house. We got two men from the Bois, and the four of us went up to him and tied him up in ropes at the mouth and feet. Then we hiked him into the dogcart—how we did it, I shall never know—and tied him to the back of it. The rest was easy. The zoo was only fifteen minutes away.

I shall never forget the picture of us moving along the Bois in the moonlight with a Russian bear tightly roped up behind us. When we arrived at the zoo, the men took him off the cart and put him into a large cage. I know he was there before the Second World War broke out, and if he is alive to-day, he is still there, big, brown, and ferocious, and, I'm quite certain, happy. And that's the story of Mr. Andersen's little souvenir from Russia—and how it grew.

## The Hammerstein Era Ends

I WAS three years in New York, and I remember I had to be very careful because the weather was still against me. There was no man in my life then, none, at any rate, that I can recall; it was just work, work, work. I stayed only one year at my sister's flat on East Fifty-sixth Street. Then Mother and Father took it, and I moved into the newly-built Ritz-Carlton, where I was among the very first guests. The manager hung up my picture in his office, because he told me he was certain it would bring him and the hotel luck. And the first big affair held at the Ritz-Carlton was the luncheon I gave for my sister Aggie when she married Edward de Witt Walsh.

I didn't sing at Aggie's luncheon that day—for one very good reason. I tried never to sing anywhere but on the stage. That was my world as an artist, and I never saw any point in stepping out of it and into another. And while I was singing at the opera I was never seen in a restaurant or night club. I always felt that if people wanted to see me, they could buy a ticket to the opera. I wanted to be absolutely unknown outside the theatre. I so hated to be pointed out and pawed and have everything going out of me that belonged in the theatre. I could never bear to have people stare at me and say, 'Oh, that's Mary Garden, look at her!'

'Sing me a bit of *Thaïs*, Mary,' Father said to me one day.

'Papa,' I replied, 'I'm going to sing *Thaïs* at the opera house next week. Hear me then.'

He laughed, and understood.

And I never practised in the hotel or flat where I was staying. I always managed to have a studio. I didn't want to bother people and I didn't want them to bother me. My studio hours were from ten to twelve in the morning. In New York my studio was located in the Manhattan Opera House on West Thirty-fourth Street, and in Chicago I used a room in the big Auditorium. Wherever I went my first concern was to get myself a studio.

I used to study about one hour a day, sometimes a little more. That was my schedule throughout my career, and I stuck to it religiously. I don't believe in people singing from morning to night, practising or getting ready for a performance. One hour a day is worth seven hours of the same thing over and over again. I've known singers, singers who were good, mind you, who had no reason to be anxious about their voice and technique, do *Butterfly* twice in one day, once in their homes or studios, in the morning or afternoon, and then at night in the theatre. What a waste of time!

My first half hour in the studio was usually at ten. I did nothing but scales. Then at eleven I took my opera score and worked on it for another half hour, once in a while an hour, but never more. That was when I was not scheduled to sing at night. The days I sang I did next to nothing in the way of preparation. Before I went on the stage I sang one or two scales in my dressing-room, and *that was all*.

I rarely went to dinners. When I was invited out, I always wrote back to my hostess asking if I could come after dinner, because I think dinners are a ruination, though I suppose a man has to eat his dinner. To me the table never meant anything. Eating and drinking have never had any fascination for me, thank goodness. And that, of course, helped keep me fit and slender.

I began the day with my *café au lait*, two cups. I confess I couldn't do without that. But no bread, no butter, no eggs, no nothing. And then I had a nice lunch at one, and that was very plain. I like eggs, am fond of shellfish, but loathe every other kind of fish. I also love everything inside an animal and nothing outside the animal except the tail. I adore oxtail like nothing in the world. I had my two green vegetables, but I never touched a salad in my life. Then a dessert, which I would take provided it was always ice cream, vanilla or chocolate. I never had coffee at lunch, and I never cared much for cakes and pastries. In the evening I usually had—and have—a cup of tea or coffee, at about seven o'clock, and nothing else.

When I sang, I added only one thing to my diet. Upon finishing my performance I went home, took a hot bath, and drank down a large glass of hot milk, with ten drops of iodine in it. A doctor in Paris told me early in my career that that was a good thing after any great exertion, and the finest tonic of all for toning up the nervous system. I have adhered to this diet of one meal a day since I began my career at the Opéra-Comique in 1900. I still eat that way, and I have never changed. Very few people can live as I did, and I don't expect them to.

I never had any real illnesses—except the usual things that singers have—like colds, laryngitis, bronchitis—but nothing that needed a hospital. My mother never had a doctor in the house, and she lived to ninety-three. So I must take after her.

I have often been asked about my clothes, and I suppose I might say something about them now. Most of them were made in Aberdeen. I have two ensembles, a red and a green. In the green ensemble there is a tartan skirt, and I take a colour out of the tartan to make my short jacket. I wear a white blouse with a high collar, and pearls wrapped around the collar. A red velvet hat matches this ensemble, Then I have Scotch walking shoes. You can't walk with high heels in the streets of Aberdeen because everything is granite. Of course, I also have my high-heeled shoes, which I wear in the evening.

In my red ensemble I have a Stuart-tartan skirt and red coat, with the red taken out of the tartan again. The buttons on both jackets should not be metal as they are on mine, but leather, to be genuinely Scotch. With this ensemble I wear a red hat with cock feathers. Both these hats are from Suzy's in Paris.

I love tailored suits and always feel dressed that way. That has been my morning wear since *Louise*. And when I returned to America and gave my talks, that was still my morning wear, my tailored suit.

I always wore tailored suits in Paris, sometimes navy blue or black, always with a short jacket and skirt. That was every single day. I have never in my life worn a dress in the morning. I sometimes wear a dress in the afternoon, and of course I dress in the evening.

I spoke earlier of my pearls. Most of my beautiful jewels are in Scotland, and most of them were gifts from my many admirers. When I was speaking in Town Hall in December, 1949, a lady came up to me and said:

'Excuse me, Miss Garden, but are those the jewels the Czar gave you?'

'Oh, just some of them,' I said.

And, of course, I never saw the Czar in my life.

The little red, blue, and purple stripes of silk on my things are my decorations. I wear them because in France you're expected to wear your decorations.

The first part of my insignia, the red, is the Legion of Honour. That was given to me when I was director of the Chicago Opera because of my services to French music.

The second, which is white with little blue stripes and a

star, is the Medaille de la Reconnaissance. That was awarded me for everything I did in the First World War.

The purple stripe next to it is a decoration from the Minister of Beaux Arts, given to me for my 'creations' in French opera.

The fourth one, which is red like the first, was bestowed on me by Serbia in the First World War.

When you wear your decorations in France you don't have to open a bag while travelling. I was in a coach one day with an Englishwoman loaded with furs. The men came in and examined every bit of her luggage. Then they turned to me and saw the decorations on my jacket. They just clicked their heels and saluted and left.

And my voice? What was it like? It depended on what I happened to be singing. It was a brilliant voice and it cut through an orchestra like steel. It was both big and piercing. I did what I liked with my voice; I was always its master and never its slave. It obeyed me, and not I it. And I used it as freely as a painter uses his brush. But, then, I never thought of my voice as distinct from the rest of me. It was never a thing apart. My voice, my acting, my whole personality were one. And it wasn't, 'Come and *hear* Mary Garden'; it was, 'Come and *see* Mary Garden.' People would say, 'Have you *seen* Mary Garden in such and such an opera?' I was a singing actress, not a singer.

My voice ranged two octaves, from C to C. It never gave me any trouble. I mean, I never had to rest because it was tired—never, never, never. At all times, my voice was absolutely at my command. Whether the critics liked it or whether they didn't made no difference to me. I liked it; my public liked it. It was the critics who differed. But criticism never meant a thing to me. When I sang my rôles and then read what they had to say, it never made any impression on me, good or bad. That's the only way to be when one is before the public.

And it didn't make any difference what I sang or where I sang. I always had my audience, from the beginning to the very last day, in my hand—just as I have it now, speaking. Then it was Salomé, Thaïs, Mélisande; now it is *me, myself*. I feel that same immediate contact with the people out there. We seem to know one another at once, as if we could never have been strangers. That was how it was with my singing: I made them feel close to me, and they made me feel close to them. And my voice was never just the voice of Mary Garden. It was the voice Mélisande might have had, or Salomé, or Thaïs. That may have baffled the critics—that it was never the same voice.

As I remember those years in New York, it was just one unbroken cycle of work, very little social life, but that never interested me much anywhere at any time in my life, and no 'romance' that I can now recall, certainly nothing serious. My life was so much more than that, and I never thought that having an affair with a man was a terribly important thing. I never *really* loved anybody. I had a fondness for men, yes, but very little passion, and *no need*; that's it, perhaps, I never had any real need for it. But nobody in God's green earth is ever going to believe that. I'm just a peculiar person, I suppose. As I often said to Mother, 'Nobody will ever believe what my private life was really like.' Out of the theatre my life was simplicity itself. I'm so different from women in general. I've seen this thing, call it passion or call it sex or call it love, bring pain and disillusionment to men and women.

My career never gave me pain. It never gave me anything but joy, and what man could give that? I've known hundreds of women to go through the other thing and suffer, oh, how they suffered! But they don't understand a great friendship with a man; they don't understand it. I had one such friendship in my life, and it was the sweetest thing I ever found on earth. . . .

One day shortly after we produced *Le Jongleur de Notre-Dame*, I heard the heartbreaking news that our conductor, Campanini, was leaving us. There is supposed to have been an awful fight over the orchestra. I think it was something like this: Mrs. Mackay, who had been behind the Manhattan Opera from the start and had brought over so much support from other Metropolitan boxholders, was giving a great soirée in her house. It seems that without asking Mr. Hammerstein's permission she engaged Mr. Campanini and the orchestra to play there. Now, that may have started the fight between Mr. Hammerstein and Campanini, I'm not at all sure, but Mr. Campanini packed up his things and went to Chicago with Harold McCormick and his wife, who was John D. Rockefeller's daughter.

I remained with Mr. Hammerstein for a short time after Campanini's departure. But something had gone out of the company. What had been brilliant and sparkling was now flat and routine. I sang *Sapho* and *Grisélidis*, both by Massenet, but there was no more enthusiasm in the house. Campanini had kept the company at an artistic peak, and now that he was gone it became just plain dull and I never went back. I returned to Paris late the spring with a contract for the following season, but I was no longer bound to it because by then Mr. Hammerstein was out, too. He had sold his Manhattan Opera Company to the Metropolitan Opera House, and they sold it to Chicago, and thus came to birth the Chicago Grand Opera Company.

So ended the great era of Oscar Hammerstein. I was in Europe when the end came, and I never knew the real reason for Mr. Hammerstein's decision. They said at the time that he was a sick man. Mr. Hammerstein was a proud and arrogant person. It was against his nature to bend to anyone, but he was a theatrical genius, and in his time of need he should have had the support of everyone interested in the development of great art. This support he failed to get, and I believe it broke his spirit. Oscar Hammerstein's obsession was to see an opera house in every great American city from the Atlantic to the Pacific. He was blessed, or cursed, with a frantic ambition. Had the resources been there to carry through his magnificent plans for American opera, we would have seen something!

# I Go to Chicago

ONE day the tenor Andreas Dippel came to visit me at my apartment in Paris. Besides being a singer, Dippel had great skill as an operatic manager, and for a while had assisted Giulio Gatti-Casazza at the Metropolitan.

'Miss Garden,' he said, 'I'm now general manager of the Chicago Opera Company, and I want you to come with us as our leading soprano.'

'What about the repertory?' I asked. 'Will I have my French operas?'

'All you want,' he said. 'McCormick took over almost the entire Manhattan organization, after Hammerstein sold out his interests to the Metropolitan.'

'That means our French repertory isn't entirely ruined and lost,' I said.

'Far from it,' said Dippel. 'And you'll have the same people singing with you. How about continuing your old contract with us?'

'What will you pay me?'

'The same as Hammerstein—fifteen hundred dollars a performance,' he said.

'Oh, no you don't!' I said. 'You'll give me two thousand.'

'We can't afford it.'

'I'm sorry; then I won't come.'

Mr. Dippel looked very unhappy for a moment, then he gave a deep sigh and said:

'You win, Mary, two thousand dollars it is.'

I asked for the additional five hundred dollars because it was hard work and well worth it. I believe any real artist of the theatre or the screen is worth anything he can get. They none of them can be paid enough for what they have to give. If you want good people for your company you've got to be prepared to pay them. Later when I took over the Chicago company, I offered Chaliapin a contract for thirty-five hundred dollars a performance, with twenty-five performances guaranteed. That was a contract worth leaving Europe for.

'What would you like your Chicago début to be in, Mary?' Dippel asked me.

'*Pelléas et Mélisande*,' I answered without hesitation.

'Good,' he said, 'we'll make it for some time in November.'

'With Campanini to conduct?'

'With Campanini to conduct.'

Dippel's visit came some time late in May. I was then singing with the Opéra, of which André Messager was director. Messager had come back into my life, but only as a friend and an associate. We were now good colleagues, working in the greatest harmony and instilling into the new company something of the same spirit that had gone into the Opéra-Comique in the early days of *Pelléas*.

Performances at the Opéra were on a Monday, Wednesday, Friday, and Saturday nights, besides a Sunday *matinée*. At the Manhattan Opera House we had opera every night except Sunday, with a Saturday *mantinée*, and this schedule was the same in Chicago. My contract with the Chicago Opera called for two performances a week, and the season was to last twelve weeks. Then we had ten extra weeks of touring.

I continued singing at the Opéra. Then I went to Monte Carlo for a short holiday and returned to Paris for a few more performances with Messager. You see, the Opéra didn't shut down for the summer.

Finally, I left for America, arriving in Chicago early in November, 1910, my début being scheduled for some time later that month. I registered at the Blackstone Hotel, and there I remained for the twenty years that I was in Chicago. I immediately got myself a studio in the Chicago Auditorium, and Isaac Van Grove became my accompanist. I was introduced to my new boss, Harold McCormick, and his wife, and when I met my dear old friend Campanini, I just took him into my arms and hugged and hugged him. What a man, and what an artist! And how he loved Debussy! How delighted he was at the prospect of doing *Pelléas et Mélisande* with me again!

'Mary,' he said, 'I could never conduct that opera for anybody but you.'

'If it were up to me, I would sing it for you alone,' I replied.

We then did the first *Pelléas* in Chicago, and both the critics and the audience took to it at once. The performance was even more brilliant than it had been at the Manhattan, and the response was exhilarating to all of us. The Chicago press was so wonderful about it all. I remember one of the critics wrote: 'Why do they say that Mary Garden can't sing? We have never heard such beautiful singing.' And I loved so much being the first to bring something new to that exciting city. They had nobody to compare me with, and they're always comparing everybody with everybody else in America.

Not long after that, Campanini was made director of the Chicago Grand Opera Company. That was something he had never been at the Manhattan; Hammerstein was that, and Campanini had only been musical director. Now he controlled everything—contracts, repertory, casting, and what artistic glory he brought to the company—and to Chicago!

During all of those years in Chicago I had very little social life; but then I never cared for social life, and oh, how it bored me and bores me still when I've got to go to dinners! Chicago, for me, meant work. I tried to bring as many new things to Chicago as I could, and there was a wonderful audience for them. We never had to worry about that in Chicago.

Among the creations that excited me most was that of Fiora in Montemezzi's *L'Amore dei tre re*. I shall never forget how Marinuzzi, who followed Campanini as conductor of our company, always came up to me after the performance and said, 'Brava, Garden!' So I suppose I was good as Fiora. How I loved that opera! I sang it in the original Italian, the only opera I ever sang in that language, and I adored every word of it. The summer before I created the part I worked on it in Monte Carlo with my accompanist Bartholemy. He came to see me every day to give me the Italian. I had no difficulty at all with the language; on the contrary, I found it easier to sing than French—the vowels are so beautiful in Italian.

Fiora! What a fascinating rôle! Her secret was that she was in love with the young king, and there was that great scene with her lover. The husband, you know, suspected something. When he went off to war, he told her that she was to stand on a high part of the castle and wave to him until she could no longer see him.

Fiora got tired of waiting, and when she had stopped, the other young king slipped in, and we had this great love scene together. Then the blind old king came in, and I put him out. But the old man wouldn't rest till he knew the name of the man I had been with. I wouldn't tell him, so he strangled me, and as I lay on the bench dead, my husband, who was wondering why the waving had stopped, came back. And when he found me dead there was a great scene with the old king.

Finally, the blind old king picked me up and put me on

his back and carried me into the castle, and in the last act I lay dead in the chapel. I was the only Fiora who ever lay there, because they usually put in a chorus girl or somebody to play dead for the prima donna. But I wanted to do the whole opera. I lay there, and the old king put poison on my mouth, so that when my lover came in he would kiss me and die, and he would then know who the man was that I loved. But instead of the lover the son came in—my husband—and he kissed me long as I lay there, and died. And the old man knew.

In the earlier scene with my lover, Montemezzi put in music for a long embrace. We were supposed to lie in each other's arms, my lover and I, and then I tore myself away because the old king broke in. And the only reason the blind king got hold of me was because my lover had left me and I was mad with passion. Virgilio Lazzari was the blind old king, and what a fight we two used to have in the strangling scene!

'Mary, look at my hands!' he used to say to me after that scene.

They were covered with scratches from my nails. How I used to fight for my life in that opera! Lazzari killed me, but what a struggle it was, and how I loved and adored it! I lived and died every minute of it. What a scrap that was, so real you'd have thought he had really killed me! Then Lazzari would pick me up, throw me on his back, and carry me off the stage.

One day Lazzari flung me on his back, and instead of lying there dead and still, I had to move my head to one side and whisper in his ear:

'Lazzari, for God's sake, change my position! I'm dying of pain.'

But he didn't budge, maybe because he didn't understand me. When the curtain went down he lowered me on the steps; I could hardly get up. He must have put me wrong on his back, for something in his shoulders went right into my back, and did I suffer! I wanted to scream and I was supposed to be dead. The audience couldn't help noticing that something was wrong. I didn't take any curtain calls that afternoon and of course they talked about it in the papers the following day.

That was a Saturday *matinée*, and, I remember I went to a tea after that and I had to walk into the drawing-room with a cane. The pain stayed with me for more than a week. I had to have massage and all sorts of things done to my back. After that the scene with the blind old king always made me nervous, because I knew that if Lazzari put me on that part of his shoulders again, I wouldn't be able to stand it. My, that man was powerful; how easily he picked me up from the bench and threw me on his back! He was such a dear, though, and the best of them all in that rôle.

The tenor doing the part of my young lover got ill for one performance of *L'Amore dei tre re*, and I had to sing it with a Spanish tenor in the company. I don't remember his name. We were standing in the wings before I went on, and the Spaniard said to me:

'I haven't had my cigar to-day, Miss Garden.'

'What's that to me?' I asked, puzzled.

He looked very embarrassed.

'Well, I have to kiss you for a long while in that scene, and I thought . . .'

I stopped him.

'Nobody kisses me on the stage—never,' I said.

Imagine, he hadn't smoked his cigar because he thought he was going to kiss me for ten minutes—actually kiss me! Well, he didn't and he was very sad, because he could have had his cigar that day; he could have had ten cigars, and it would have made no difference to me. I never let any man kiss me on the stage—not once. I always pretended that I was being kissed, and that's very easy to do. During those ten minutes in *L'Amore dei tre re* I always turned my back to the audience, and nobody knew the difference. I wasn't going to allow any man to kiss me that long, not in public.

I had had one very nasty experience on the stage of the Opéra-Comique many years before. Since it has to do with kissing I suppose I may just as well tell it here. There was a handsome French tenor singing *La Traviata* with me. While I was saying good-bye to him in the second act, he completely forgot himself. I suppose he prided himself on being a ladies' man and thought he could do anything he wanted with a *prima donna.* Maybe he could with the others, I don't know, but he couldn't with me. Oh, how disgusting it was! There I was with my back to the audience, pretending to receive that farewell kiss, and before I knew what he was up to, that wretched creature had his tongue half-way down my throat. If we hadn't been before an audience, I'd have slapped his face. Instead of that, I went into M. Carré's office after the performance.

'That man must never sing with me again!' I said.

I must have looked very serious, for Carré never asked me why, though he may have suspected, knowing the man better than I did and perhaps having had other complaints about him from the others, but he never let him sing in any opera with me again. What made me so furious was that he thought he could do that vile thing in public and get away with it. I'll say now that I never, never fell in love with any singer who was supposed to be my lover on the stage. They none of them meant anything more to me than friends or colleagues in the same company. When the curtain came down, I was no longer the woman they loved.

To return to Fiora . . . I created the rôle the same way I created all the others—as I felt it. I didn't *study* Fiora; I *was* Fiora. Some people think you have to have some sort of life of your own that is like the life of the rôle you're playing in order to do it right. That's nonsense. You can portray a character completely without having anything at all parallel to her in your private life. You never bring your own life into a rôle, because what happens to you personally has nothing to do with that rôle. When I was on the stage I was Fiora, not Mary Garden, who lived at the Blackstone Hotel.

Every one of these women I sang had a special quality of her own, and in every one of them I had a different singing voice. In Fiora the quality was passion and terror, and I put these things in my voice. I should like to say again and again that I used my voice the same way a painter uses his brush. He throws the colours he wants on to his canvas. I threw colour into my rôles in the different tones that I sang.

Fiora was full of the red passion of Italy. Salomé was vice personified; the Jongleur was sexless; Louise was *l'amour libre*; Mélisande was mystery, secrecy; Sapho was the cocotte of Paris, common, and I made my voice that. Aphrodite was a cold, brilliant diamond, her quality being that she wanted what she couldn't get. There was no love in her at all, just longing for the unattainable. She wanted the pearls from the statue in the temple, and she had to have them before she would go to that man's studio and give herself to him. And when she got them she faced him in a gesture of surrender. But he turned to her and said: 'I don't want you.' And suddenly she was like a tigress. There my voice turned wild and dark with anger, the same voice that had been cold as a diamond.

Then, when I had to die, because they found the religious jewels on me, and they brought the poison, my voice became that of a child. I was afraid to die, and I put a child's fear into my voice. The hesitation I had before I put that cup of poison to my lips! What a beautiful death! Can I ever forget that moment?

# My Season as an Impresario

THERE was another rôle I loved in my Chicago years, and that was Monna Vanna, the music by Henri Février, after the book by Maurice Maeterlinck. How I lived every moment of it! This is the way it went. Our part of the country had lost the war, and our enemy, Prinzivalle, to give us peace, demanded that I, Monna Vanna, come to his tent nude under a coat. My husband Guido was furious when he received the offer.

'I will never let you go!' he shouted.

'I am going,' I said resolutely.

I flung a cloak over my nudity and went to this man's tent, this Prinzivalle whom I didn't know. I entered the tent with dignity and fear—until finally I saw that the enemy was a childhood friend of mine, Ginello.

And my voice became the merest whisper when I said, '*Tu est* Ginello?'—a whisper of surprise—and all my thoughts went back to when I was a child. I couldn't sing and I couldn't speak at that moment. I gave only a whisper, and yet my voice went all over the house. There was nothing *vocal* in it, no resonance at all. I just threw those words out in a hush, a dramatic hush, and they went to everybody in the house. The surprise of meeting Ginello just took my breath away. I could have shouted my surprise and spoiled it completely. What a situation! and how beautiful! I knew then there was no harm coming to this man's tent, and I said:

'Ginello, you will return with me to my husband.'

And we left the stage to come back in the third act to Guido, and then my voice was something else again. For my husband wouldn't believe I had not given myself to Prinzivalle. When I saw that he was going to kill Ginello, my voice, which had been a hush, became full and tense with drama. I turned to my husband defiantly.

'I've been lying!' I shouted. 'He did take me!'

And then he believed me, just like any man, always ready to believe what he wants to believe.

'Give me the key of the dungeon!' I demanded.

And I let Ginello out, my childhood friend who had risked his life and shown such generosity of spirit, and the two of us passed through that dungeon to a new and happy life together.

My wonderful friend and colleague, Lucien Muratore, sang *Monna Vanna* with me, and nobody has been able to do the rôle of Ginello since. I went once to hear the opera in Paris, and the man singing the part of Ginello was more like Ginello's valet than Ginello himself. He had absolutely no idea of how to be a prince. If I remember correctly, when Muratore and I sang *Monna Vanna* in San Francisco we took in 31,000 dollars at one performance, and I believe that all four performances I was in brought something like 100,000 dollars.

Marinuzzi, my new conductor, had succeeded Campanini, who died in 1919. Now, Marinuzzi was a great artist, but nobody could touch Campanini, *nobody in the world*. He was the most consummate artist in every way, not only as a conductor. He had faultless taste in choosing operas and in filling the rôles with people who were absolutely right for them. When he died, the company gave him the most marvellous funeral in the Auditorium in Chicago. I was supposed to be singing a concert in Cleveland that day, but I came back to Chicago for the funeral.

They had Campanini's body in a coffin in the middle of

the stage. All the curtains and backdrops were up, and the rest of the stage was one mass of flowers. The artists of the company sang and the orchestra played, and then we were all permitted to go up on the stage and pass in front of the coffin and look at him. When I went up there and gazed down at Campanini, he looked like a child of five. His tiny hands were folded over his breast, and between the fingers of those baby hands he held the baton he had used in all those glorious performances. And what a tiny head! It has never gone out of my mind how shrunken Campanini looked in that coffin of his, shrunken and wasted away. The great Campanini had diminished to a little boy. The artists passed in front of him and said 'Good-bye,' and everybody cried, everybody but me. I didn't cry at all. I just looked down in wonder at Campanini lying there. I was so fascinated by the way he had melted away to nothing, that tiny man in the coffin. After that, the curtain came down slowly, and that was the last we saw of Cleofonte Campanini.

Marinuzzi must have been with us three years, from 1919 to 1921. There was a second conductor, a Frenchman named Charlier, who conducted performances I was in till the end of the first season after Campanini. I did Prokofiev's *Love for Three Oranges* and *Carmen* with Marinuzzi, and everything else with the Frenchman. Were there fights and scandals? How should I know, I who never went to the theatre but to sing and rehearse or else to sit in the orchestra and hear an opera I wasn't singing in. I never knew very much else about a theatre. I rarely heard what was going on backstage and never cared. When my work was finished in a theatre I departed. Nothing interested me outside my rôles, the people I was playing them with and who was conducting them. I never went backstage when I wasn't in a performance. I was a singer. I had nothing to do with the administration, and it never interested me, not, that is, till I became a director myself, and then only because I had pledged to give my best. I suppose there were squabbles—I tried never to let them touch me. My work sufficed.

Marinuzzi had succeeded Campanini only as conductor. Campanini had been general director, too, and to succeed him Mr. McCormick brought in a man named Herbert Johnson. Well, in the ninth years of Mr. and Mrs. McCormick's sponsorship of the Chicago Opera, they let Mr. Johnson go. I was in Monte Carlo at the time, and when I came back to Chicago there was some trouble in the company. All I know is that Mme. Ganna Walska was to sing, and then she didn't sing and went away. I never knew why, and I shall not even try to guess. On my arrival in Chicago I was told about Mr. Johnson's dismissal by Mr. McCormick.

'Mary,' he said, 'this is going to be our last season. Will you be my director?'

'Why me?' I asked. 'I've never administrated an opera company. I'm a singer. Nobody would take orders from me.'

'You have nothing to lose and nothing to gain.'

'Then why should I do it?'

'We want to go out in a blaze of glory, and we need your name.'

I couldn't refuse this very, very great friend of mine who had supported us so faithfully and often against much opposition and wavering.

'I'll do it,' I said, 'but on one condition.'

'You don't even have to name it, Mary,' he said. 'I agree.'

'I don't want the company to know I'm going to be director for just this one year,' I said.

'I see,' he said; 'just to keep them in line. An excellent idea. You can count on my co-operation.'

The following morning the papers all came out with the announcement that Mary Garden was going to be the director of the Chicago Grand Opera Company, and that was just like a meteor falling in the middle of the Auditorium. Because, I suppose, they all thought that everybody

Salomé

Mélisande in the Balcony Scene

who wasn't French would now have to go. And, of course, that was the rankest nonsense. I knew nobody could run an opera house in America without Italian repertory. Americans adore Italian opera and Italian singers, and I don't blame them. When I finally made out my plans for the following season, I gave sixty per cent. of the repertory to the Italian opera, twenty per cent. to French opera, a little less than twenty per cent. to German opera, and what was left went to two Russian operas, Rimsky-Korsakov's *Snegurochka*, which we did in Russian, and Prokofiev's *Love for Three Oranges*, which we did in French.

When I first saw the score of *Love for Three Oranges*, I knew I'd have to produce it. I believe the music was sent to me by Prokofiev himself; I've forgotten how it happened. The opera fascinated me the moment I looked at it, the rich fantasy and iridescent music. I wrote at once to Prokofiev, who I think was in New York at the time, asking him if he would come to conduct it for us in Chicago. He did, and it was beautiful. Everybody said it was just like going as a child to see a lovely fairy tale.

As for *Snegurochka* it was Serge Diaghilev who advised me how to produce this charming work. We spent many hours together over the score that summer in Venice. He showed me all the cuts they had made in the Russian performances, and I made them all for my Chicago season.

'You must produce it without "stars," ' he also cautioned me. 'Just a good cast of singers.'

And that was the way it was finally given in Chicago, becoming one of the greatest successes of the season.

Later, in Monte Carlo, I used to go with Diaghilev to the rehearsals of his famous Ballets Russes. What a gruelling ordeal of work those dancers and musicians were subjected to! Rehearsals usually lasted from nine in the evening until three the following morning.

Diaghilev went over every step, every gesture, every nuance.

I was exhausted just watching them, and yet none of them seemed to mind. It was part of their life to be striving endlessly for the perfection that was in Diaghilev's mind.

Diaghilev sat alone in the theatre at every performance, his hawk-like eyes on everything. I remember how once he ordered one of the dancers to remove a tiny flower in her hair because it wasn't the right colour. I don't wonder it was the greatest ballet company in the world.

'Don't you ever rest?' I asked him one day.

'My dear Mary, there is all eternity to rest us,' he replied.

My first problem in becoming director of the company was to engage a great conductor. Marinuzzi had refused to conduct French opera for me, so I told Mr. McCormick that I didn't want to keep him, and he let him go. Then I thought of an Italian conductor I had heard in Paris at a theatre called the Vaudeville, where I created the opera *Cléopatra*. I never forgot the man because I don't think I had ever heard an opera conductor like him, unless it was Campanini himself. But I couldn't remember his name, so I wrote to my old accompanist, Bartholemy, who wrote back, telling me his name was Giorgio Polacco. The moment I got Bartholemy's reply, I sent Polacco a cable asking him to be my musical director. I liked his response; it was prompt and to the point. Without asking any questions about what he would be paid or what he would be expected to do, he cabled back, 'I'm sailing.' Polacco arrived in Chicago and immediately took over the musical direction of the Chicago Grand Opera for the year I was there. Always with the exception of Campanini, Polacco was the finest conductor I ever had . . . and he loved the French works.

No sooner did I start managing the company, when a peculiar situation began for me. I found myself getting a great many anonymous letters. Knives would reach me by post, then revolvers, and once I got a box of bullets, and in the box was a letter that said, 'Remember that there should be twelve bullets in this box. Count them. There are only eleven. The twelfth bullet is for you.' Well, I kept the bullets as a souvenir. I thought the whole thing was very funny, and I told Mr. McCormick about it, but he refused to see any humour in it. I was with him one night when I was preparing to leave for the theatre.

'Mary,' he said, 'you've got to have a detective.'

'What for?' I asked.

'For your safety. He'll ride with you to the opera house and stand at the door of your dressing-room.'

'But that's ridiculous,' I said. 'I don't need any protection.'

'There's no telling what might happen,' Mr. McCormick insisted.

'But there's nothing in the world I'm afraid of,' I said. 'Every policeman in Chicago is a personal friend of mine. Do you know what would happen to anyone who tried to do anything to me?'

'That's all very well, Mary,' said Mr. McCormick, 'but we'd all feel a lot easier if you took this man along with you.'

Mr. McCormick wouldn't take no for an answer, so that night when I went down to the theatre, the detective was in my car with me. We became good friends, he and I, and he told me many wonderful stories as we rode to the theatre. I couldn't get rid of him after that; he had his orders, he kept on telling me, and he was with me in my car and outside my dressing-room till the end of my season.

Who wrote those letters and who sent those revolvers and bullets and knives I have never known, and I don't much care. I have no theory at all about it, and it made no difference to me. Then I began getting more anonymous letters, saying, 'So you've got a detective with you now. Don't worry, we'll get you just the same.' But I went on living just as if it was my last day. I took it all as a huge joke. I knew that all such letters are sent by cowards and I knew perfectly well that nothing would happen to me. And it never did, but Mr. McCormick must have been getting anonymous letters too, and that may have alarmed him about me.

The irony of it all at the Chicago Opera was that they thought I was going to be their boss for ever. You see, Mr. McCormick never let on to them that I was to be there for one year only. I must say I had a difficult time with the men in the company; the women singers were charming and co-operative, but the males were just a pack of jealous boys. I've never seen such jealousy in my life, and I was told that some of them began plotting to take my place, not knowing, the dears, that I would be out of there in a few months. It all amused me intensely. I'm afraid that one of my conductors began resenting me, too. I feel I must tell this little bit about him, merely to show the sort of thing I had to contend with as director.

The question came up one day as to who was going to sing a particular rôle. He wanted one artist to do the part, and I wanted another. We had a heated argument over it, and he became very ugly. Then one night when I sang he was conducting. As a rule, he conducted to perfection, attentive to every detail, and giving it his heart and soul. But this night he came into the pit with his hands in his pockets and conducted in such a scandalous way that I was almost tempted to call down the curtain.

The other members of the cast all came up to me and said, 'Mary, what's the matter with the conductor to-night? Why don't we stop the performance?'

They knew I wouldn't do anything like that.

'Do your best,' I said, 'and we'll get through somehow.'

Which we did, and as I was undressing to go home after the performance, he came into my dressing-room in a rude manner, with his hat on his head.

'Well, what do you think of to-night's performance?' he asked sullenly.

'In all my career I have never heard anything so frightful,' I said.

Then he turned to me, a mean expression on his face.

'You're nothing but a dirty spy!' he snarled.

When he said the word 'spy' I saw two red balls in front of my eyes. I had nothing but powder puffs and cold cream and rouge on my table, but if there had been a knife I'd have taken it up and killed him. I took him by the collar and threw him out of my dressing-room. I must have had superhuman strength at that moment . . . that man never entered my dressing-room—or home—after that. But on the stage it made no difference. I respected him as an artist, and I wasn't going to let any personal feeling interfere with that.

After my year was up, Samuel Insull, who had now taken over the company, came to see me one day, asking about this conductor.

'Shall I keep him or shall I let him go?' he asked.

'Don't ever let him go,' I said. 'He's one of the best there is—anywhere.'

'All right, I'll hold on to him.'

If I had been a different type of woman I'd have said, 'Let him go,' but he was a great conductor and he stayed on with Insull.

That fight happened some time in 1922. Twenty-five years later, in 1947, I was living in Aberdeen. One day my maid came to me and said, 'Miss Garden, there's a box that's just arrived from America. I can't carry it, it's too heavy.' I went with her, and together we brought it up and opened it. There were eighteen pounds of coffee and fifteen pounds of tea, and with them a New Year's card bearing the name of my Chicago conductor. It surprised and amused me. I wrote back thanking him for his kindness. Then, when I was in New York late in 1949, he telephoned, asking if he could come up and see me. I was really awfully fond of him, and I never bore him a grudge for that ugly episode in my dressing-room. . . . Well, there he was, sitting in my room again, an elderly little man, crying like a child.

'Oh, Mary,' he said, 'there's been nothing in my life like the days I conducted for you in Chicago.'

I was so dreadfully sorry for him then that we became very good friends again. There was always a great charm about him, and for all the things he may have tried to do to me, I never lost that admiration I had for him as a fine conductor. When I think of it all now, I suppose that, like all other men, he resented the fact that he had a woman as his boss.

Frankly, I didn't enjoy being director. I never liked coming upon anything that wasn't completely mine or completely under my control. If the theatre had been my own, then I could have said what I wanted and what I didn't want, and taken in whom I liked and let go whom I didn't like. It wasn't my company, and I was doing it just as a courtesy to Mr. McCormick. He offered me a free hand, but I didn't take it. He gave me a blank contract as director.

'Mary, you fill it in at your price,' he had said to me.

'I'll accept no money except my pay as a singer,' I replied. I wanted no salary as impresario.

What a to-do the papers made over my being director! I had a taste of something I never want a taste of again. It didn't take up much of my time, but they gave me decisions to make that I didn't like—which artist would sing which rôle, and so on. There was always conflict in my mind. I wanted to change the whole thing and put the right people in the right place, but I didn't want to make enemies. I didn't have absolutely full control, you see.

If I ever had complete charge of an opera house, the chances are I wouldn't get anybody to sing for me. I would be very emphatic about some things. I would never have a curtain call. I would never allow an encore. I would never permit a claque. There would be only art in my theatre. I would put every artist in the operas of his own school and language. I would have the finest singing actors, the most magnificent *décor*, the best orchestra I could get, and the greatest conductors. But that costs money, and money you can't get for grand opera. I would try to have everything in youth. I'd like that in my theatre, everlasting youth. I'd love to make great artists, to mould them in the rôles they sing. I would want them to know when to stop. I knew when to leave, but too many of them don't. Then, I would get a great impresario, someone like Albert Carré, who was always in everything. Oscar Hammerstein was a great director too, and even if he didn't direct everything, he knew how to get great stage directors. I would have two or three of the best stage directors in the company, and I would pay good money to everybody, because great artists deserve the best pay. . . .

The newspapers said that the company lost one million dollars during the season I was director. I don't know, because I had nothing to do with the business end of it. It was news to me. It may very well have happened, but I don't know. I do know we finished the way Mr. McCormick wanted us to finish—in a blaze of glory. That's what he asked for, and that's what he got. If it cost a million dollars, I'm sure it was worth it.

When my year as director of the Chicago Opera was done, I breathed my breath of liberty again. My motto has always been liberty, just that one word. I put liberty into my work; I put liberty into my life, and I put it into my 'loves.' That's the one thing that I never allowed to go from me. I knew I could never again direct people. The whole experience had detached me from my freedom. But I never regretted it, because I never regret what's done.

When I finally stepped out, Mr. Insull asked me to be co-director with him.

'I don't want a third of a director's share in any opera house, let alone half,' I said. So he took it on alone, and brought back Mr. Johnson as his business manager.

# My Unspeakable Turk

WHILE on tour during my Chicago career, I stopped somewhere in the Middle West, and there I met the warden of a prison who asked me, 'Would you like to sing at our prison?' Of course I replied, 'I'd adore it!'

Well, I went over to the prison, sang my songs. When we were coming out I saw a great big table with lots of beautiful wooden animals spread out on it. Standing beside the table was an old man with pink cheeks and pure-white hair. The warden went over to him and said:

'This is Mary Garden; she'd like to meet you.'

The old man turned around to me and smiled, and the warden said to him:

'Will you give Miss Garden one of your animals?'

And the old man gave me a little wooden horse that he had made.

'Thank you so much,' I said to him. 'I shall never part with it.'

When we left the room, I turned to the warden.

'What is that dear old man in prison for?'

'Murder.'

'Murder?' I cried. 'What? That charming old man! But whom did he murder?'

'His wife.'

'But why did he do that awful thing?'

'Well,' said the warden, 'it seems this wife of his nagged

him for twenty years, till one day he went out and bought a revolver and shot her dead—and that's why he's here.'

I still have that little wooden horse, and when I look at it I say to myself, 'Don't you ever nag anybody!'

Nagging is awful, but the people who do the nagging love it. I don't think I have any of that in me, and I don't have any kind of jealousy in me. Maybe that's what makes most people nag—jealousy. They should stop when they feel the impulse to nag.

It's a dreadful thing, this constant hacking away at someone, someone very close, and someone who can't get away. It's continual, nagging: it just goes on for ever, till the person being nagged can't do or say anything right any more. I suppose twenty years of that sort of punishment is more than even a normal, peaceable man can take. You must be born a nagger, just as you must be born a genius—it's a special gift . . . or curse.

On another of my many tours with the Chicago Opera Company through the West, my sister Aggie came along with me. We had our private train, and after each performance we went to a comfortable bed, then off to the next city.

Well, my sister was very dainty, and she had beautiful red hair that looked like a halo around her pretty little head. Her night clothes were all silk and lace, smelling of some divine perfume.

On the particular night I have in mind, I just couldn't resist putting a string of my favourite pearls around her neck. She looked simply ravishing.

As for me, my only thought was to get to my bed as quickly as possible. I must have looked a sight, with my face covered with cold cream, a knitted cap on my head for fear of a draught, and a big woollen shawl all around me.

I remember my sister, who was majesty itself at that moment, looking at me in disgust and saying:

'Mary, what an awful-looking woman you are! Shall I tell you something? If this train is wrecked to-night and both of us are killed, I shall probably be buried as the beautiful Mary Garden.'

'And I?' I said, tightening the shawl about my shoulders.

'You will be buried as Mary Garden's maid,' replied my sister.

With that comforting thought, I kissed my sister good night and went soundly to sleep.

Those were fascinating days, singing in different cities before new audiences. At that time it was all very primitive, as many of the cities we sang in had no opera house.

I remember our first visit to Dallas, Texas. That was long before they built their beautiful new opera house. We were put in an immense building on the fair grounds that must have seated several thousand people. It was always my habit, whenever we arrived in any city, to look over the place we were going to sing in. When I looked into that enormous hall, I could feel something clutch at my throat.

When I entered, the orchestra was already there rehearsing. With the first blast of the instruments, hundreds of birds flew out from all parts of the building. The musicians had to get popguns and pop the birds out of the windows.

And then there was another amusing incident in a city where the company played for only two nights. A circus was performing in the hall where we were to sing. For the two days that we took over the hall, the animals were housed in the cellar.

The first evening we were there, we gave a performance of *La Bohème*, and it was during the first act, in the middle of the beautiful love duet between Rodolfo and Mimì, that a great big red tongue came wriggling up through a hole in the stage. The giraffe, one of the animals confined in the basement below, evidently wanted to know what was going on above him and found a hole in the ceiling through which he tried to satisfy his curiosity.

For a few moments, Campanini and the singers were frightened out of their wits, and then convulsed with laughter. The management immediately sent a man down into the cellar to remove the inquisitive giraffe. The singers told me later that they never knew how they managed to finish the first act.

I was almost killed in Chicago one day. There was to be a great charity affair at the Auditorium, and they were auctioning off the boxes.

'Mary,' the directors said to me, 'you've got to go to the Stock Exchange and sell some of these boxes.'

'It will be a pleasure getting those billionaires to loosen up,' I said.

So I went over to the Stock Exchange. There was a platform for me to stand on, built quite high, so that I could look down at the men and say:

'How much will you offer for this ticket?'

There I was selling the boxes for our benefit, when all of a sudden a revolver dropped at my feet. Before I knew what was happening, a great big policeman came up, took hold of a man who had climbed on the platform and was standing at my back, and dragged him off. Then another policeman walked up to me and said:

'Miss Garden, I think you'd better go.'

I went, and I didn't sell any more boxes, but I said to myself: 'I've got to find out why this man wanted to kill me.'

He was a dreadful-looking man, with long grey hair and shabby clothes. So I sent a friend of mine to ask this man who was now in prison why he wanted Mary Garden put out of the way. All he could get out of him was this one statement:

'She talks too much.'

I wonder what he would have done if he had been alive and free during my lecture tour.

Which reminds me that I had come very close to losing my life in 1912 at the hands of an unfortunate young girl who, completely unknown to me, had contracted a morbid infatuation for me through my impersonations. While on tour, I was to sing a *matinée* of *Faust* in Philadelphia. Mother was ill in New York, and I promised to come back directly after the performance to have dinner with her. I told my secretary not to let anybody come into my dressing-room; I wanted to be sure to catch the five o'clock train to New York. He kept everybody out, and when the performance was over and I was getting ready to catch my train, he said:

'Miss Garden, there was a young lady who insisted on seeing you, and when I told her she couldn't she went away in a very disagreeable manner.'

'Had you ever seen her before?'

'No; she was a total stranger to me.'

I didn't give the episode another thought. That was Saturday afternoon. I returned to New York and dined with Mother. My next performance was the following Tuesday night at the Metropolitan, in Massenet's *Thaïs*. Well, Tuesday morning, as I lay in bed, I opened my newspaper and there on the front page, in large letters, I read:

GIRL KILLS SELF OVER MARY GARDEN

I became instantly ill, because I hadn't the faintest notion what it was all about and it was a terrible shock to my nerves. I sat up, stunned, wondering what in heaven's name it all could mean. And there was *Thaïs* to sing that night! I remained in my room all day, tense and distraught. No one can possibly imagine what I went through during those hours before I left for the Metropolitan. I had never experienced anything like it. It was all so unnerving that perhaps another woman might not have sung that night. I tried to give myself courage.

'Mary Garden,' I remember saying, 'you're perfectly innocent and you're going to sing to-night!'

How I sang that night at the Metropolitan Opera House, I shall never know. But sing I did, and I suppose every single, solitary person in the house had seen the headlines and was just as tense and bewildered as I was. Then the following day the papers came out with a letter from the girl's mother.

'Miss Garden never knew my daughter,' the letter read. 'My daughter had never even met her. She had developed a mad infatuation for her from hearing her sing. She went to Philadelphia to hear Miss Garden in *Faust* and then went to her dressing-room but was not permitted to speak to her. This was not the first time my daughter had become infatuated with a celebrity. She was a very high-strung girl, and I wish to repeat that Miss Garden was in no way at fault.'

When I read that I suddenly remembered what my secretary had said to me in Philadelphia about the girl who had insisted on seeing me in my dressing-room. I called him at once.

'Can you recall anything else about that girl?' I asked. 'Did she make any threats?'

'I didn't want to tell you this before, Miss Garden,' he said, 'but when that young lady was leaving, a revolver dropped out of her muff.'

'Why in heaven's name didn't you tell the police about it?'

'I thought it might upset you,' he replied.

So, more than likely, that girl had come to Philadelphia with the idea of doing away with me, and when she was not received, she went back home, brooded over it for a couple of days, and then shot herself in her mother's garden.

I have always felt strongly about people coming into a dressing-room during a performance. I never liked it, rarely permitted it, and never understood why anybody, not excepting the impresario himself, thought he had the right to. I myself never went and never go behind the stage to congratulate anyone that I admire. I write to them instead. I never pushed myself into any singer's dressing-room. It just went against me to invade anyone's privacy or have anyone invade mine. I almost never go up to people in public places and say, 'Aren't you so-and-so? I'm so glad to meet you. I've admired you for so many years.'

After the performance I didn't mind having a few people coming to my dressing-room, though, frankly, I preferred going home to bed. But during the opera, except on very rare occasions, I absolutely refused to see people. This is an order I gave and an order I'd like to see given everywhere. To-day, no one can get into the dressing-rooms of the Opéra-Comique between the acts, except with a search warrant. Whether that was because of my practice or not, I don't know; but it's a good rule. I regard it as an imposition and an interruption to come into an artist's dressing-room in the middle of an opera.

Then another thing: if I had an opera house of my own I never would let the orchestra be seen. I would cover it as they did at Bayreuth, maybe the very same way, with leaves. It is so beautiful! Seeing the orchestra destroys the illusion. What's more, I'd never have a curtain call. After you've had a great act and finished with a great drama it looks ridiculous to come out and bow. As far as the public is concerned, the singer should remain in character even after the curtain has fallen. That would be my policy, NO CURTAIN CALLS, and of course nobody at all would come to sing for me. How they all love to go out and bow! And I'd never permit flowers to be brought on the stage. Flowers were always brought up to my dressing-room, baskets and baskets of them, but never on the stage. If I had a theatre of my own, I'd do just that.

I'd make it such a gorgeous opera house, if it were mine! No scraping, no bowing, no claques. But, then, I'd have to have people who understood what I was aiming at. Except for the little friction of my one year as director of the Chicago opera, which was really nothing at all, I never had any cabals or serious conspiracies against me.

During this period in my life I became engaged, without my knowing it, to a Turk.

He was from Constantinople, a bey, very rich and very indiscriminate in his pursuit of women. It could as easily have been any other woman in the world as myself. He liked them all, and that was one reason why my dashing young Turk never became my lover. *Mon Dieu*, what an awful man, what a gambler, and of course I adore a gambler and gambling!

I met my pursuer at Aix-les-Bains, where Father and I stopped for a short holiday. He was the fiancé of a great English lady, who was desperately in love with him. But he had no moral scruples whatsoever. When I met him he took a frantic liking to me. There was his lady at Aix-les-Bains with him, and he utterly and absolutely turned his back on her.

My Turk and I used to go down to the gambling rooms together. I never played there because I didn't care for baccarat. Roulette is the only game I play.

'You bring me luck,' my Turk used to say to me.

I used to sit there and he would win terrific sums of money. And if I happened not to be there, he would lose, and that's why he believed I was responsible for his luck. Well, we saw a great deal of each other at Aix. Then I left abruptly for Paris.

I wasn't in Paris very long, when my ardent young Turk came dashing after me, this time with his father and mother, whom he had brought over from Constantinople to meet me. They were both very pleasant people, and I remember the father wore a fez. They had brought with them from Constantinople a most gorgeous ruby ring.

'This is for you,' said my young Turk, giving me the ring.

And, of course, foolish me thought it just a nice kind present. I hadn't the remotest suspicion then that all three of them regarded it as a bethrothal ring!

After his parents left, the Turk returned with redoubled ardour to his campaign, only to be rebuffed again. My, was that man angry! I remember there was a thing in Paris at that time called *les fêtes des fleurs*. Everybody had carriages full of beautiful flowers, and as they passed they threw the flowers at one another. My handsome Oriental passed by in his carriage, his face black with rage. I saw this enormous bouquet in his hands and as he drew near he flung it at me, and of course it was a bouquet full of water.

That was just before I left for America, and he was beginning to realize he couldn't get the better of me. I remember saying to myself, 'If he treats this charming lady whom he intends to marry the way he does, what in God's name would he do to a wife?'

The day I left for America, my Turk came to bid me good-bye.

'I'm coming to America soon to marry you.'

I just shrugged my shoulders to that and said nothing.

There I was in Chicago, not long after, and I was taking my bath, when my maid came in with a cable. It was from my undiscourageable young Turk.

'When shall I come?' it read.

I didn't let a minute go by, but cabled right back, 'Never!'

Then he got mad and cabled again: 'Send me back my ring.'

And of course I realized, with a shock, what that little ceremony with his parents had been. And that was the hardest thing I ever had to do, returning the ring, because it was the most glorious thing you ever saw. I didn't dare send it back myself, not anything so priceless, so I went down to a jeweller and had him send it for me.

What a cruel and callous man that Turk could be! Imagine, he once brought his fiancée to dine in my home, and when we were sitting at table he turned to her and quite casually said:

'It's Mary I'm going to marry, not you,' and that poor girl cried and cried, and I felt so sorry for her and had the devil of a time assuring her the Turk would never marry anyone but herself.

Yet he had a terrific personality, that man, tall, dark, magnificent, and very, very masculine. Oh, my, yes; but he wasn't for me. He had the sort of charm that no matter how hard you tried you couldn't avoid being attracted to him. A woman who had no intention of succumbing had to be very careful with him.

He got back his ruby ring all right, and married that charming young English lady. It must have been twelve years after our little friendship that I met her on the street in Paris. She was very cordial and asked me to come up to lunch, and I went. They had a lovely home in Paris, and of course when the Turk saw me he began reminiscing about the past. Suddenly he said to me:

'Come into my bedroom, Mary. I want to show you my new radio.'

And he looked at his wife and said, 'Do you mind, darling?'

He had a great big radio which he played from morning to morning, for that man never slept. He didn't need sleep, and that was something I could never understand.

And when I went into the bedroom with him, he turned to me and the very first thing he said was:

'What's your address and telephone number, Mary? I've got to see you!'

And I wouldn't give it to him.

We had a charming lunch. They seemed to be very good companions, but my young Turk hadn't changed a bit. He was the same unscrupulous pursuer. There had to be something new around all the time. He could never rest on any one thing, or fasten on any one woman. So I never went to see them again.

It had been a marvellous 'romance' while it lasted, which was about two months. Marvellous because it was my first touch of the Orient. I didn't know their ways of living, and it all fascinated me, but only for a while. It just didn't make any difference what kind of skirt he passed. He ran out to every woman. I didn't like that, so I was never serious with him.

A man like that could never have won my love. Then there was his charming fiancée. I had no intention whatsoever of marrying him. I suppose, when I look back on it, that it interested me to play around and see how far he would go. It was never an *affaire*, not with a type like that.

I've been asked to give a picture of the ideal lover. I don't know how to give it. Perhaps any man capable of lasting devotion would be the ideal lover, but I don't suppose there is any real fidelity in the world, not in a man. I don't think any man can be faithful to one woman. The temptations are terrific. A woman puts much more into a romance. She gives fidelity much more readily than a man. She yields everything. What does a man yield? Nothing in the world that I can see. Some men are less animal than others and less promiscuous. That's all. I have never seen the man I would marry. You see, the *grande passion* never came into my life, and perhaps the right man passed me by.

Lovers don't often stay that way for long—a year, perhaps two, before it burns out. But friendship lasts. The friendship between a man and a woman is the most beautiful thing in the world. It is very rare, but when it comes it is a great thing. I had only one such friend in the world, and that friendship was the sweetest thing that ever came to me. That was Clarence Mackay, a devoted friend who never failed me.

During the First World War, I was in Aix-les-Bains for the summer. There was a small military hospital there, and the wounded were all lying around naked, waiting for supplies. Everything was lacking in that hospital. I remember the first day I went over it with the doctor in charge.

'You see, Miss Garden,' he said to me with a sigh, 'we haven't very much of anything here. We need linen, aprons, medicine, bandages, chloroform.'

I immediately cabled my friend in New York:

'I'm interested in a military hospital that lacks everything. Will you send something to help them out?'

My friend sent me 50,000 francs immediately, and I gave the money to the hospital, adding a little of my own.

Then we got a special funicular and took the men up to the mountains. We had them lie in the sun, and oh, how thankful they were that they could get away from those hospital beds! I remember my chauffeur used to carry the ones without legs on his shoulders. . . .

Then one Christmas morning in Paris I looked out the window and there, standing before my house, was a magnificent new Rolls-Royce.

That was my Christmas present from this sweet friend of mine in America who had never sought or expected anything in return but my friendship. How different from my young Turk, who could no more think of having a woman as a friend than he could think of going to a monastery!

I have always said that I had my friendships in America and my acquaintances in Europe. I don't think a woman like myself could have had a friend like Clarence Mackay anywhere else in the world.

Then Mr. Mackay died, and that was a black day for me. I remember going in to see him during the last few days.

I remember something bothered me in his room and I couldn't tell what it was, until I saw a crucifix on a dresser.

'There is something about that crucifix that disturbs me,' I said to him.

'I quite understand,' he answered feebly from his bed. 'That crucifix contains a piece of the cross on which Jesus hung.'

And I remember it gave me a turn, because I saw that my friend believed it with all his heart. Then he died, and with his death I lost something I cherished dearly.

## My Longest Romance

IT was during my second year in Chicago that I met him. There then began the longest 'romance' of my life—a relation that brought happiness to neither of us and considerable torment to him.

I was invited for luncheon one day to one of the clubs to meet certain gentlemen of Chicago. I remember it was snowing fiercely outside, and we were all waiting for the last guest to come, when I looked up and saw him in the foyer, taking off his coat and goloshes. I knew at once he was the one I wanted to meet. It was very strange; it had never happened to me before, not quite this way. I don't like calling it love at first sight, because I'm certain I never loved anyone in my life and I am impatient with that sort of nonsense. But I found my heart pounding, and I was tingling all over. Yet, I didn't know who this handsome gentleman was. He came in in his breezy, charming way, and someone said, 'Miss Garden, Mr.—— ——' and for the rest of the afternoon we sat near each other at the table and talked.

He had never heard an opera in his life; he knew nothing about books; he had never travelled. Almost the only thing that man knew was the dollar sign before his eyes, and he knew that so well he had built up one of the biggest fortunes in America. He was a man of middle age when I met him; not tall, but not small, with beautiful eyes and a very attractive face, and he had a great sense of humour. While we sat there at lunch, he turned his head toward me and

I turned my head toward him and we paid no attention to anyone else.

'Have you ever heard an opera?' I asked him.

'I have never heard an opera in my life,' he answered.

'Why don't you come and hear me in *Thaïs?*'

'I can't afford it,' I remembered he said. 'If I go, I'll have to buy myself a seventy-five cent seat.'

'That's better than nothing,' I said. 'I hope to see you someday in your seventy-five cent seat.'

At the next Saturday *matinée* of *Thaïs*, I got a bouquet of flowers, with a card saying, 'I decided to take my seventy-five cents and buy myself a seat. I shall be in the audience this afternoon.'

Well, when I ran out on the stage as Thaïs, throwing my flowers, I saw him in the front row of the orchestra. I shall never forget his face—it was very red and all eagerness. Now, that was unusual, my seeing him there. I hardly ever pay any attention to the audience, not till the last curtain.

Later he told me what he did when he returned to his office. There was his desk loaded with letters and papers and things for him to sign, and he took his cane and just swept over the desk with it, and everything flew all over the floor. Why he did that I don't really know, unless the thought came to him that everything that had happened to him up to that moment suddenly meant nothing, and that something strange and exciting had now entered his life.

Then one day he came up to my suite at the Blackstone Hotel. I shall never forget that visit. He came into my room like something that shouldn't be there, nervous and fidgety and cautious. And I said to him:

'Why do you enter my room with bars in front of you? Take them down and come here and sit and talk with me like a human being.'

He laughed, and said: 'Miss Garden, you're right. There

were bars in front of me from the moment I rang your bell. But they are down now.'

Suddenly, he was standing before me, his face red and serious.

'I haven't slept since I first saw you,' he said. 'I love you.'

'I think I'm going to love you,' I said.

And he took me into his arms, and I knew something serious had come into my life.

He stayed about an hour and then left. He came very rarely to visit me at the Blackstone—always with those bars in front of him, as if had no right to be there, like a child who'd done something he shouldn't have done. It was a peculiar attitude. It wasn't guilt, no, nothing like that; or fear; he was as brave as a lion. I think it was this: in all his life he had never learned to be himself. He was that way only in his home town, however. Later, whenever I met him anywhere else, he was quite different. There was his reputation to consider, and this wasn't part of the picture he had built up of himself.

'I'm sailing next week for Europe,' I told him one day.

'What boat, Mary?' he asked.

And I told him. Two days later he was back at the hotel, a ticket in his hand.

'Mary, here's my passage on the boat with you,' he said.

'You go right down and give it back!' I said sternly.

'Why, what do you mean?'

'I mean just that. You can take another boat.'

'But, Mary, we'll be together.'

'There's no point in your taking the same boat.'

'I don't understand.'

'It's simply this: I prefer to be by myself when I cross the ocean.'

And that was the simple truth. I hate people I know being on the same boat with me because I never get up when I cross the Atlantic. I've crossed it maybe forty times, and I have never seen a dining-room. Most of the time I stay in my cabin. I always have my cabin and a drawing-room, and I usually go out only at night when everybody is eating and I have the boat to myself. It was always like that, and I was making no exception for him.

He took it like a sport and went down and changed his ticket. He arrived in Paris a week after I did, and when he came to me we began taking glorious drives through France in my motor car. Then we stayed in Deauville, and it was there in my villa that we understood there was nothing and nobody in the world but the two of us.

Everything interested him now. He was like a big boy who had suddenly come upon something beautiful and desirable. This was all strange and fascinating to him because he had never known anything but business and money. A man who lived next door to him once said to me, 'I never needed any clocks in my house because I always knew the time by the way he came and went.'

So you can imagine what it was like for him to fall in love with a woman like me, how completely his life changed, and how, later, it made him suffer. How wretched he became, because, I suppose, he could never have me the way he wanted me, to possess and dominate me in every way!

'Mary,' he once said to me, 'I wouldn't want my worst enemy to suffer the way I've suffered—suffered knowing you.'

'That's wild talk,' I said. 'I think I've been very nice to you, and you have no right to say that.'

And how jealous that man became! When I was stopping at the Ritz-Carlton in New York, he would wake me up at two and three in the morning by long-distance telephone.

'Mary,' he would ask in a grave, accusing tone, 'who's in that room with you?'

'Don't be ridiculous,' I would say; 'you know I can't bear to have a man in my bedroom at night. That's always been for me alone.'

Fifteen minutes later he would call again.

'Mary,' he would say, 'I must know who's in that room with you.'

In desperation I would tell the Ritz-Carlton operator that if any more calls came for me at that hour, I was not to be disturbed. As time went on he became more and more jealous. He would follow me in his private train on all my tours. I never knew where he would turn up, maybe in San Francisco, maybe in Denver. One day he appeared in Kansas City, and that was something to remember. I had had my suite at the hotel arranged for me, and when I arrived the manager came up to me.

'Miss Garden,' he said, 'I'm very sorry, but all we have available for you is a very small room.'

'What about my reservation for the large suite?' I asked, puzzled.

'Oh, Mr. —— has that.'

I telephoned him immediately.

'What are you doing in my suite?' I said furiously.

'Why, Mary, is this your suite?' he said. 'I'll get right out.'

'You needn't bother. I don't need it, and I don't like this at all.'

I think I got terribly interested in him in the beginning because he was so unspoiled. He had been living his life on a straight line, with nothing but business to interest him, and he knew so little of life in general. There was something untouched about him that fascinated me, much more than his love for me, for I must confess that his love got to bore me terribly. He knew that he never in the world would capture me.

He also knew that there was one thing in my nature that he couldn't fight against, that was my loathing and detestation of anything that meant destruction. I never destroyed anything in my art; I was always building, never tearing down. And I certainly would not destroy a home, and he knew that. There was his wife, and there were his children, whom he was very fond of. Then I knew that even if I had let him divorce his wife I could never hope to break through that crust of family life which had formed over him. No woman, no matter how she loved a man, and he her, could do that. And he knew I would never marry him, even if he were a free man.

'I'll never conquer you, Mary,' he said to me once.

'Why must you men always talk of being conquerors?' I replied. 'Can't we belong to one another without conquest?'

'Let's go away together, Mary.'

'Where to?'

'Oh, we'll find some little island to live on for the rest of our lives.'

I laughed in his face.

'But, my dear man,' I said, 'when we get to that island, and we've seen every inch of it, I'll have nothing to look at but you, and then I already know everything about you. So I'm quite sure we'd never be happy on that island.'

There were times when I felt that if he had been a free man, I say *if*, and alone, and not so wrapped up in his business, I might have married him, with his great love for me; but I always knew really that I wouldn't, when the time came for a decision, because he didn't have anything in him to interest me but that unspoiled naturalness of his.

He had never read a book; he had never travelled. Living with a man of that kind can get very tiresome after a while—at least for a woman like me. He needed the other part of his life to fill in; he loved his factories and his reputation, and, without being aware of it himself, he loved his home. Men are never aware of that till they lose it. And then there was his vice.

In 1913 my father and I rented a great mansion in Scotland called Strichen House. It was the most gorgeous place you ever saw, about fifty miles north of Aberdeen. With the house we had 11,000 acres. We leased it for four years, Papa and I, for the shooting. When my friend came over to see me in June, I was alone with my French servants. Papa wasn't coming up till July, so I asked him to stay a week with me. He looked as pleased as Punch when he arrived, and almost the very first thing he said was:

'Mary, I'll buy it for you.'

'I don't want it, thank you,' I said.

And he never could understand why I didn't want to own it. To begin with, I wouldn't have taken that property on my back for anything in the world. And then I never wanted to own anything in my life. Private ownership never interested me very much. But a man like him, with his immense fortune, couldn't be expected to understand that.

It was at Strichen House, two or three days after his arrival, that I discovered that he was a hopeless alcoholic.

In the morning he used to have his breakfast out on our magnificent lawn. He had brought his butler over from America, and I used to look out of my window and watch him giving his master breakfast. Then in the afternoon I used to take him by car to Aberdeen to buy things we needed in the house, and I remember I went into a shop one day and I hadn't any money. I said, 'Have you fifty cents to give me?' and he, the big, confident, multimillionaire, just adored that.

One day we came back from Aberdeen. We had dinner, and I never saw him again till the following morning, because he got dead drunk at table. I had never seen him touch a drop of whisky before that; I had assumed he was what every close friend and associate assumed him to be, a complete abstainer. For three years he had hidden this thing from me, and now he drank to his heart's content, and I said nothing. The butler finally came to put him to bed, and I knew why he had been brought along.

That drinking became a nightly ritual. Now, that's

tiresome, and I might just as well have been alone. For the remainder of the week that he was there, I never saw him after dinner. That was a dreadful realization, and it completely broke me away from him. He didn't know then, but came to sense it later. When he returned to America, he asked my sister Aggie to lunch with him at the Ritz-Carlton, and almost the first thing he said to her was:

'Mary doesn't love me any more.'

And of course Aggie didn't understand then.

I just can't stay hours with a man who doesn't know what he is talking about. Nobody with a brain like mine can ever do that. So, when I came back to America, I saw him in an entirely different light. I knew his vice was consuming and ruining him, and in the end it killed him.

When we saw one another after that, it was very calm on my part and very boring. There was nothing in it for me any more. What intimacy we had had ceased after the third year—entirely. But his love went on, tormenting him more and more, making him insanely jealous and suspicious. He was finished for me, but even though he told my sister that, he didn't know how finished he was. He used to come to New York to see me all the time.

There was no sex in his love now; it was just a mad, hopeless love. He had his love and he had his liquor. Not once did he refer to his drinking, and I never mentioned it myself, but he knew that I knew.

The following year, the war broke out. I was at Strichen House, and he cabled me from America, asking me if there was anything in the world he could do for me and did I need money. I sent back my answer: 'I need nothing, thank you.' Then I went over to Paris and did my military work, for which I was awarded the Medaille de la Reconnaissance that I always wear on my dress, and the following year I went back to Chicago. Very soon after that I had another taste of his jealousy.

I promised Chicago that I would sing *Thaïs* with that magnificent baritone, Titta Ruffo. The day after the papers printed that, I had an out-of-town telephone call from my friend.

'Mary, I don't want you to sing with that Italian,' he said.

'I'm very sorry, but I'm going to sing with *that Italian.*'

And, of course, I sang *Thaïs* with Titta Ruffo. That made my friend wild, because I suppose the papers were full of this great artist, and the thought of Ruffo's making love to me on the stage had become an obsession with him. I wanted very much to sing with Ruffo, not only because of his beautiful voice and technique, but because I was curious to see what an Italian would do in my French works. But it proved to be such a disaster that we never sang together again. Ruffo was just out of place in that opera; it was so hard for the Italians to invade my French repertory and stay there.

'Mary Garden put Ruffo in her pocket and we never saw him,' the papers said the next day.

Ruffo was perhaps the greatest singer of them all, but completely out of his element in an opera like *Thaïs*.

After that, my friend's drinking got worse.

He had managed to hide his vice from the world because he was a night drinker. He never drank anything in the day, and I was told by his butler at Strichen House that wherever he went he had his whisky hidden in his room. I remember the luncheon he gave for some friends from home the following year at the Carlton Hotel in London, I was there with him that day. I watched how he turned his glass down when they brought around the champagne. I was sitting next to him and I just gave him a look and turned the glass back up, because that was such pure hypocrisy and I didn't like to see it, not with what I knew. He then put champagne in his glass and drank everybody's health. You see, he was with his friends, and they knew nothing about this fatal weakness of his.

Later he sent me some beautiful jewels, all diamonds, and he sent them through the post. I must say he never really interfered with my work, or rather I never let him interfere. Nobody could do that. He did try in every way to take me out of my world, but he never succeeded, and he couldn't, at any price. He made offers of all kinds to make me give up opera, but that was like asking me to die. Shortly after that week at Strichen House he asked me again whether I would marry him if he got free, and I gave him a very big 'No!'—now that I knew about his vice.

All I remember of that year is that it was very tiresome. He never once apologized for his drinking, and never even admitted he drank; it is quite possible he thought I didn't know how helpless an alcoholic he was, but I think he did. The thing was completely beyond his control; how it had begun I have no idea, but I do know it had become his master. He just couldn't do anything about it.

One night I came back to the Blackstone Hotel from *Thaïs*. It was about midnight, as I remember, and there he was at my door.

'Mary,' he said, 'I want you to come home with me.'

'What new nonsense is this?' I said, very much annoyed.

'I want to show you my house. It's not far out of town. You've never been in it.'

'I'll do nothing of the sort,' I said. 'I'm tired and I'm going to bed. Now you go home alone.'

'But, Mary, I've always wanted you to see how I lived. My family is away and this is a good chance.'

That made me furious.

'I'll never enter your home. That's your wife's home, and I'm never going to set foot in another woman's house.'

I wouldn't have gone into that house even if I had married him, not me. I would have lived anywhere with him, if he had been my husband, but not in the house that had been his home. But he went on insisting.

'Mary,' he pleaded, 'you've just got to come.'

'All right,' I said, 'I'll come with you up to the door, and then I'll come straight back to the hotel, but not into that house.'

So we drove many miles to his house, and he left the car and I said 'Good night,' and drove back to the hotel.

Later, when I gave up spending my summers at Monte Carlo I took him with me to Corsica. He stayed a week. I showed him around the island, and he was simply amazed at its glorious beauty. As I remember, he did very little drinking in Corsica; he may have done it quietly, in his room, after dinner—I don't know. But it was one of the most pleasant weeks we ever spent together, perhaps the best of them all. We went everywhere in my car. I took him on top of the mountains and down in a boat under the rocks, and when he saw all the bats flapping about he was scared to death for the first time in his life.

'You wanted to buy me eleven thousand acres of ground last summer in Scotland,' I said to him one day. 'Buy me Corsica. That would please me enormously.'

But he never offered me the island, and I would have loved it.

Many years later, when the crash came, he lost everything. At least, they told me he did; I don't know how true this is, but when he knew that the bottom was falling out of everything, they said he just opened his safe and said to the men, 'Go ahead and take everything you can, boys!' He even lost that beautiful house of his. Well, he came to me in Paris after that, and he said to me:

'Mary, did you ever see a man smile that lost . . .?' And he named a sum that staggered me.

'No,' I replied. 'I never knew a man who had that much money, and if I had it and lost it I would just die.'

'Well, I had that much, and I've lost it all, and I can smile.'

And he didn't look like a broken man. That was his charm.

Then one night I was singing at the Opéra-Comique. When I came home from my performance they told me someone had called long distance; that it was very urgent and that I should come at once. I knew it was my friend, but there was nothing I could do. I was deep in my performances of Alfano's *Risurrezione*, singing three times a week, and I couldn't give up my work to go, not for anybody. A few days later I picked up the Paris *Herald* and saw that my friend had died.

And that was the end of what might have been a perfectly beautiful thing in my life, but became a very ugly one, ugly for the two reasons I have given, one because he couldn't have me the way he wanted me, and that made him miserable and jealous and tiresome; two, because of the drinking. I don't think he drank because he couldn't conquer me. He just loved liquor. And it wasn't only a matter of not being able to marry me, much as he plagued me on that point, but of not possessing me.

I suppose he did gain something from knowing me. I know he began writing articles for the newspapers and interesting himself in things that interested me. There was nothing extraordinary about what he wrote; the extraordinary thing was that he wrote at all; nobody understood why. I remember he came right out with it one day: 'Mary, I'm going to begin to write.' And, what was more significant, he began to read, too.

After that first *Thaïs*, he almost never came to the opera. He neither understood nor cared for music and was jealous of everybody who made love to me on the stage and of everybody he thought made love to me in real life, which, of course, was perfectly ridiculous. There were no others, certainly not during the first great period of our friendship.

When I read of his death, I was naturally sad, but I wasn't surprised. He was worth while, and he should have lived;

Marguerite in Gounod's *Faust*

Carmen

but he chose to destroy himself. During the last years of his life I know he was an extremely unhappy man. After he died, I returned to Chicago. One day a woman asked to see me at the Blackstone Hotel. I asked her to come up.

'Miss Garden,' she said, 'I was with Mr. —— when he died.'

'Did he suffer much?' was my first question.

'No, he died like that; he rolled his head over on his pillow, and I looked at him, and he was dead.'

'Do you remember his last words?'

'He said to me, "I'm not going to die, am I, nurse?" And I said to him, "Oh, no, Mr. ——. Whatever gave you the thought?" And he said, "You see, I mustn't die because there's something very important I've got to do for Mary." '

'That was all?'

'Yes, Miss Garden.'

The nurse had no idea at all what he had meant, and neither did I.

And that ended the one love of a man, if I have any right to call it love, that came into my life—a love that brought no lasting joy to either of us.

## Billy Sunday, Andrew Carnegie, and Richard Strauss

❁

WE lost one performance of *Salomé* in Chicago, and it wasn't the fault of the police. It was Mrs. Harold McCormick. This is how it happened.

We had scheduled four performances of *Salomé*, and all four were entirely sold out. The first three performances went smoothly. The house was filled to overflowing, there was tremendous excitement and not the merest hint of interference from any quarter. The fourth performance promised to be just as brilliant—and just as jammed—when I got word from Mrs. McCormick.

'There will be no fourth performance of *Salomé*,' read the message.

So I on with my hat and over to Mrs. McCormick's house.

'My dear Mrs. McCormick,' I said, 'I've given three performances of *Salomé*, and you've occupied your box for each one of them. Why can't I give the fourth?'

'It's you,' she said solemnly.

'But what have I done?' I asked, baffled. 'You accepted three of my Salomés. Why won't you accept the fourth? What *have* I done, Mrs. McCormick?'

'Miss Garden, the truth came to me in a flash when I went home after your third performance.'

'And just what do you mean by the *truth?*' I asked.

'I said to myself, "Edith, your vibrations are all wrong." '

And Mrs. McCormick crossed her hands over her breast, and I saw that there was no use talking any more. I went to Mr. Insull.

'I'll have to change the programme if you don't get her to permit the fourth performance,' I told him.

'I'll see what I can do,' he said.

Well, he went over to Mrs. McCormick and pleaded with her to change her mind, and all he could get out of her was the same answer:

'My vibrations were all wrong.'

So I had to change the programme and put *Pelléas* in place of *Salomé*. Of course, that wasn't what the public had paid to see, and though they took it like sports, there must have been great dissatisfaction in the house. Then the next thing you know, the papers took it up, and of course the police began to wonder whether, after all, there was anything here they should look into. Pretty soon they stepped in, too. I remember a policeman came to see me one day.

'Will you tell me why *Salomé* shouldn't be given?' I asked him. 'What's wrong with it?'

The good man looked very embarrassed.

'Come on,' I said, 'you can tell me. I'll try not to blush.'

'Well, Miss Garden, we've heard that you rolled around like a cat in catnip and that you had very little on.'

'They never complained about that in New York or Philadelphia,' I retorted. 'Somebody must be seeing things in Chicago.'

Just about then I received a telegram from Milwaukee. 'Come to us with *Salomé*,' it said, and of course we packed our things and went down and gave our fourth performance in Milwaukee to a house of ten thousand people, and what a magnificent reception we had! We performed *Salomé* in Convention Hall. Since they had no dressing-rooms, they built special papier mâché rooms for me and the other principals. The chorus had to go down into the basement to dress.

I remember I went to the hall very early, as I usually do wherever I am singing, and I was waiting there in my papier mâché dressing-room, all bejewelled and bewigged and dressed, when I thought I heard someone put his fingers through the wall. The fumbling stopped, and then after a while I heard it again. I opened the door, and there stood a great, big, red-faced Irish policeman.

'What are you doing, poking your fingers in my dressing-room?' I demanded.

'I'm looking for Mary Garden,' he said guiltily.

'*I* am Mary Garden. What do you want?'

'But you're dressed, Madame,' he sputtered.

'Certainly, I'm dressed,' I said. 'What did you expect?'

'Is that the way you sang *Salomé* in Chicago?'

'Most decidedly it was!'

'Well, what are those blankety-blank fellows in Chicago making such a fuss about?'

'I'm sure I don't know anything more about it than you do,' I said. 'Have you ever heard *Salomé?*'

He gave me a very Irish expression which I've forgotten, but which amounted to an emphatic 'Oh, no!'

'Well, then,' I said, 'you better go out and get a seat and listen and enjoy yourself and don't criticize it, because you're going to hear the most beautiful opera that's ever been written. And then come back and tell me what you think about it.'

But my big, red-faced Irish policeman never came back.

So we went on and sang *Salomé*. I didn't get a chance to look out into that enormous hall till the end of the opera, and when I finally saw what I had been singing into, my vocal cords just screamed for mercy.

We took *Salomé* on tour and went everywhere, and of course there were always people from the pulpit saying things about me and warning everybody about *Salomé*. And Billy Sunday! What didn't he say about me? I remember he was preaching in his tent when we arrived in one city.

'I'm going to hear Billy Sunday,' I said to one of the men of the theatre.

'Oh, you'd better not, Miss Garden!' he warned.

'Why not?' I said. 'I want to see what he's like.'

'But don't let him know who you are, because he's been saying all sorts of things about you, and something dreadful might happen.'

'I'm going over to listen to his sermon,' I said, and I went—alone.

Billy Sunday wasn't screaming about me that afternoon; it was the Vanderbilts and all their money who were getting it, and I can still see him flying over a table and chair, roaring and hollering like mad. I never in my life saw anything so ridiculous. After it was all over, I went back to see him.

'Mr. Billy Sunday?' I began.

'I don't think I know you, Madame,' he said.

'I am Mary Garden.'

He was so confused he couldn't say anything, this man who had been ranting for hours.

'What have you been preaching about me and *Salomé?*'

He looked very put out.

'I'm not going to tell you,' he said.

'But I must know,' I insisted. 'I'm sure people are telling you lies about me. What have you said about *Salomé*, Mr. Sunday?'

'Miss Garden,' he said very seriously, 'that's a very sinful opera.'

'Mr. Sunday,' I replied, 'it's all in the way you take it. And now will you stop talking about me and have you got a drink of water?'

It was so awfully hot that day, and there were thousands of people sweltering in the tent.

'No,' he said, 'but will you come on out and have a drink with me?'

And the two of us went into the nearest drugstore and sat on those high seats and ordered an ice-cream soda.

Oh, my, he was funny, Billy Sunday! I liked him, and when I left I said:

'I'm not afraid of you, Billy Sunday, or anybody, and I think the best thing to do when you hear about people saying anything against you is to go and face them.'

'Miss Garden,' he said, 'I agree, and it's been a pleasure meeting you. I guess I've been hearing lots of lies about you.'

For a few years Billy Sunday and I corresponded with each other, and I remember his letters were just as comical as he was, but I never saw him again after that ice-cream soda.

Then there was an episode on a concert tour. I can't remember the city. I know it was in Ohio, just a small place, and I was supposed to give a concert there that night. Well, I arrived late in the afternoon, and my manager went over to the hall to see if the piano was all right. An hour or so later he was back at the hotel, a frown on his face.

'Miss Garden,' he said, 'something's gone wrong.'

'What do you mean?' I asked. 'Isn't there a piano in the hall?'

'I don't know what's in there. The hall is locked, and we can't get in.'

'That's odd,' I said. 'You go over to the local manager and find out what's the matter.'

I looked at my watch.

'It's getting near seven o'clock, and I want to know what to do about that concert.'

He was back in a short while.

'It's no use, Miss Garden,' he said gloomily, 'I think we'd better start packing. You're being padlocked.'

'And just who is responsible for this?' I demanded.

'The minister. He's been preaching against you.'

'Do you mind telling me what he has been telling these people?'

'I'd rather not.'

'Don't be a fool. I want to know.'

'Well, he told them, "Anybody who buys a ticket to hear that woman is going plumb to hell." '

'So nobody bought any tickets,' I observed, 'and they shut down the hall. And now they can all go to heaven.'

'What'll we do, Miss Garden?'

'I'm not going to sit here worrying about this town's morals,' I said. 'Go and see if there's anything worth hearing to-night.'

My manager returned later to tell me there was a sort of operetta being sung somewhere.

'Go over and buy a box,' I said. 'I want to see what the people of this town are like.'

It was a very nice show they put on that night, and the singing was quite pleasant. The young man doing the main part must have found out I was in the house, because he suddenly stepped out before the curtains and put up his hand to quiet the crowd.

'Ladies and gentlemen,' he said, 'we have a great artist in our midst to-night. This woman came over here to sing for us, but she was not permitted to do so. So, instead, we are singing for her. Her name, ladies and gentlemen, is Mary Garden. Will you all stand up and give her a hand?'

And the whole house stood up and gave me a long ovation. When the little operetta was over, we all went home, and I must say I have never regretted going to that little town, even if it was the only city in the United States that banned any appearance of mine. And it was all because of *Salomé*.

But what had it to do with *Salomé?* Will someone kindly tell me? Because all I did was to sing and act in it. It wasn't *my* opera. And when I think of what goes on in *Faust*, and the free love in *Louise*, and the Lesbianism in *Aphrodite*, *Salomé* strikes me as pretty tame by comparison. Think of the incest in *Die Walküre!* Yet nobody ever seriously thought of padlocking Wagner or any woman singing Sieglinde. I suppose what they held against *Salomé*, the men of the pulpit, was that it was Biblical. But I'm not sure.

I was supposed to sing *Salomé* in Russia shortly before the First World War broke out, and I would have, if the Czarina hadn't got word of it. One of the great impresarios of Europe came to see me one day in Paris, offering me a contract for St. Petersburg. He was positive the Russians wanted *Salomé*. I agreed to go. But when he was brought in to see the Czarina about it, it was thumbs down. She was a fanatic about religion, and it seems that the very thought of *Salomé* in St. Petersburg revolted her. So the impresario wrote me that the deal was off. I was fearfully sorry, because I would have adored going to St. Petersburg.

My brief encounter with Billy Sunday reminds me of someone else who was very disturbed by another opera I sang. That gentleman was my distinguished countryman, Andrew Carnegie, whom I had the honour of knowing in America. The offending opera this time was *Louise*.

Carnegie and I once crossed the ocean in the same ship. We had many talks together and in one of them the conversation turned to opera.

'Miss Garden,' said Carnegie, 'there is one opera of yours I would never go to hear.'

'Which one is that?' I asked, intrigued.

'*Louise!*'

I was astonished.

'But, Mr. Carnegie, why?' I protested. 'It's one of the greatest masterpieces of our time.'

'Perhaps,' he said, 'but it's a bad, bad story—that girl and her young man. Not for me, thank you.'

And I said, very innocently, 'You don't believe in free love, Mr. Carnegie?'

And he said, 'Oh, no, Miss Garden!'

'Do you mind telling me, Mr. Carnegie, which opera you consider proper?'

'*Faust.*'

I said nothing, but I thought to myself. 'That's a rather spicy story, too.'

But, then, you see, once a work of art is established, it becomes pure. So, I suppose, in a hundred years the Andrew Carnegies and Billy Sundays will find *Louise*—and perhaps even *Salomé*—safe and inoffensive. They will be 'classics' then.

I was very fond of Carnegie, however. What he felt about modern opera was his own business. I found him charming and a Scotsman with great pride in the country of his birth.

I was once asked to sing Scotch songs at a Robert Burns dinner. That gave me great joy, and amid all those bagpipes blowing merrily away, it was Andrew Carnegie who escorted me on his arm to and from the platform.

I often wonder whether he forgave me for my Louise and Salomé for those Scotch songs.

Which reminds me that I went to Garmisch in 1910 to see Richard Strauss about *Salomé*. There had been some kind of quarrel at the Opéra in Paris. I had signed a new contract with them that year and I was going to create *Salomé* on my arrival in Paris. Then, one day, André Messager called me into his office.

'We can't give *Salomé*, Mary,' he announced gloomily.

'But why not? Is it the police?'

'No. It's Strauss himself. We're having a fearful fight with him—over nothing, really.'

'But that's childish,' I said. 'If I know Strauss at all, he couldn't possibly object to anything we're doing here.'

'Do you know him personally?'

'Why, yes,' I replied. 'I met him in Chicago while I was singing *Salomé* there. I found him very charming and co-operative.'

On my way out of M. Messager's office I said to myself, 'I must find out what this is all about.'

So I got into a train and went to Munich. From there I took a car and went on to Garmisch. When I got to Strauss' house I rang the doorbell, and he opened the door.

'Well, Mr. Strauss,' I said, 'how do you do?'

'What are you doing here?' were his words of greeting.

'I've come to talk about *Salomé*,' I said.

'So I suspected,' he said. 'Won't you step into my garden?'

And the two of us went into his charming garden and sat down at a table under a tree and drank tea.

'Mr. Strauss,' I began, 'I've come all the way from America to sing *Salomé* in Paris, and they tell me I can't do it because you are having a fight with the people of the Opéra.'

Strauss smiled and said nothing.

'I want to know why I am being prevented from singing *Salomé* in Paris?'

'Oh, well, let's forget all about the fight,' he said.

'I'm perfectly willing to, but will you permit us to do *Salomé?*'

'I think it can be arranged.'

'Will you give me your permission in a letter?'

'Gladly.'

'And you won't tell me what the quarrel was all about?'

'I thought we had agreed to forget it,' said Strauss. 'It was a matter of no consequence at all. I have something of real interest to tell you, however.'

'About *Salomé?*'

'No, about you.'

'Yes?'

'I'm writing an opera for you.'

'How exciting!' I said. 'What's it to be called?'

'*Der Rosenkavalier*, and you're going to be a boy in it.'

'How did you happen to think of me for the part?' I asked.

There was a glint of boyish mischief in Strauss' eyes.

'My librettist, Hugo von Hofmannsthal, saw you in Paris and wrote me that you were just the wench to do it because you had such beautiful legs.'

'Well, I never!'

And we both roared with laughter.

'Is the opera done?' I asked.

'Almost,' Strauss replied, and I remember he wrote that all out in a letter later.

Well, I went back to Paris and showed my letter of permission from Strauss to the directors of the Opéra. They immediately put *Salomé* into rehearsal, and then Paris saw something it had never seen before! There was never a triumph like that *Salomé*. I sang it on the average of three times every ten days during June and July. Then I went away in August, and when I came back in September I began singing it all over again.

I believe it was early in 1914 that I got a letter from the Opéra-Comique telling me to come over and sign a contract for *Der Rosenkavalier*. I went over and saw my old friend, Albert Carré, and then I went to Heughel, Strauss' publishers, and signed my contract to create the rôle of Octavian at the Opéra-Comique.

After I signed my contract the publishers gave me a copy of the score of *Der Rosenkavalier* and I took it home with me and began to study it. And I remember it wasn't very long after I began working on the music that war came and *Der Rosenkavalier* was never given. No German operas were done during the war. When the fighting had ended and they again began to give German repertory, *Der Rosenkavalier* was finally given in Paris, at the Opéra. And when I saw it there I knew that I would never have liked to do Octavian.

Oh, I didn't care for that opera at all. So I was just as glad that I hadn't created it at the Opéra-Comique. Everybody said I would have made a wonderful Octavian. Perhaps. The rôle didn't appeal to me at all. Making love to women all night long would have bored me to death.

So that was the last time I saw Richard Strauss, in his garden at Garmisch, discussing my legs. I never found out what the squabble over the Paris *Salomé* was about. Maybe it had to do with financial terms. Anyway, it was settled amicably over a cup of tea under a tree, and Strauss sent me a beautiful picture of himself with his name on it.

Then there was the curious story about me and Lucien Muratore. Who started it and how it started I never knew. Neither of us ever found out what it was all about; but did we have one battle royal of a press fight! You would have supposed from what appeared in the papers that we were sworn enemies, out to get each other by fair means or foul. One of the papers went so far as to have Muratore say, 'If Mary Garden were a man instead of a woman I would shoot her.' They quoted me as harbouring equally tender thoughts. It was just a newspaper feud, but it ran on and on and neither of us thought it worth while to put a stop to it.

A few years ago I was dining with him in Paris.

'Muratore,' I asked him, 'what was all that trouble about that you and I had in the Chicago papers?'

'I don't really know, Garden,' he said. 'I never could find out for sure. Someone did tell me that you were rude to me on the stage in *Carmen*.'

'Was I?'

'If you were, I never noticed it,' said Muratore.

'I don't think I've ever been rude to anyone—on the stage,' I said. 'If I wanted to be rude to you, I'd have left it to when the curtain fell.'

Muratore laughed.

'But what a row that was!' he said. 'And all over nothing.'

'You never really wanted to shoot me, did you, Muratore?' I asked.

Muratore made a villainous face.

'Maybe I did—who knows? And maybe you deserved it.'

And we both laughed ourselves sick over it.

I sang a great deal with Lucien Muratore because, I suppose, he was so much like me. He knew and understood every single thing I was doing on the stage.

Muratore dressed every one of his rôles to perfection. He used to go to the greatest trouble to get the very best clothes. When he dressed he was absolutely in the period. He was a great reader and an intellectual, and there wasn't an epoch he didn't know.

He knew how to act and he knew how to sing. I never bothered him on the stage, and he never bothered me. When I did something new and unexpected, Muratore would always be the first to compliment me.

'Oh, Garden,' he would say, 'that was wonderful, what you did to-night!'

'All right, Muratore,' I would reply, 'we'll keep it in.'

I sang *Carmen*, *Faust*, *Roméo et Juliette*, *Salomé*, and *Monna Vanna* with Muratore. He was superb in every one of them, always thoroughly in his rôle, the way I was in mine. He was never himself, always the part.

Whenever I was on the stage with that man I never once thought of him as Lucien Muratore. That was the kind of artist he was.

Another tenor I sang with was Ansseau. That was a voice! Muratore had a voice like mine. He coloured what he was singing with his voice; he was as little interested as I was in just standing there and singing. But this man Ansseau *sang*. What glorious tones were his! I believe singing with me ultimately gave him a new outlook in opera.

'I don't know what I'd do on the stage without you,' he said to me once.

'Nonsense,' I said; 'you'd still be the finest tenor there is.'

'No,' he said. 'The truth is I've become a different person on the stage. I find myself forgetting I am Ansseau.'

Ansseau had the tiniest waist for a man. I used to say to him:

'Thank God, I can put my arms around you! Don't you ever get fat!'

You know what most tenors are like. I always had great difficulty in putting my arms all around them.

## Samuel Goldwyn Signs Me Up

I WAS living in Versailles in the summer of 1913. One day, while lunching with some friends in the dining-room of my hotel, I saw a gentleman and a lady come in and take a table in front of me. I was facing the gentleman, who was tall and extremely handsome, and I soon caught him staring at me in a way I didn't like. I changed my chair so that my back would be to him, and that was the end of that.

The following year, after the war broke out, I was having dinner with a great friend of mine in Paris, when this same gentleman came into the restaurant. My friend rose to greet him and presented him to me as one of the great naval personages of our time.

'I've seen you before,' I said. 'Where?'

'At Versailles,' he said. 'You turned your chair around because I kept looking at you.'

'Why, of course,' I exclaimed; 'I remember now, you flirt! What were you doing in Versailles?'

'I was on my honeymoon,' he said, and I remember that gave me a start.

'What are you doing in Paris?' I asked.

'I'm here on naval business,' he said. 'I expect to remain two or three months.'

After that we began to see a great deal of one another. I don't think I'm exaggerating in the least when I say he was just about the handsomest man I ever saw. He was then fifty, very tall, with a gorgeous figure and pure grey hair, and that uniform of his was something too lovely for words. When he marched down the middle aisle of the Opéra-Comique in that uniform—and that was every night I sang—people would turn around and say, '*Mon Dieu, qui est-il?*' I can still see him walking down that aisle.

Of course, the inevitable happened. He was an Englishman and very, very correct, but he tumbled over like a house of cards, and that just fascinated me. Soon he told me he couldn't live without seeing me. Then, one day, he was suddenly called away to war duty, and I went to Bordeaux to bid him good-bye. I don't think I've ever had a more tragic farewell than when that man left.

Did I love him? I may have, in my own cold way. I was flattered more than I was in love. It made no real difference to me whether he came to see me or not. He was so very cold to every other woman. But that good-bye! It wasn't going to be for long, really, except that it was wartime and you never knew if you were coming back.

I never saw a man, a great man and a great officer and an Englishman, lose such complete control of himself. He just cried tears of agony, like a child, because he was going away. I'll never forget it. He said very little. I suppose he was suffering too much to say anything, really.

In 1914, while the submarine warfare was at its height, I was about to go back to Europe, when I received a cable from my naval officer.

'Don't return on any boat but a Spanish boat,' it read.

So I had an opportunity to see Spain. . . . I was lucky to get a place on the *Alfonso XIII*, sailing to Vigo. It was just a six-thousand-ton yacht, but I had the good fortune to get a small room for myself. There was just one chair in that room, no carpet on the floor, and no running water. When I wanted to wash, I was brought hot water in a small jug.

The day we sailed I caught a glimpse—and a whiff—of the

kitchen as I went down to my room. I resolved then and there that I would eat nothing that came out of that kitchen. Luckily, friends had sent me several baskets of fruit. So the ten days it took to reach Vigo, I ate my meals out of those baskets.

Eight of those ten days I spent in bed. And while *Alfonso XIII* tossed and tumbled in stormy weather, I amused myself watching the oranges and melons and pineapples roll out of my baskets and fly around the room. I used to place mental bets on which piece of fruit would get around the room first. It was always the pineapple that won.

As we sailed out of New York Harbour, I was standing at the rail of the *Alfonso*, waving good-bye to everyone, when an American gentleman came up to me.

'Are you Miss Garden?' he asked.

I said I was.

'I have been appointed to save you should anything happen at sea,' he went on.

'That's very comforting,' I said. 'Just what do you think might happen?'

'If we should be torpedoed by a submarine,' he replied, 'there might be a struggle for a boat, and you might be stabbed or drowned.'

'That's a cheerful thought,' I said. 'I'm most grateful to you, but I hope it won't be necessary.'

There were many interesting people on board—Mrs. Morgan, with her two beautiful daughters (later to become Mrs. Vanderbilt and Lady Furness); Nijinsky, with his wife and little daughter and their ballet, on their way to dance in Spain.

I had met Nijinsky a few years earlier, when Serge Diaghilev and I happened to be in Venice at the same time. Diaghilev invited me to lunch one day to meet Nijinsky. He took me to one of those picturesque Venetian restaurants, where Italian food was of the best, and there we waited for the dancer. A half hour went by, and, all of a sudden, Nijinsky, with his dark skin, almond-shaped eyes, and the waist of a wasp, came floating into the room, ordered in a quick manner something in Russian, which turned out to be a watermelon, and ate it in complete silence. Then he bounded up from the table and floated away again.

My steward, whom I took for the captain, in his dark-blue uniform, gold braid, and diamond studs, spoke no English or French. The stewardess, who was also no linguist, was the fattest woman I ever saw. All she could say was '*Coma, coma, coma!*' Both were desperate because I ate nothing. They would poke their fingers down their throats and try to make me understand what 'eat' was in Spanish. But they never succeeded. I had seen the kitchen.

I spent eight full days in my cabin. On the ninth day, I finally went up on deck. I saw Nijinsky and never would have recognized him as the beautiful will-o'-the-wisp I had seen in Venice.

On the tenth day, we arrived in Vigo. We had a delicious lunch of shellfish; at any rate, it tasted delicious to me after my ten days of self-imposed fruit dieting. And then off to Madrid in the train.

When I entered the Ritz Hotel, I ran into some French friends of mine from Paris who were there on military duty, and we dined together. They got an American correspondent whom they knew to take us to a celebrated café to see the night life of Madrid. Many of the performers were Andalusian gypsies; I have rarely seen such grace, beauty, and dancing anywhere. They also sang their folk songs—weird, melancholy, and haunting.

And that's where I saw what a real Carmen was. She came to our table and put a rose down in front of one of the men and gave him a look. That was all that was needed. She didn't pull up her skirts or pull her shawl down from her bosom. She just gave him a look, and he knew perfectly well what she wanted. That is the real Carmen; not the kind that shows her legs and breasts. It helped me understand the character of Carmen, and when I came to do the rôle, I based it on that episode in the Madrid Café. I used to give my baritone Baklanoff that look, and he would look right back at me with those eyes of his, and that was the end of it.

If any of the singers who do Carmen had ever been to Spain they wouldn't act the way they do. I saw one Carmen who spat oranges in Don José's face.

If ever I put on *Carmen* as director of an opera company, I shall do it the way the Ballets de Paris do it. That is the true conception of *Carmen*.

There is one detail of the Card Scene in the third act that I believe is more effective the way I did it. Two of the girls are reading their fortunes. *Carmen doesn't read cards*. She shuffles the pack and she opens it to death. When she sees that, she puts her cards together again. *And she stands*. Carmen doesn't sit and she doesn't put her mantilla on the floor and lie on it.

Then when Carmen says that it is death for both of them, she sings to the audience not what is in the cards, but what is in her mind. It is a beautiful thing, that little bit of business. Finally, when she gets through with that, she opens her cards again. She still sees death, and she closes them.

Now, instead of that, I have seen singers spread their things on the floor and put out their cards. But Carmen isn't reading her fortune!

The next day before leaving for Paris, I went shopping and got myself some lovely coloured combs and fans for my performance of *Carmen*, which I was scheduled to sing the following week in Paris for soldiers who had been blinded in the war. I never knew so many men to come up and speak to me in the street as I did in Madrid. They would just stop every ten feet of the way and talk to me. . . .

Then I went on to Paris and saw those dear boys brought into the Opéra-Comique, each one accompanied by a nurse. It was a sad and harrowing sight to watch their young faces all attention to hear *Carmen* because they couldn't *see Carmen*.

Later in the war, my naval officer went away and I never saw him again. But I knew a lady who had dinner with him in London some years ago. The conversation got around to me—how, I don't know—and he said to this lady:

'Mary Garden was the only woman I ever loved in my life.'

With all other people that man was like ice; he was very just, but not liked, really. How his men felt about him I don't know, though I suspect none of them cared for him. Yet they must have known that he would always be fair and that if he said anything he must mean it. He was a perfect seaman of the higher rank, one of those men whose life is the lonely, detached life of the sea . . . and cold. But he wasn't cold with me. Underneath that ice he was a man of a clinging and romantic nature. But it made little difference to me when I didn't see him any more.

I repeat, I never missed them, any of them. I had other things in my life, my work, my books. I liked all those men for their companionship. That was all, really. Nobody ever took me from my work, not a man who lived. That was my life and my passion, my work. That's what I really lived with. It wasn't any individual; it was my work that made me live. I'm very sorry if I made any of these men suffer. I didn't ask to make them suffer. If they broke down and whined and whimpered, they had only themselves to blame. There never was anything in the world to take the place of my work—nothing and nobody. That's how I was. I'm a very proud woman, and I never could and never wanted to change myself, certainly not for the love of any man.

It was some time in 1916, when I was at the height of my career, that Samuel Goldwyn came to see me in New York.

'Miss Garden,' he said, 'we'd like you to do a motion picture of *Thaïs*.'

'That interests me very much, Mr. Goldwyn,' I said. 'Where are we going to make it?'

'The desert scenes in Florida and the rest in Jersey City,' he said.

'What will you pay?'

'One hundred and twenty-five thousand dollars, for which we expect you to work ten weeks.'

'I find that highly satisfactory,' I said. 'I only hope you have a director who knows something about Egypt.'

'Don't you worry your pretty head about that,' Mr. Goldwyn said. 'If he doesn't, he'll learn fast enough.'

Well, I went over to Jersey City and began work on *Thaïs*. For a while it was interesting—till I discovered that the gentleman putting it on not only knew nothing about Egypt, but had no intention of finding out. From then on it was just torture for me.

They had me do things that I'm sure neither Thaïs nor anybody else in any other part of the world would ever have done under any circumstances. I remember I was supposed to be walking in the garden, and along my path were thirty parrots on their perches.

'Scratch their heads!' the director shouted to me.

'You're not serious!' I protested.

'Scratch their heads!' he demanded.

'All of them?' I asked.

'Each and every one of them.'

And scratch their heads I did; for a hundred and twenty-five thousand dollars I suppose I would have scratched the heads of all the parrots in the world.

Then there was a woman who was rather important in the company; I've forgotten her name, but I haven't forgotten her, and I'm sure she hasn't forgotten me. One day I brought a few roses for one of the directors, a perfectly innocent gesture, for he meant absolutely nothing to me. But when this woman saw that she jumped on me like a tigress. I remember that for some reason or other, during a discussion of the story on the set, I said to her:

'But, Madam, I'm playing Thaïs, and in this part of the story I'm supposed to act like a saint.'

She gave a very nasty laugh.

'*You* a saint!' she snarled at me; 'why you . . .!'

And that started the most awful scene I ever got caught in. I began to cry, and then we strode toward one another, arms upraised, and poor Mr. Goldwyn had everything to do to keep us apart. Some years later I met that woman again in Paris. I was with my naval officer when she came into the restaurant. After surveying the tables, she saw me and walked over.

'How do you do?' she said, giving my naval officer an appraising glance.

'I beg your pardon,' I said very sweetly. 'I don't think I know you; in fact, I'm certain I've never seen you in my life.'

And the woman turned her back and rejoined her friends.

'Don't you really know her?' my officer asked, when she had gone.

'Of course I know her, but I don't want *her* to know it.'

We finished the film version of *Thaïs* in less than seven weeks, after which Mr. Goldwyn came to see me.

'Mary, you owe me three weeks,' he said.

'What have you in mind, Mr. Goldwyn?'

'How about making another film for us? Just a small one this time.'

'I'd be delighted. What's it to be called?'

'*The Splendid Sinner.*'

'That's me, I suppose.'

'That's you, Mary,' said Mr. Goldwyn.

I made *The Splendid Sinner* in three weeks, and I hope nobody in God's world will ever see it again. I have heard many films called the worst ever made; I am sure those who make such judgments never saw *The Splendid Sinner.*

I remember I had to shoot a man in the film, and I had to go off to war as a nurse. But I was a spy, really, and the Germans finally got me, and the next thing you knew I was standing before a firing squad. I shall never forget how Mr. Goldwyn would personally examine every one of the guns to be sure there were no real bullets in them. Oh, mercy, when they shot me! That was something the like of which has never been seen on the screen again. But shoot me they did, and I died, most conspicuously, in my uniform of nurse. When I had finished my ten weeks, I said good-bye to the movies for good.

If they had been talking films, I suppose I would have been all right, because then I could have talked and brought out some sort of character. And I would like to say here that every actor and actress in the motion-picture business earn every sou they make. They can't ever ask too much—sitting there from nine in the morning to six in the evening, with paint all over their faces, and living and never getting out of that atmosphere. What a tiring métier it is, beginning and beginning all over again, until you don't know what you're doing.

In the silent days we didn't say anything; we just looked. That's why there was no place for a woman like me. I had to talk. Just marching around and moving my hands smothered me as an artist. The young ones like Mary Pickford—they went on and charmed people with their sweet youth and prettiness; but a great actress had no place in the motion pictures during the silent days. Now they can talk and act and give out their sentiments. But in those days you could do nothing but walk around.

That was in Jersey City in 1916. I didn't see the film *Thaïs* till they screened it one day in Nice. It had been shown in New York, but I don't think it was a hit; I don't see how that monstrosity could possibly have been a hit with anyone in his right mind. The French all went to see it when it reached Europe, and the only reason they went was because they liked me. Oh, but it was bad! It was no more *Thaïs* than I was Cleopatra! I never saw *The Splendid Sinner;* I can stand anything, but that, I'm certain, would have finished me.

I feel the same about my records; I just loathe them. I can't bear it when someone plays a trick on me and turns them on. I made them at a time when we were singing in wax. We had to stand in front of a small hole in a great enormous piece of wax. The wax flew all over the place. We were supposed to sing, and someone would say, 'Go in front!' and 'Go behind!' I just couldn't do it. I was an opera singer, a singing actress, and I couldn't put that on records. To-day you can stand in a room and have perfect liberty to sing and be yourself. Then it was mental and physical agony.

The recordings I recall most vividly were those I made with Claude Debussy of a part of *Pelléas* in 1902. Those were on cylinders. We were invited to make them shortly after the success of *Pelléas*, and unless I've forgotten, I believe we put one or two of his songs on cylinders too, but I'm not sure. We both went down to the Pathé studio in Paris to make them. I sang, and Debussy accompanied at the piano. Some years ago, a man wrote me that those old *Pelléas* cylinders had been put on records and were selling very well. I can't understand that.

I do know they were dreadful, those cylinders. I can think of only one value that the records made from them could have. People have a chance to hear Debussy at the piano, and the women who sing Mélisande should listen to those records over and over again. For they would then understand the tempo to take. Otherwise, those records are worthless. Debussy didn't enjoy doing them very much. But then he never enjoyed anything, really, except writing music.

The only record of mine that I would knowingly permit anybody to play in front of me is one I made of the lovely song, 'At Dawning.' I'd like to find it some day and take it home to my sister in Aberdeen.

## Alfano and *Resurrection*

❁

VICTOR HERBERT'S *Natoma* was 'the first American grand opera.' So they said, but I myself considered it a very excellent light opera, nothing more. I sang it in Chicago with John McCormack, and there was an American girl named Lillian Grenville in the cast, too; but most of the others were French, and they had to sing in English, and, believe me, that was a scream.

I remember one day I went to rehearsal. As I came in I heard those Frenchmen trying to pronounce some of the English lines. I just lay on the piano in hysterics. The basso was supposed to say 'a woof of royal wool,' but he got his tongue all tied up in his mouth, and he couldn't say it, and I couldn't hold back my laughter. Then another Frenchman had trouble with the line, 'Look the mustang in the eye!' What that sounded like I can never hope to show you.

We had Mr. Herbert worried for a while about my dagger dance in *Natoma*. I must say it was a lovely thing as I did it. While I was dancing my dagger dance, off in another part of the stage one of the men was abducting a beautiful young girl. What bothered Mr. Herbert was that while the girl was being kidnapped, nobody would notice me.

'Won't it hurt the dance?' Mr. Herbert asked Joe Redding, the man who wrote the book of *Natoma*.

'Hurt it?' Joe replied. 'Why, Victor, that man could be taking his pants off and nobody would see him when Mary's on the stage.'

I was an Indian maiden and John McCormack was a lieutenant of the Navy, and I loved him and he didn't love me—in the opera, of course. So I had to rush down the stage and throw myself at his feet and say:

'I love you! I love you! Don't leave me!'

And poor John put his hands on his knees one night and looked down at me and whispered:

'My God, Mary, you scared me to death!'

One night in New York, when John and I were at the height of our American careers, I went to the Hippodrome to hear one of his concerts.

When it was over, I went backstage to see him and found him acknowledging the tremendous applause he was receiving. As he caught sight of me, he rushed over and seized my hands.

'Come on out, Mary, and take a bow,' he cried. 'You need it. You are so little known in America!'

John loved his little jokes.

I suppose I ought to say something about another American opera I created, an opera that nobody in Chicago liked but that I thought had moments of great beauty. I admit I was responsible for staging it in Chicago, and I think I would do it all over again, knowing it would be an absolute flop, if only to give an American composer a chance to have an opera produced by a big company, and that, as everybody knows, is a rare thing indeed.

The name of this young American composer was Hamilton Forrest, and his opera was *Camille*. I believe Mr. Insull had already come in as director of the Chicago Grand Opera, a post he was to hold for ten years. I was again just an artist in the company, and what happened off the stage was no longer any of my business. I was free again, free to give everything that was *me* and *in me* to my beloved rôles.

Hamilton Forrest had once worked as office boy in Mr. Insull's utilities. Well, he came to me one day with a very interesting symphonic composition. It was not for the theatre, but a sort of small symphony. The young man played it for me on the piano, and I thought there were many fine things in it, very new, too.

'Why don't you write an opera?' I said to him. 'If you do and I like it, we'll give it at the Auditorium.'

'I've already been thinking of one,' he said.

'Splendid!' I cried. 'What's the theme of it?'

'A modern version of *Camille*,' he said.

'Good for you!' I exclaimed. 'But I think you ought to write it in French. It just won't do in English.'

'I was planning to leave for Paris soon, Miss Garden. I'll work on it there.'

'I expect to be back there some time this summer,' I said. 'Come and see me.'

When I finally got back to Paris, Forrest called on me. The score was almost finished. He played it for me, and I went over the text, and it appealed to me very strongly. I urged him to finish it and promised to persuade Mr. Insull to allow us to put it on the following season. On my return to Chicago, I went to see Mr. Insull.

'Is it a good opera?' he asked.

'I think so,' I answered. 'But I also think we owe it to him as an American composer. They don't get much of a break, you know.'

'Your word is good enough for me, Miss Garden.'

'I think you also owe it to yourself as a matter of pride, Mr. Insull,' I said.

'I don't follow you.'

'You may not know it, but this young man was once your office boy.'

'That settles it, Miss Garden. Anybody that can work for Sam Insull and then go ahead and write an opera deserves to have it produced. We'll put it on just as fast as you can get it ready.'

I think *Camille* was the hardest music we ever struggled with. It just screeched with modernism. At our first orchestral rehearsal the men put down their instruments and groaned, it was so fearfully difficult. And poor Emil Cooper, who conducted! What a wretched time he had! He put all his soul into it, but he said that never in his life had he conducted anything so difficult.

We gave *Camille* in Chicago, and I was Camille. That American tenor, Charles Hackett sang it with me, and he and I just sweated blood till we got to the end of it. What fiendish music it was! But it had a great many striking things in it, and I remember how gratified I was when I got a telephone message from Edward Sheldon, the man who wrote the play *Romance*. I believe he then was paralysed up to his eyes, and he must have heard a broadcast of the opera —if they were broadcasting then—because I don't know how else he could have got to it in his condition. Sheldon adored *Camille* and complimented me on producing it, and for a while we went on exchanging letters. So *Camille* couldn't have been all bad.

There were other people who thought there were a few good moments in *Camille*, but I'm afraid none of those people were in Chicago. It was a pretty dismal failure there. I just wanted to give an American a chance, and I wanted an American 'grand opera'! It interested me greatly to do it, but it didn't interest the public at all. Maybe Forrest was too young, and maybe I should never have asked him to write an opera. I still don't think it was a total loss. But that was the end of *Camille*. There's absolutely nothing else to say about it.

One of my favourite creations in Chicago was Katusha in *Resurrection*. The book was by Tolstoy, and the music by an

Italian named Franco Alfano, and that was one of the most satisfying experiences of my whole career.

I got to know about *Resurrection* one summer in Monte Carlo from my accompanist, Bartholemy. He came to me one day and said:

'There's a second-rate opera company playing in Nice to-night. They're doing an opera by a friend of mine, and I'd like you to hear it. Would you care to go?'

'I'd be delighted,' I said. 'You know I'm always looking for new things.'

We went down to Nice to hear it, and I saw immense possibilities in the opera. I immediately cabled Chicago:

'I've found a new opera. Will you buy it and give it to me to do next season?'

They wired back one word: 'Yes.'

They must have had confidence in my judgment, for they bought it immediately and began distributing it to all the artists. I began to study *Resurrection* in Monte Carlo. I went back to Chicago with my rôle all learned, and I found them all ready.

Oh, how I adored that opera! That poor girl's innocence, her disillusionment with men, her crime and imprisonment, and the final resurrection of her soul. Each act was different, each about a different woman, really, yet about the different woman that is potentially in all women, and to each act I gave a different voice. Perhaps that fascinated me most of all, how I managed to be so many women and so many voices in one opera. Of course, it was a great triumph in Chicago, and so I said to myself: 'Paris has just got to hear this opera!'

When I returned to France, I went to the directors of the Opéra-Comique.

'I want you to produce Alfano's *Resurrection*,' I said. 'It's a splendid opera, and I'm sure the public will adore it.'

'We should like to oblige you very much, but we can't give you a promise,' I was told.

'I don't understand.'

'Well, you know this is a government theatre, and as such we are not allowed to produce more than one foreign opera a year.'

'That's simple,' I said. 'That one foreign opera has got to be mine this year.'

'But it's not quite that simple, Mlle. Garden. You see, we have already contracted with another Italian composer.'

'Then there's nothing more to say.'

'But won't you come back and sing *Pelléas et Mélisande* for us?'

'All right,' I said, 'if you promise to give me everybody who created the opera with me . . . and André Messager as conductor.'

'We shall do everything you wish, if only you'll come back.'

'In that case, I'll give twelve performances of *Pelléas et Mélisande*—for nothing.'

I think I owed it to the Opéra-Comique. I had made my name and reputation in that beautiful institution. Of course, I had my own ulterior purpose. I was never one to be discouraged by a momentary rebuff. Well, I gave the twelve performances I had promised—all without pay—and when the curtain came down on the twelfth I went to see the directors again.

'Now, you've got to give me Alfano's *Resurrection.*'

And they threw up their hands—and did.

I wrote to Alfano, and he came from Turin to hear this work of his given for the first time with the greatest artistry. It was even more brilliant in Paris than it had been in Chicago.

Alfano had been a poor man till then, but now he made enough money to build himself a little house in San Remo, all covered with roses, and he had me down as the first guest to dine with him and his wife.

'Mary,' he said, 'this is what you've given to me by bringing my *Resurrection* to the attention of the world. Nobody would have heard of my opera if it hadn't been for you.'

I never saw anybody so happy as Alfano and his wife in the little dream cottage they had built from the proceeds of his opera. I turned to his wife Marthe, an attractive French girl.

'You must come to Paris to hear the opera,' I said.

'No,' she replied. 'In my prayers I've always said to God, "If ever I have a home of my own, I'll never leave it," and I never shall.'

She was a very religious girl, and she never once saw her husband's opera—or set foot off her little property.

Then when Puccini died, before he could finish his last opera, *Turandot*, the great house of Ricordi gave Alfano the honour of completing it. And when Alfano had placed the last note on paper, all the Puccinis and all the Ricordis came down to hear him play it on the piano. And while he was playing the last act of *Turandot*, something dreadful happened. The poor man had a hæmorrhage of the eyes and went totally blind.

I was then living in my villa in Beaulieu, near Monte Carlo. When the news reached me, I wrote to him asking him to come over to my villa and we would talk about it. I was already thinking of a famous occulist whom I had met in Corsica and who was then living in Nice. When Alfano arrived at my villa, I told him about this Corsican doctor, and the two of us drove down to Nice to see him. I saw the oculist alone for a few minutes before he examined Alfano.

'I want you to promise me something, Doctor. If he can never see again, don't tell him.'

The doctor agreed, and I waited outside while the examination went on. When they came out again, Alfano was clapping his hands like a little boy, and shouting:

Cleopatra

Thaïs

Katusha in Act I of *Resurrection*

Katusha in the last act of *Resurrection*

'Mary, Mary, where are you? I'm going to see! I'm going to see!'

I took the oculist aside.

'Is that true, Doctor?'

'Yes, Miss Garden, Mr. Alfano will see again.'

I kept Alfano at my villa till his nerves were stronger and he was completely relaxed. He had been living in such a frightful state of tension since he was stricken. Then he went back to his wife, who wouldn't leave her little house in San Remo. I was so happy to have given him back his peace of mind.

That *Resurrection* of Alfano's is an acting opera. It is drama, and therefore you have to find someone who not only sings but who knows what drama is. That person must be able to bring these two things together. When we find her, we might have *Resurrection* again. What a rôle, Katusha! The contrast of absolute innocence and absolute crime, so entirely different, the way I did the part. And the pictures they took of me as both Katushas—you'd never suspect they were the same woman.

## The Curtain Falls in Chicago

IT was after I became director of the Chicago Opera Company in 1922 that I had my first contact with Lina Cavalieri since our Hammerstein days. She was then married to that splendid French tenor, Muratore, and Mr. McCormick had engaged her to sing for us. As her director, I sent word one day, asking her what night she wanted to make her début, what rôle she wanted it to be, and whom did she want to conduct. She sent back a reply that she wanted to sing Tosca with Georges Baklanoff and that Giorgio Polacco should conduct. Well, at noon the day of her début I got a message from her doctor, saying that she was ill and couldn't appear. So I had to arrange for another singer in my company to do Tosca that night. If I remember correctly, it was Rosa Raisa who helped me out that night, a lady of great charm.

The following week I sent the same letter to Mme. Cavalieri, and at five in the afternoon of the day she was supposed to make her début I got another message from her doctor. Mme. Cavalieri was ill again and couldn't possibly sing that night. That was that. This time I changed the programme—from *Tosca* to *Pelléas et Mélisande*. And Lina Cavalieri never sang with us. She had been engaged to sing at fifteen hundred dollars a night, but she never sang. I recall speaking to Baklanoff one day about Cavalieri.

'Mary, she'll never sing Tosca,' he said.

'But why? That's supposed to be one of her great successes.'

'She's afraid.'

Cavalieri was perfectly beautiful; of course, she wasn't in her youth any longer, but what a lovely figure and face that woman had! Muratore married her, and I'm told they were very happy together. Some years later they gave concerts together in Paris, but I never saw her again.

Although Mr. Insull had been quite sweet about allowing me to go ahead with the opera *Camille*, he and I never really struck it off together. There was one little thing that happened in his office when I first knew him that showed me why we'd never work together. I went up to see him one day, and there, hanging on the wall facing his desk, was an enormous painting of Adelina Patti.

'Mr. Insull,' I said, 'what makes you keep Adelina Patti up there? It's been so many years since she stopped singing.' And then, jokingly, I added, 'Why don't you put me up there?'

He looked at me, and in all seriousness said:

'Miss Garden, I hate modern opera. I like the old things.'

That was that. I knew he and I were in two different worlds and that we would never see eye to eye about an opera house. Well, Samuel Insull built himself a dream opera house in Chicago, and up on the forty-seventh floor of this enormous building he put his office. The idea was sound, I suppose, commercially. There were forty-seven stories of offices to pay the annual deficit of the opera company he was sponsoring. But he made several fatal blunders. To begin with, he went and built his opera house in the wrong part of Chicago. The crowds wouldn't bother to go there because it was out of the way. Then, it wasn't really an opera house, but more like a convention hall. We had absolutely no communication with the public.

How different from the Chicago Auditorium, which was beautiful acoustically. We were always in complete communication with the three thousand people sitting there. And they, in turn, always felt they were very near to us. I said once to Jean de Reszke, 'You've been singing all over the world. What do you consider the finest place to sing in for acoustics?' And without hesitation he replied, 'The Auditorium in Chicago.'

But the opera house that Mr. Insull built had forty-seven rows of seats, with two enormous dark walls on each side and not a single box along them. The only boxes were far off at the end of the rows of seats, and nobody could see anybody else. They just couldn't reach us, and we couldn't reach them. When I looked into that long black hole, I said, 'Oh, no!'

There was something else too, perhaps the worst drawback of all. I saw very soon what Mr. Insull had in mind. That was to turn the opera into a utility, like all his business. You can't do that, of course, without destroying the very spirit of art. Nobody ever did and nobody ever will make a business of grand opera. It's just impossible. . . . So, when I finished my career in America, I finished it in that opera house, and it happened to me quite suddenly.

I was doing the *Jongleur* on that particular night. While the others were singing and doing other things in the opera, I sat by myself on a bench in one corner of the stage. Before I knew what I was doing, I was talking to myself, or rather to the little boy whose part I was playing.

'Dear little Jongleur,' I said. 'You've performed all your little stunts. Everything you had you've given to the Virgin. Now your work is done.'

Then I turned to myself.

'I, Mary Garden, have given twenty of the best years of my life to my work here in Chicago, and I've given everything to the people as well as I could, and now I think I'll go.'

When the final curtain came down, I went into my dressing-room, dressed myself to go home, and without saying good-bye to anybody I left, and I never went back. I walked out of that vast hall without seeing a soul. I told nobody of my decision, and when I was back in Paris they cabled me to return the following season.

'My career in America is done,' I cabled back.

And then Samuel Insull suffered his fall from glory, and the opera house was closed. So, I suppose, it was just as well that my decision came when it did. I never went back to America—as a singer. I sang awhile longer in Paris, mostly Alfano's *Resurrection*, and then I stopped altogether.

Painters and sculptors and architects and poets can stay in their métiers for a hundred years, if they live to that age, but nature tells a singer when to halt. Yet, very few of them ever heed the warning. They prefer to have others say it for them that it's time to quit. I chose to leave when I knew I could still continue if I wanted to. The public is a marvellous inspiration to anybody before it, but it is very cruel if you go beyond the moment you should stop.

Oh, what I've heard people say about other singers! I didn't want them to be saying those dreadful things about me! 'The poor thing! She's finished, and she doesn't know it!' I've heard it, and I didn't care to have them saying it about me.

What did I notice at that particular performance of *Jongleur* that made me decide to give it all up? Nothing to worry me, really. I was in good voice that night, and I felt as artistically vital as I had ever felt. It was just this: when you've sung for thirty years as I did, and you've given all the great modern operas written in France—sixteen of them—and you've had almost nothing else in those thirty years but your career, the day comes when you say:

'I've done enough; now I'll live!'

There was nothing in my last performance of Alfano's *Resurrection* in Paris that made me say, 'I can't do it any more.' I will confess this much, however: my voice was still firm, but I had been using it steadily for a good many years, and frankly I was apprehensive of what might happen—maybe the following month, maybe the following year.

'This is the time,' I said to myself; '*now*, not later.'

And when once I had made up my mind, I never had any regrets, never. I heard hundreds and hundreds of singers after that, some very good and some very bad, but not once did I say to myself. 'Oh, why did I give it up so quickly!'

There was no jealousy, no nostalgia. I closed something up here, the music box in my brain, and I never opened it again. That was the end of me as an operatic being, and that was in 1934 in Paris. I had begun my career in Paris and I ended it in Paris. It was rounded and complete. I had never sung in any country but France and Belgium and America, except for a few performances in London and one performance of *Pelléas* in Cologne. The truth is I never had time to go anywhere else. My contracts usually took up ten months of every year. The other two months of the year I used for my holidays.

And during those two months I forgot completely that I was a singer, or that there was an opera house, or that there was music in the world. Those two months I went to live with nature. At first it was Monte Carlo, then Corsica. I adore mountains, their mystery and their grandeur, and I adore the sea, because, I imagine, I was born beside the sea. I just love to be in it. I also love the heat and the sun and I got all I wanted on Corsica. And I love the cold and the snow of my own country.

I am at home with nature, but I don't like going into a motor car and lunching somewhere on the grass and then driving back. I love to take books with me up into the mountains, and I love to plunge into the sea and feel the sensuousness of going into water and being alive there. . . .

I had to have those two months during my whole career, and I always tried to spend them alone. I suppose that's why I lasted as long as I did. There is so much to see and feel in nature—to watch the many ways the sun sets and the many ways it rises. When I cross the ocean I usually stay in my cabin, but I always go up and watch the sun rise and then go back to my bed again. I used to go up to the highest mountains in Switzerland and look at the sky at night. I never knew there were so many colours in the stars.

What were my thoughts with nature? Just the glories of the world around me. I had no anxieties, no troubles, no anything that would break in on the beauty of those two months I had alone. When my sister went to Corsica with me, she didn't like it at all; she complained about the heat and the mosquitoes and everything else. But I never felt the heat, and I never knew there were any mosquitoes on the island.

I never felt anything but the wonder and the peace of being with nature and myself. And how it thrilled me on Corsica to see all the haunts of the boy Napoleon, and how I studied the life of that amazing man and read all the books about him I could get my hands on! But it was nature I was with all the time. People can't be great who don't love nature, yet oh, how many people spend their lives passing it by!

I remember once my sister and I took a funicular up the Alps. We saw the whole range of mountains, and there was Mont Blanc stealing up into the sky. I said to my sister:

'What a lot of ants we are! Look at those mountains. They stand up for centuries and centuries and never change—just like genius.'

I looked forward to those two months of vacation; but that doesn't mean I was ever depressed or bored during my ten months of work. I loved every moment of my working career, and in all those thirty years I always said to myself before I went on the stage:

'There's one person in that vast audience who has made a sacrifice to come and hear me, and for that one person I'm going to give my best.'

I never had anything but pride and glory in my work, and I never once said: 'Oh, God, I've got to sing again to-night!'

I had the same enthusiasm for my work that I had for those two months of vacation. I never was bored for a moment, and I never knew what loneliness was. I don't understand people when they tell me how lonely they are. How can they be when they have books and nature—and themselves?

What were my impersonations like? I think the one word that best describes them is improvization. My performances of the same rôle were the same and they were different. It depended on the mood of the moment, how I or, better, how the character felt. Usually it amounted to nothing more than this: I took my character and I gave it to the public. Sometimes I would keep it that way and sometimes I wouldn't. I mean, of course, the mood of the woman I was singing, not *my* mood. She always had a mood, especially Salomé, though not so much Mélisande.

You see, these women I became all had moods, and I had to find that mood, and perhaps the very next time I would find another mood. Just what mood depended on how they came into my brain, and I suppose that's what made me different from anybody else. Most of the others sang; they didn't create the mood of the woman. They were singers who never lost their identities, whereas I was never myself on the stage. I was always the woman I was singing. I was always completely convinced of the woman's motivation. If only singers had it all in their heads and not only in their vocal cords . . . Those who saw my Mélisande saw something strange and inexplicable. I couldn't begin to explain her; I could only live her, and it was the music that gave me that. Others sang the words; I sang Mélisande.

The change of mood would depend entirely on how I picked up the character in the first act. Then I carried that mood through to the end, which was perhaps not the same mood as the one I had had before. The secret was in how I caught the moods of these women at the start. I began to notice it in my early work. 'My,' I would say to myself, 'I played a different mood of Thaïs to-night.' It might have been a very suave mood. Then the next time I'd make her very arrogant, very Thaïs, very powerful. And the time after that she might be very *amoureuse* and *câline*.

I, Thaïs, was tired of life. All my lovers had ceased to interest me. There were all these different moods when I was with them. Finally, I met the monk and I now knew what I wanted, but I wouldn't permit myself to think it. So I sent him away in furious anger when he dared to say I would become a religious woman.

But I thought over what the monk had said, and when I came back in the next act it troubled me. Nobody interested me then. So I followed him into the desert, not freely, but because he pulled me away from this life. I hadn't really walked out. And now you saw the change from arrogance to humility in me.

I was in the middle of the desert with him, tired and thirsty, and when I asked him for water he didn't give it to me. But he did go and get me some fruit, and I wouldn't take the fruit. And I went a little bit further into the desert because he commanded me. And that was the only time I obeyed anybody. I was dead with fatigue when I reached the convent, and I lay down on a beautiful bed surrounded by the religious women.

And then the monk came to me and said: 'I've been telling you lies; there *is* love in the world; there is *nothing* but love in the world, sexual love!' And he got on his knees and took me into his arms, and I suddenly came to myself and threw my arms into the air and cried out, 'I see God!' and the monk could do nothing more with me. . . .

And Salomé—I was just a child of fifteen, born in vice, and I saw Jokanaan and I said to myself, 'I want that man!' But he wouldn't have anything to do with me. And then I went over to the bench and lay down with my head to the public and my hands on my face and never moved. It was my eyes that heard what Herod was saying.

I asked myself, 'How shall I get that man?' I looked like a lioness at that moment. . . . The dance of the seven veils just had to be mine, not a dancer's. I, Mary Garden, wouldn't allow any but my own mentality to go into Salomé. A dancer would have kicked up her legs and 'danced,' and that had nothing to do with the drama that I was living.

That dance was a drama between the cistern of Jokanaan and the throne of Herod. Finally, I stood before Herod like a mischievous child, and I said, staccato, 'I want the head of Jokanaan!' . . . And when they brought me the head, instead of taking it out of the soldier's hands and turning it to the audience and looking at it, I used to lift it to the very top of my head and then bring it down quickly, and that was the first time my eyes looked at it. When I put it over my head, that was my victory. When I looked at it, that was my lust. . . .

And then I kissed the mouth of the head, and I was wild with sensuality.

'Now I can do it!' I said to myself, and then I spoke to the head: 'You didn't let me touch your skin; you wouldn't let me touch your hair.'

Finally I kissed the lips, and that was my *jouissance*. When Mary Garden went home from Salomé she was dead; nobody understands that, and I don't understand it myself. That girl had a deeper effect on me than any other rôle. . . . Salomé was never mad; she was sane, in her vicious way, all through the thing; that lust of hers gave her a passionate logic. I'll never forget how I was drunk with gratification of the senses when I kissed the mouth.

Then when I was completely *épuisée*, I fell on the head, and Herod, that monster of vice and sensuality, even he couldn't bear the sight of it and he shouted, 'Kill that woman!'

Salomé has to be young. I don't see a big woman doing the part, a big woman with large breasts and hips. She was like a cat playing with a mouse. With her so young, the whole thing couldn't be ugly; morbid perhaps, but not offensive. And I kept Salomé young. I wore short hair and short dresses, and, oh, I was quick! Salomé was poetry, vice, youth, all mixed together. I remember I played it in Brussels, and a certain countess came to my dressing-room after the performance.

'I was never so embarrassed in my life, Miss Garden,' she said. 'I could stand watching it in my own house. But with a houseful of people around me—never again, my dear!'

Then I recall how Oscar Hammerstein was making plans for a Boston engagement and he announced that he would put *Salomé* on the programme. Till he heard from Boston. 'If you perform *Salomé* here,' they wired, 'we promise to put every one of you in jail.'

'Mary,' said Mr. Hammerstein to me, 'I've got a good mind to give *Salomé* in Boston, just for the pleasure of seeing you behind the bars.'

Later, when I was in Paris, London cabled me.

'Will you come over to do Salomé at Covent Garden?'

'I'd be delighted,' I replied, 'so long as you don't place any conditions.'

'You can have everything but the head,' they cabled back.

And my answer to that was, 'No head, no Salomé.'

Was I supposed to be screaming for something for one hour and a half and then not get it? I couldn't face that. So they cabled me again.

'Will you sing Carmen at Covent Garden?'

'Gladly,' I answered, 'but I must know who is going to sing with me and who will conduct the orchestra.'

They then cabled their agent in Paris:

'Break off negotiations with Garden. We will not tolerate dictation.'

And so, after that disastrous experience of many years before, I never sang again in Covent Garden. I was asked three times, and three times some obstacle was in the way. I never sang at the Metropolitan, and the reason is quite simple: I was never asked.

I never went into the Metropolitan except as a ticket-holder or with a visiting company on Tuesday nights, when there are no regular performances. When I was asked to come to America, it was by Oscar Hammerstein for the Manhattan Opera House. I was perfectly happy with him, with my contract, with my repertory, and with the French singers who came over with me.

There just wasn't any French tradition to speak of at the Metropolitan. What would I have done there? But why speculate on it; I was just never invited to sing there. I have been asked if I ever thought of an eventual Metropolitan début when I left America to go to Paris to study singing.

The answer is 'No.' It was never my goal, and I never lost any sleep over it. *The truth is I never had a thought in my mind of what I was going to be.* I had no fixed purpose in going to Paris except to learn how to sing. The idea of going on the stage never entered my head. There was nothing, absolutely nothing, in my life up to that point to persuade me or anybody else that that was my calling.

## Lion Hunting and Voice Hunting

IN 1934, while in Monte Carlo, I became a hunter of lions . . . almost. I met a man who passed his whole life hunting lions in Abyssinia. My sister had somehow got to know him, and she presented him to me. I don't think he ever cared for women before, but he fell for me, all six feet four of him. There had been only lions in his life, and now there was me. My, what a baby that man was; kind and sweet and amusing, but a perfect child. We had a romance, yes, but just for that brief summer in Monte Carlo. We went swimming together, though most of the time he was telling me about the wild beasts of Africa. He would just sit there and enumerate all the different things he had killed.

According to himself, he was the only outsider who was allowed to hunt lions in Abyssinia, because he was such a good friend of Haile Selassie. That all fascinated me because it was a life so utterly unlike mine. I remember he used to bring all his guns to my house and scare the liver out of me. It was all quite pleasant while it lasted, nothing very important in my life or his. My holiday soon came to an end, and my friend packed his guns and went back to his lions. I often wonder where he is, and even whether the lions of Abyssinia finally bagged *him*. He was the biggest man I ever knew, and the biggest baby . . . and he looked like one.

Just after my man with the guns departed on his latest, and perhaps his last, lion hunt, I returned to New York and found myself plunged in a hunt of my own, far riskier, I'm certain, and more difficult than his. One day my great friend Robert Rubin of Metro-Goldwyn-Mayer came to see me.

'Mary,' he said, 'I suppose you've seen Grace Moore in *One Night of Love.*'

'I have,' I said.

'Well, I won't ask you what you think of it, but it's a terrific success, you know, and we're thinking of making a great number of musical pictures.'

'You're not planning to engage me to sing,' I said. 'I've finished, you know.'

'I know, Mary,' he said; 'but what we have in mind is quite different. I think you'll like it.'

'Frankly, I want something to do; I don't like being idle.'

'We want you to find voices. Look anywhere you want—Italy, France, New York, Hoboken; you'll stay in Hollywood part of the time, and we'll have them brought in to you.'

'I like that, Mr. Rubin,' I said. 'All you want me to look for is voices?'

'Just voices, Mary. You leave the rest to us.'

'I accept.'

Well, I began my big hunt for voices. I went to Rome and I went to Milan and Paris and Brussels. I heard dozens and dozens of singers. Nothing much came of it all, and then they gave me an office in Hollywood, and one day brought to Mr. Mayer a young and beautiful Chicago girl to hear. I auditioned her.

'That's a beautiful voice, Mr. Mayer.' He said, 'I'm going to make a recording of her voice.'

A few days later Mr. Mayer was back in my office.

'Mary, that's a beautiful voice all right, but she won't do.'

'Why not, Mr. Mayer?'

'No sex appeal.'

'But I'm not supposed to be looking for sex appeal,' I said. 'That's your department.'

Then there was a young boy whose voice hadn't changed

yet. How beautifully he sang all those coloratura arias! They took him and a tenor I had found. But where they went and whether they ever got on the screen, I don't know. I never heard anything more about them. Towards the end I was listening to everything from the cradle to fifty. In the sumptuous studio he put at my disposal, I heard voices from ten in the morning until five in the afternoon.

I shall never forget one woman, influentially sponsored, who arrived at ten-thirty one morning in full décolleté to sing the rôle of Santuzza in *Cavalleria rusticana* for me. She flew around my studio like a moth, finishing on the floor, with one fearful high note. At that moment, the office boy who brought up my letters came in, took one look at Santuzza, dropped my letters, and fled. I asked him the next day why he had run away.

'Why, Miss Garden,' he said, 'I thought the lady was dead.'

Frankly, the people I enjoyed most in Hollywood were the taxicab drivers. I had to use them every day to go to Culver City, and they would say the nicest things to me.

'We like you because you're real human,' one of them turned around to remark one day. 'We even got a name for you, Miss Garden.'

'Tell me,' I said.

'We call you the Lady of the Good Scent.'

I was quite flattered. They were all my friends, those taxi drivers. But, then, I have always been a great favourite with the real people of the country. They were my great triumph throughout my career, the people. I adore them, their genuineness and simplicity, their warmth and their instinctive joy in what is good and beautiful. That was another thing I loved about Corsica, the naturalness of the people, and their rugged pride.

During one of my lectures in 1949 I was asked what I

liked most about America. Without a moment's hesitation I replied:

'Its people.'

I might have said, 'Its women!' What the women of France and England could do if they had that power! . . .

Speaking of Hollywood cab drivers reminds me of a perfume that was named after me, and I suppose I should say something about it. I had finished my season here and was sailing back to France one day. We were still in the dock and a bell was ringing, telling everybody who wasn't sailing to get off the boat, when a young woman rushed up to me with a piece of paper in her hand.

'Oh, Miss Garden,' she panted. 'I'm so glad I've found you! Wouldn't you like a perfume called after your name?'

'I think I'd like that,' I said in all innocence.

'Do you mind signing this?' she said.

And I signed it, and she thanked me and went away. I sailed to France. Well, I came back the following season, and I was walking along Broadway, and there at the top of a building, in electricity, looking down at me and those thousands of people on the sidewalks, was my face!

'What in God's name is this?' I said to myself.

That was the Mary Garden perfume. So I told Father about it, and he got a lawyer interested in it. The lawyer looked into the matter and came back to Father with a report.

'Did your daughter ever get any money from the company?' he asked him.

'Not a cent,' said Father.

'Well, the name of that perfume was copyrighted almost immediately after she signed that piece of paper on the boat.'

'Is there anything she can do about it?'

'Nothing at all, except never to put her name to anything again unless a lawyer first looks at it.'

The perfume became a terrific success, and I was told many years later that I probably would have got from thirty to forty thousand dollars a year from it for as long as it was popular. Everybody made money on it, even the boys in the drugstores who sold it, but I, Mary Garden, who gave it my name and my face, never got a single sou! But, I suppose, it was my fault. After that I was careful about what I signed.

The perfume was called Gardenia, and I know it was a great favourite with the Negro people. I remember when I used to travel by train, the redcaps would say to one another, 'Oh, there's the lady of the perfume!'

I was never the lady who sang!

# I Live Through the War

MOTHER and I were almost trapped in the Nazi occupation of Paris. We left the city early in June, 1940, of the war and arrived in Scotland on the thirteenth—I had every intention of going back to Paris and the French government had stamped its permission on my passport. Then the Germans were in Paris on June 14th, and I never got back.

I shall always regret having left Paris, because I should have liked very much living through the Occupation. It might have been very tragic and it might have killed me, but it would have been interesting to live through something I had never experienced in my life and I would have liked that challenge.

Well, Mother and I left Paris on the ninth, were in London on the tenth, and in Aberdeen on the thirteenth. There was I thinking of getting right back to Paris, and I stayed nine years with Mother in Aberdeen.

When the war was at its height my sister Aggie and I took care of the soldiers who came to Aberdeen. What a woman Aggie was! There were one hundred soldiers staying in the village, and she had to take care of all one hundred of them. She had them up to the house almost every day. There was an enormous billiard room in the garden, which Aggie turned into a canteen, and there they came for nothing. Sometimes she had all one hundred of them to tea, and they were served cakes and buns. Aggie's maids gave them all the food they wanted. She would answer their letters for them and even send money to the wives of many of the men.

Aggie's soldiers would then go to the front, and another regiment would come up to Aberdeen, and Aggie would do the same for them. She continued this for four solid years—out of her own pocket. And then the refugees came in from the Scottish cities that were bombed. Aggie took many of them in. The canteen, which had been a billiard room, was now converted into a bedroom for a woman and her four children. Aggie had a bathroom put in and a kitchen too, and she made beautiful curtains for them. A beautiful little home now stood in the middle of Aggie's garden. Then one day she went down to London with me, and when we got back the woman and her four children were gone, and so was everything in the little house, everything but the four walls.

I stayed in Aberdeen with Mother much of the time, but when I wasn't with her I lived in Banchory, which is eighteen miles outside of Aberdeen, on the River Dee, where you catch some of the best salmon in the world. The officers stopped there at a hotel called Tor-na-Coille while the soldiers occupied little huts of steel that were built all over the gardens, about two hundred of them. My sister Amy then lived in Torphins, which is about ten miles away. She has six hundred acres with the most marvellous gardens. Well, I would go up to my sister's place and fill baskets with her glorious strawberries and plums and take them to the soldiers in Banchory. And I would take down to them the first salmon that arrived from the River Dee.

Then one Christmas I went to the general and said: 'General, I want to give these soldiers something for Christmas, and I don't want to give them anything to eat. What can I offer them?'

'Well, Miss Garden,' he said, 'I'd rather let them speak for themselves. Suppose I ask them.'

So the general asked them, and each and every one of those soldiers said they wanted to go to the theatre in Aberdeen. During those two particular weeks I have in mind Noel Coward was playing in Aberdeen in *This Happy Breed* and *Present Laughter*. So I went down and got a hundred and fifty orchestra stalls for the first week and a hundred and fifty stalls for the second week and gave them to the soldiers as a Christmas present.

Noel Coward told me afterward that he had never played to such an audience; they were all so sweet and enthusiastic and attentive. They had all gone down in camions from eighteen miles away, with their hair brushed and all their buttons polished—to see Noel Coward. There was a woman who played with Coward named Judy Campbell, the loveliest thing I ever saw on the stage. When the boys went into the camions to be taken back, the officers asked:

'Is everybody in?'

'Everybody but Judy!' they shouted together.

So that is what I did as long as they were there in Banchory. A great many of the officers played beautiful bridge, and we used to have many bridge parties. They were all delightful people, and the day they had to go to the front was always a fearful wrench for me. I had made a great many friends among them, and some of them did not come back.

And then I entertained a lot of American boys who came up for their leave in Aberdeen. They wandered out to Banchory, and the moment they went into the hotel, Miss Musgrave, who was in charge, would tell them that Mary Garden was stopping there. So, they would ask to see me, and I would take them to Balmoral Castle and show them other interesting places in that part of my country. Then one day three American colonels arrived in a jeep and of course they insisted on taking me for a ride. I never want to go into a jeep again. I went away looking very lovely, with a beautiful veil and hat, and I came home with no veil, no hat, and my hair flying everywhere.

Later, I took a great interest in a naval hospital called King's Seat. One day they brought in some badly burned American boys who were taken off a ship that had been blown up on its way to Russia. The nearest port was Aberdeen. The American Consul of Edinburgh, who was a great friend of mine, asked me to please go over and see if there was anything in the world I could do for those boys.

'And don't forget to take a lot of spectacles,' he said. 'Many of them lost their eyeglasses in battle, and I hear they have nothing to read with.'

Well, my sister and I gathered up all the spectacles we could buy, borrow, and steal and took them up to the hospital, and they fitted the sight of the men very well. I have never seen such happy faces as when those men saw us come in with our arms loaded with spectacles. Then we were introduced to them.

'Here's Mary Garden, come to see you, Sonny,' someone said to a boy lying in one bed. 'She wants to know if she can do anything for you.'

He was a very young boy, with great big eyes, and he looked up at me and said, 'Oh, not the real Mary Garden?'

And I said, 'Yes, the *real* Mary Garden; she's come to see if there's anything she can do for you. Is there anything you'd like?'

'Yes, there is something I want,' he said.

'What is it?'

'I want to go home.'

And he asked me for the only thing in the world I couldn't give him. I often think of him in America, and I hope he's well and happy.

I had great fun with the Americans when I met them on Union Street. I would take them into my favourite tobacco shop and give them all the cigarettes they wanted.

On November 2nd, 1944, something very sacred was given to my people of Aberdeen. It was a gift of an American combat flag to our beautiful St. Andrews Cathedral—a gift from none other than General Eisenhower.

The Very Reverend Provost Kinnell had asked General Eisenhower for one, and it was sent at once. Provost Kinnell had to find an American soldier to carry the combat flag at ceremonies that were arranged. A tall, young American officer, Captain Jack A. Teufel of Chicago, was then on leave in Aberdeen. Provost Kinnell met him one day, and to Captain Teufel went the honour of bearing his country's flag down the centre aisle of the crowded cathedral. As the flag was presented to Provost Kinnell, Captain Teufel announced:

'General Eisenhower presents this United States colour to be preserved as a memorial to the association in arms of the American and British people in this war for freedom.'

Then the Provost handed the flag to Dr. Ashton Oldham, Bishop of Albany, who was visiting Britain at the time and had come to Aberdeen to dedicate the flag to the cathedral.

After the dedication, Dr. Oldham asked the Bishop of Aberdeen and Orkney to accept the colour.

'With a glad heart,' responded Bishop Hall.

As the Bishop placed the flag on the high altar of the cathedral, the American anthem rang out on the organ, and for a few sacred moments everyone wept.

I wrote to General Eisenhower, thanking him for sending us such a precious relic despite all his endless preoccupations and worries. I received an answer. I am certain he would not mind my giving the last paragraph of his letter here.

'Letters such as yours are always most welcome,' he wrote, 'because they are additional evidence to me of the strength of our national partnership.'

Think of it, it was the middle of the war; the dreadful decisions that man had to make; yet he had time to write me an answer! That is the quintessence of good breeding, because nobody answers letters to-day.

One night the bombers came over and killed 148 men in a café. They were all sitting and drinking—poor people, all of them. Once, while I left Mother to visit my sister, we heard that the bombers were over Aberdeen again. I wanted to know what was going on and tried to telephone. But the lines were broken. Then someone arrived from Aberdeen.

'We've just had a bad raid,' he reported.

'Where was it?' I asked.

'Tartin Church.'

And that was four doors from Mother's house. I rushed back to Aberdeen. What a sight awaited me! All those enormous blocks of granite with their wonderful colours had been thrown into the air and had come down on Mother's house. They had broken through her skylight and come down her stairs. They had knocked down the chimneys and destroyed her gardens. Oh, the blocks and blocks of granite we had to dig up out of Mother's garden!

And I found Mother in her room, in bed, nervous and terrified, but unharmed. She had been alone in the house when the horror came!

The bombers had flown in from Bergen, Norway, which is just across the water. They told me that the Germans who came over with their bombs were always looking for Balmoral Castle, but they never touched it. We had a great many raids in Aberdeen. I remember one German came down on the top of our great skating rink, an enormous building. The plane stuck in the middle of the roof, half of it in and half of it out, and the man was dead in his plane. They never touched Union Street, and they never touched things of Aberdeen that were vital to the war. Their bombs always came down on houses and churches. They never knew and they never cared where they fell.

Then the war ended, and as soon as I could I went back to

Paris to see about my things. I had an apartment in the Rue du Bac, and in it were almost all of my precious belongings, paintings and statues and glassware. I immediately looked up my maid Françoise, who is still with me, and learned that most of my stuff was safe, and this is how it was.

The Germans had occupied my apartment, not the soldiers or the officers, but their families, which had come to live with them in Paris. But before they moved in, Françoise had acted. She got herself a pushcart and went into the apartment one night and took out all my pictures and statues and beautiful linen and glassware. She put them into the cart, and half of them she stored away in a room she had rented and the other half in her own apartment. There was one moment of terror for her when the Germans called her in for questioning.

'Where is Mary Garden?' they asked.

'She has left the country,' Françoise answered, and they didn't trouble her again.

When I returned to Paris I found Françoise in her lovely little walk-up apartment, brave and calm as usual. She had lived through the Occupation, and it must have been awful. Quite simply and undramatically, she told me how she had saved my things. It never seemed to dawn on her that she had risked her life. Françoise has been with me for thirty-five years, faithful, devoted, and thorough.

I never went back to the apartment on the Rue du Bac. What I valued most had been rescued, and I felt certain that the Germans had left nothing worth while behind of what remained of my furnishings. And my five motor cars—I had no business owning five, of course—were all gone. The Germans took them all—the Rolls-Royce, the Packard, the Pierce-Arrow, the Chrysler, and the Mathis. The Mathis was the only one I ran myself; the others were much too big. I never bothered to have any of them traced.

What was my greatest reunion in Paris? My reunion with

the city itself. What an inexhaustible city! I went to the Opéra-Comique; I went to the Opéra, and I went to the Comédie-Française. I saw all the haunts where I used to sing and have my triumphs—and loved every moment of it. But I felt absolutely no desire whatsoever to go back to my work; that was done. I had no regrets and no sentimental longing to have it back again. I never, never had any desire to return.

Then I went to *Pelléas et Mélisande* and saw the new *décors*. They had thrown out all the old sets and had engaged some woman to do new ones, and they were dreadful. They had nothing to do with Debussy's music. When the curtain went up on the death of Mélisande, I was so shocked I thought for a minute I was at Elizabeth Arden's, having my face cleaned. What a frightful thing to see! Now I hear they're not content with this *décor* and are going to make new scenery again. I hope it's an improvement.

I stayed about a month in Paris, at the Hotel Lancaster, which is where Mother always stopped when she visited me in Paris. Mother would never stay with any of us when she came to visit. That was her freedom and her independence; she wanted her own room and she wanted it in a hotel, where no one could invade her privacy. We were all that way when we visited each other away from home.

Then I went to Versailles to see if the war had touched it, and I found that not a blade of grass had suffered. I suppose they thought they were going to live there one day, so they never harmed it. I went back to Paris and from there returned to Aberdeen. I don't know if I'd ever live in Paris again. You see, I like my own country too much now. Yet, if I were to open a studio, I'd open it in Paris. 'Why don't you teach modern French opera?' everyone tells me. I might, though I have no intention right now. But if I ever do, it will be in Paris.

I went back to Aberdeen and stayed with Mother. I no

longer had a home; I had no desire to go back to my apartment on the Rue du Bac. I was, really, a refugee, I now had Mother's home to share with her; that was all. That was in 1946. Then in 1948 I rented an apartment of my own in Aberdeen, and that gave me the wonderful feeling of having a home again. I went again to Paris and brought back my pictures and statues, and as I tell this story I am about to move into my own place. My sister is furnishing it for me, and I have only now received a cablegram from her:

'Can I buy a Frigidaire for you?'

'Yes,' I'm cabling back, 'a Frigidaire by all means.'

'I'll have a nice fire lit for you and the coffee on the table when you come back,' she wrote the other day.

So, you see, when I go back to Aberdeen I shall walk into my own home. No cats, no dogs, no garden to keep. I can take the key and shut the door and go where I please, and the first place I mean to go to is Africa.

Then I lost Mother in 1948. . . .

I should like to pause here for a few moments and say something about Mother and the other members of my family.

We were all born in Aberdeen, all except my sister Helen, who was born in America. As far as we could see, the family, for several generations, was from Aberdeen on both sides. We were Scotch through and through. That, I think, is what makes me so independent.

Father and Mother never said boo to any of us. We did what we wanted, and not once did Father ever write to me in Paris to come back home. He never doubted that I could take care of myself or that I was old enough to know what I wanted. He knew, too, that he couldn't stop me once I had made up my mind. We were all like that. Father never interfered, and neither did Mother.

We were very near to one another, but not bound. There

was no jealousy, and no domination of any kind, and in our own way we loved one another. What it amounted to was this—each of us wanted her own liberty and her own life. What it must be like to be chained to anyone!

Father's full name was Robert Davidson Garden. He was one of the greatest athletes of his time, a strong and handsome man, and he died when he was ninety. Father's father was one of the biggest landowners in Aberdeenshire. He kept the most marvellous animals. All except Father died young on his side. Both his father and his mother died in their sixties, which is very early among us.

Besides Father, there were a brother and two sisters, one of whom was called Agnes, and it was after her that my sister was named. This aunt of mine married a business man who traded in China, and it was there that she went to live and died. I used to be told that she was the only one in the whole family whom I resembled in any way. They say, too, that she was a great musician and played the piano very well. I never heard her.

Father was an engineer in Aberdeen. Like so many other people, he wanted to see America, and did. After all the children except Helen were born, he went over by himself, decided to stay, and one year after he left Aberdeen he called for us to come over. Father later became an American citizen.

Mother's sorrow was that she never had a boy. All four of us were named boys before we arrived—all 'Robert'—and we all turned out to be girls.

The first of these girls was my sister Amy, who married Colonel Bower of Aberdeen, a big lawyer who was in the First World War, serving with the famous Scottish regiment, the Seventh Gordon Highlanders. They have no children.

The second was Mary, and you know about her.

The third was Agnes, who married a very handsome American named Edward De Witt Walsh, who died in 1917.

He was in the Stock Exchange. They, too, had no children. Aggie is a very witty woman, full of fun and beautiful in a way. I have been more with Aggie than with the others. She lived mostly in America, but after her husband died she returned to Scotland and took back her British nationality. I believe that was in 1920. She has made Scotland her home since then.

The fourth and last of the Garden girls is Helen, the only one to be born in America. Helen married a Frenchman associated with the Tobler Chocolate Company. He was killed in the First World War. She had two boys by him, the only one of the four sisters to have children. Helen became a French citizen, but after her husband's death she resumed her American citizenship. She loves the country she was born in and is American to the backbone.

Helen lives in Megève, in the Haute-Savoie of France. That is the greatest ski-ing place in France, and both her boys are excellent skiers. My sister had them educated in Switzerland, and both speak four languages perfectly. They are very interesting boys. One of them lives with her in Megève, and the other is in business in Paris. Besides her house in Megève, Helen has a villa in Cannes. When the Germans came in with the Italians in the last war, she took up her bag and her dog and walked to Megève. She got there three weeks later.

Helen went to school and college in Maryland. She had one of the most beautiful soprano voices I have ever heard, not brilliant like mine, but sweet. I have no doubt that she would have made a great singer, if it hadn't been for one thing. She could sing beautifully, but only when alone or with just the family around her. Appearing before others made her so nervous her vocal cords just tied up in knots. What a beauty she was, too! I am certain she would have made a perfectly wonderful actress in the silent-picture days.

And Helen loves animals like no one else I have ever known. There isn't a dog or cat in the whole village of Megève that doesn't know her. Every morning she puts pieces of cheese and meat into her little basket, and as she marches down the street every dog and cat is there, waiting for her to give them something to eat.

There's a garage in Megève, and the owner of it keeps a huge and ferocious dog chained and fenced there. Nobody in Megève would come near the animal, nobody but Helen. One day she went right in there and gave that dog cheese. What's more, when the dog had puppies, Helen went in and took one of them up, and that big brute just looked up at her and smiled and seemed to say, 'Don't you think that's a beautiful child I had?'

I saw that dog when I was visiting my sister. Ooh, what teeth she had! Well, that garageman said to Helen one day:

'Madame, if anybody steals something from my garage I'll know it is you, because nobody else in this village could pass that gate and live.'

We are quite a variety of nationalities, we Garden sisters. Helen was born in America, became French, and resumed her American citizenship. Aggie became American and then was Scotch again. Amy married a Scotsman and remained Scotch.

I never married and I never changed my British nationality. I have always used a British passport.

Before she married, Mother was Mary Joss, the fourth of five children. My grandfather on Mother's side had enormous granite quarries in Aberdeen. My grandmother was quite an aristocratic woman. They were all Sir this and Lord that in her family, and many of the men were in the British Navy. Mother, as they say, was very well born.

Some day I want to go to Africa to visit the grave of Mother's brother, John Joss. Early in his life he went to

Africa and became associated with the Kimberley Diamond Mines, where he was a great friend of Cecil Rhodes. He often came back to Aberdeen to see his mother. He died when he was forty.

Mother's eldest sister, Isabella, married a captain who sailed his own ship. It was called *The Star of Africa*. He had had it built for himself, and when it was finished he took Aunt Isabella on as his bride. Together they sailed from Aberdeen to Africa. The captain was lame, having fallen from a mast and broken his leg. For years he did all his trading between Africa and India. He was a very thorough and provident man. He had his meat alive with him on board—cows, chickens, pigs. That was the way he and Aunt Isabella sailed the seas, like Noah.

Well, the day came when the captain was ready to retire. Returning to South Africa, he was rounding the Cape of Good Hope, when his ship struck the famous Albatross Rock near Cape Town, and every single, solitary person—and beast—on board was drowned. They found the body of Mother's brother-in-law, but they never found anybody else.

Mother's two sisters both lived to be well over eighty. Mother herself died at ninety-three.

She was the most beautiful woman ever seen in Scotland—great big brown eyes, a gorgeous form of a face, the most exquisite figure, and a beautiful mind. I never heard Mother say an ugly word about anybody. I never knew Mother to be ill; certainly I don't recall that she ever had a doctor in the house except as a guest. I must take after her in many ways. One great difference, however, is that I adore books, and Mother never read a book in her life. I am more like Father in that respect.

Mother was very proud of her beauty—and her youth. Actually, she never grew old, for when she arrived at the age of thirty-five, she stopped counting.

'Mary,' she said, 'I was never thirty-six and I never shall be.'

And it was the same thing with her passport. When she went to Europe with me, we would go down and have our passports looked at. But I never would go in with her because the way her passport read would have made her one year old when I was born!

'Mother, you're going in alone,' I would say.

'Nonsense, Mary,' she would reply. 'I don't look a day older. They won't dare question the year of my birth.'

'Yes, Mamma,' I would say, 'but they will say that *I* was never born.'

Father and I both loved to read the biographies of great men of the past, like Cæsar and Napoleon. Mother could never understand that.

'Why in goodness' name,' she would say, 'do you and your father like to read about dead men?'

Father's library meant nothing to Mother. When he died he left it to me, and it is one of my great joys and comforts. I have never gone a day of my life without reading, good reading, like history and biography and the letters of the men and women long dead who still reach our minds with theirs. Father also loved poetry, and there we differed, for I can't bear it. A poem makes my mind wander. I feel restless when I hear or read poetry; it has to be put into music before it has any interest for me.

Father was also very fond of the ladies, quite the incorrigible flirt, but Mother didn't mind it at all, because she knew he worshipped her. Mother had all her comforts, and from the beginning to the end life for her was just as she wanted it.

Mother loved to travel. Father used to meet her at the boat when she came back from Europe.

'Where are the newspapers, Robert?' was her first question.

'Why so interested in the papers?' Father would ask.

'I've got to see about the next sailings,' Mother would reply. 'I want to go back to Europe.'

Mother was always ill, crossing the ocean, but absolutely happy in the air. I have always hated flying. I don't like being cooped up and I don't like to have straps around me. I have a horror of being shut in. I always hated corsets, and I never wore them, except in *Carmen* and *Louise*. You've got to wear corsets there. I never needed them for myself.

Thaïs

Aphrodite

Cherubin

Ophelia

Fiora in *The Love of Three Kings*

## I Return as a Speaker

I HAD always said I never wanted to be near my parents when they died, because it would have been too dreadful a sorrow to go through. I was in Paris when Father died, and that made it easier to bear. But I was alone with Mother when she died, and I never knew in my life what personal grief meant till then.

A great many people have enormous grief to bear in their lives, but it had never really touched me, and now I didn't know how to cope with it. I got into a fearful rut when Mother died. I didn't care for anybody or anything. Everyone around me was nervous about my state of health and mind. I lost interest in life, and that was the very first time anything like that had happened to me. Everything had grown black and dismal. Then suddenly this call from America came. . . .

Four years before, a project was being considered to bring me over for a lecture tour. I was quite willing to do it. Then the manager wrote back and said that there was no use in coming because I was entirely forgotten. I was inclined to agree with him. And now here was Carleton Smith of the National Arts Foundation.

'We want you to come back to us, Miss Garden,' he said.

'But they tell me I'm forgotten in America.'

'Nonsense,' he said, 'your name is still a household word in every part of America.'

'Mr. Smith,' I said, 'there's no use bringing me over; no one will know me, and many of them think I'm dead, anyway. I'll let you know next year, if you're still interested.'

Then he wrote me a letter, 'Have you decided?'

And I wrote back, 'Yes—I shall come.'

And I went back on a pure gamble, for I had never thought I would take up any kind of work in America again. And having returned to America, to the life and beauty and youth of America, to my amazement, far from being forgotten, I was greeted with more enthusiasm than I ever received when I was singing there. The great joy of my first tour was this exciting realization: I was remembered!

I never dreamed that I would be able to live again with the American public. And now this experience was bringing me back all the life and all the energy and all the *joie de vivre* again. And for the first time I was appearing before the public as myself. In those twenty years of my career in America, I was never Mary Garden. I was my rôles, but never myself. My first talk was in Washington, and there I saw at once, from the great enthusiasm of the people who came to hear me, that I was not forgotten.

Think of it, in this busy world, with all the changes and the war, these days when people are so easily forgotten, they remembered me! I only went over for three months, to see if this thing could be a success or not, and it was a greater success than I ever dreamed; even greater than my career, because now it was a personal triumph. I don't have to be Salomé, the Jongleur, Mélisande, to reach the people. I draw them to me now with a warmer feeling than in any opera that I ever sang—the warmth of their love for me and the warmth of my love for them. Because I adore the people.

And the women of America—it was they who made me in my work and it is they who made me in my talks. They were so warm and sensitive and loyal. One thing that interested me especially was the questions. They were so amusing and so intelligent, and I enjoyed that part of my programmes more than the 'lecturing.'

And then I returned to my divine Chicago, after eighteen long years. What a reception! I shall never forget the moment I walked on the stage of Orchestra Hall. They just stood up and screamed, and I couldn't open my mouth for five minutes. I've never seen anything like it, and I was perfectly amazed. *They had not forgotten me.* Then one of the papers came out the next day with a great announcement:

'Mary is looking for a job.'

And, of course, I never answered it, because that was the furthest from my mind. I'm not looking for a job. I'm perfectly peaceful in my own country, and I'm not out of work. I didn't think of my talking tour as work; it was a reunion, a family reunion with the people who loved and remembered me for the artistic joy I had brought them. It was the most entrancing and exhilarating experience of my life, renewing my friendship with the great American public.

And the flowers they brought me! In Indianapolis they had little girls dressed in Scotch costumes bring them up to me, and then I opened a flower show for them, and just as I set out for the ceremonies there stood a good-looking young Scotsman with his bagpipes and he piped me all along the railway station to the show. Then there was a man in Kansas City who for two years grew a special chrysanthemum that he named after me, and he came to me with a bunch of them and said:

'Anywhere you are in the world, Mary Garden, you will get a bouquet of these flowers for the rest of your life.'

All these things outside of my talk just charmed me. And there were always invitations to teas, dinners, and parties, which, with few exceptions, I never accepted, because that was the way I had always lived. And then I didn't stay long enough in any one place. The talk was sometimes one hour and a half, and frankly I got a little tired. I spoke without notes and I had to know what to say.

The first of my 'lectures' (I prefer to call them talks, because 'lecture' frightens me and everybody else) was in Washington, and I shall never forget the thrill of being back on a stage before a responsive audience. Two of the three colonels who took me out in a jeep in Aberdeen were there, and they came up and spoke to me afterward, and we all had a good laugh over it. . . . I didn't feel then it was a rôle, but I begin to feel it now, a very interesting rôle, the rôle of Mary Garden. It was the first talk I had ever given in my life. I walked out on the stage, and everyone stood up. That put all the enthusiasm into me that I needed. I must have given a good talk, because they all laughed and we had a great time together.

'But this is easy,' I said to myself. 'It's going to be fun. I've come to do something I never thought I could do and I have the public with me.'

They had never known me before, because I had never let them know me. I had never let anyone know me, really. They had known Mélisande and Salomé and Louise and Thaïs about as well as they could ever know them, but in all those thirty years of singing and acting they had never seen and heard Mary Garden. I just wasn't in those characters; there was absolutely nothing that was the real me that became part of them. If they had lost their hearts to Thaïs and Mélisande, it was because of Thaïs and Mélisande, not because of me.

Now it was *I* who took them into *my* heart, and it was *I* who gave *my* heart to them. I find it hard to define. It was the very first time that they have ever seen me as I am; I never wanted them to see me before, except in the theatre. It was as if I had been some mysterious masked wonder and had suddenly thrown off my disguise and said:

'Ladies and gentlemen, I give you myself.'

And then I had a charming twenty minutes with President Truman at the White House. When I went in I found a vital, youthful, beautifully dressed man sitting there behind his desk and looking as if he were a great athlete.

'Why, Mr. President,' I exclaimed, 'how young you are!'

He thanked me and smiled.

'You know,' I went on, 'we people before the public have the most dreadful pictures in the papers. Why, you're a young man!'

He had the most glorious blue eyes I ever looked into. I said to myself, 'I wouldn't like those eyes to be angry with me.'

We spoke about music.

'Mr. President,' I said, 'you should have an opera house in Washington. This is the capital of the United States and this is where America's great national opera house should be.'

'Yes, Miss Garden,' he replied, 'I realize that very much, and I regret it.'

'All the great capitals of the world have their opera houses,' I continued. 'Every one of them but Washington. I'm going to put that in my next lecture. Do you mind, Mr. President?'

And he said, 'Go right ahead; I'm all for you.'

Then I spoke about his daughter.

'I think it's wonderful the way she's going at her career,' I said.

And he said, 'Have you heard her sing, Miss Garden?'

'I haven't had the pleasure yet, Mr. President,' I said. 'But nothing would interest me more. She must love her work, because as the daughter of the President of the United States she doesn't have to do it. I admire her, her courage, and her determination to sing.'

'You've made me very happy saying that, Miss Garden,'

the President replied. 'Margaret will be very pleased to know you feel that way about it.'

Then I spoke of the opera house again.

'Will you promise me to think of building one in Washington?'

'Yes, of course, Miss Garden,' he said. 'But I couldn't get the money for an opera house.'

'You can get billions for Europe,' I said. 'You raise money for libraries and money for your armed services. Why can't you get money for music?'

'I'd have to ask Congress,' said the President.

'I'd like to go before Congress and ask them myself for an opera house in Washington,' I said.

The President just laughed.

I didn't stay any longer because I didn't want to bother him. I just wanted to see him and know him and have a few words with him. And then when I arrived back in New York I got the most beautiful photograph from him, with his signature on it. I considered it a very great honour indeed . . . the President just sent it to me. I never asked for it.

The only other times I had been in the White House before that was when I sang at soirées for Mr. Hoover and Mr. Taft. They were terrific things, those soirées, and I remember Mr. Taft introduced me with these words:

'Ladies and gentlemen, I have the pleasure of presenting Mary Garden, who is a household word.'

Everybody laughed. I felt I was something like Sapolio.

In Chicago a great many members of my old chorus came backstage to me after the lecture. There were also others who had sung small rôles with me, and many of them I couldn't remember or recognize. I felt just like a child talking with them. They were absolutely new to me and remote. We had been close at one time, and now I was so far away from them.

Something had happened to many of them, or perhaps

nothing had happened to them. They hadn't had any great interest in their lives. They talked about the long ago as if their lives had ended then. But the long ago never interests me; it is here and now that absorbs me, and I adore the future. But it was nice to see them. They were all so sweet and enthusiastic.

Then I met many of my former colleagues in New York, mostly women. It was so strange. They didn't seem to fit in with opera or music or anything exciting any more. They no longer had any hold on the life we had shared. They seemed to have stood still and lost touch. They were so utterly detached from me.

But the public was never detached from me. They recognized me at once, and I them, especially the women. Oh, you women of America, you made my modern French operas, yes, you made them; you were so eager to know about the new things. When we went about the country it was my modern French masterpieces that you took, and the one that headed the list was *Thaïs*. Oh, how you wanted that opera, and how you dragged your poor dear husbands to the opera house, and how they liked it once they were there!

It was the women of America, not the men and certainly not the critics, who made me, and I love them and take my hat off to them. It was they who understood my art and the secret of modern French opera. But they don't realize their force in this country, the women. Some day they shall, and then, perhaps, we shall have a great renaissance of music, opera, and all the arts in America.

After all, the men of America, what do they like? Business. They talk business, they love business, they live business. We must look to the women for leadership in the arts.

One night my sister was seated in the orchestra of the Opéra in Paris, watching me in a performance of *Thaïs*. Next to her was an American couple, and she couldn't help overhearing their conversation. The man was in a fearful humour.

'I didn't want to come here, and you know it,' he was saying to his wife. 'I wanted to go to the Folies Bergère.'

'Well, you're here now, darling,' she said very sweetly, 'and you're going to hear Mary Garden in *Thaïs* with me.'

The man just groaned and then sat still. Soon the opera began, and my sister said that when I came in he kind of took a bit of interest.

Finally, when I threw off my robe and stood there before the monk, this American said to his wife:

'Gee, this is grand! Give me your glasses.'

And my sister said he didn't give the glasses back to his wife all evening.

That's the typical American business man—and husband—for you!

The men of America have to be educated to love grand opera, and there's not enough grand opera in the United States to educate them. That's why I say it's a shame, in a great country of 150,000,000 people, to have only one opera house with a long tradition to furnish this education. That has to change, if grand opera is to come back. Motion pictures, television, and radio have taken the place of grand opera in the minds of the American people—for the moment.

In our day we were the ones who were talked about; we made the news; we interested the public. Now it is the movie actors and actresses and their divorces and what they say and what they do—not the grand-opera singers. But once we get the great singers again, opera will be back in the people's hearts again and in the news.

In my mind, as I sit here, there is only one Kirsten Flagstad. Now, if we had fifteen like her in the world to-day, we might have grand opera again on the same scale as before.

The truth is, opera has always gone in cycles. There were Patti and Lilli Lehmann and Jenny Lind and Tamagno in one cycle; and they faded away.

Then there were Melba, Eames, the de Reszkes, Plançon, Schumann-Heink, Maurel in another great cycle; and they vanished, too. Next came Caruso, Farrar, Chaliapin, Muratore, Galli-Curci, and myself, and in time we too faded away.

Another cycle is due, but not soon. You will first have to put the interest of grand opera into the minds of the public again and somehow take them away from that irresistible entertainment, the motion picture. I *do* love the motion picture, but it can be very dangerous for the other arts. And opera couldn't be brought to the screen, not really. Television is another matter. If and when opera returns, it may do so that way.

When I saw the opening of the Metropolitan on television I said to myself, 'We have it!' Grand opera may recover its place of authority through this great medium. It will be brought into every home in the United States, when it is perfected. People will then learn to understand grand opera and want to hear it regularly. I sat and watched the whole of *Der Rosenkavalier* and enjoyed every minute of the performance as if I had been in the opera house.

Grand opera is the highest form of theatrical entertainment, and it deserves to be brought into the homes of the people for their taste. And then when the new cycle begins, we shall have the singers, new, young, attractive, enthusiastic singers. And we'll need new composers, too. The composers I sang for were all of the turn of the century. Since then no great operas have been written, except maybe one, Shostakovich's *Lady Macbeth of Mzensk*. How I would have liked to do that!

But new operas also have to come, and I should imagine that with the enormous mélange of nationalities in America they might come from there. But I don't know. And never in the world can you translate the old operas into English. The new operas will have to be in their own languages. I should like very much to hear a grand opera in English. Perhaps it will come.

You take that little jewel of a thing, *South Pacific*, that may be the beginning for American opera. Because that's a miniature grand opera. Someone will now come and write something bigger, and someone after him will add something else, and we'll have a grand opera one day. They will then take that opera and sing it in their own beautiful English language. That is one way that I say grand opera might come to America—the way of beautiful lyrics and beautiful music and beautiful story, and on television.

And the young American singers will have to be ready. . . . During my lecture tour I spoke again and again about my career. There were hundreds of questions about how I made my début, how I began. And I told them how I began at the top, not at the foot of the ladder, and that fate was with me. That was my privilege and my chance. Not everybody can do what I did and not everybody is given the opportunity—to begin, with little warning, in the middle of an opera.

But I was ready, I was ready, and that's what half of them aren't to-day. They rarely have a goal nowadays, or when they have, they must get to it in a few weeks or months. I have always stressed three years of hard, unremitting work. I have emphasized my three don'ts: no drinking, no smoking, no men for those three years. After all, three years are nothing in the life of a young girl. When she gains her name, she can do what she likes. Then everything she says and does is news. But those three years belong to her work. In that time she must also learn a language other than her own. If possible, she should go to Europe.

*And she must have a goal.* She must concentrate on one

school. I began with the modern French repertory. Later, when I dipped into the Italian repertory, I was already a personality in the world. Finally, I looked into the German school. I could afford to go exploring then. For three years that girl's eyes must be fixed on one goal. After that she is ready for anything in grand opera. The sacrifice is hers, and, so, of course, the reward. Those who do it will find it worth while. I did.

## This Was Never Make-Believe

THERE was always a strange drive in me, an impulse that I can't describe. I'm not Salomé this minute and I can't put it into words. You would have had to come to me during the performance and asked me what I was doing and why, and Salomé would have told you . . . perhaps. Now I'm just Mary Garden sitting in my bedroom, and I don't know what she did on the stage.

I never was a singer. God gave me this creative gift—I suppose that was all there was to it. I can't explain it in any other way. I used my voice to colour my rôles. Salomé was blood red. Mélisande was melting ice; there was sex, but without her knowing it; she was quite true to her husband. But it was dark—she would say, 'I never see the sky here'—and Pelléas was light and nature and the trees and flowers, and perhaps that was why, when with him, she was troubled.

What made me want to do what I did on the stage? I don't know. I had it the first time I stepped on the stage as Louise. Albert Carré saw it at once, and he always said to me, 'Garden, do whatever you want, because you can't do anything wrong.'

I never knew how I did those things, because I myself, Mary Garden, never did them. I never felt the lust of Salomé in my life. And I was never drunk, yet there was Katusha, in Alfano's *Resurrection*, hiding her bottles in her prison bed and getting drunk on vodka. At that moment I *was* drunk. There I lay on the floor when the prince came in, and he left me because he couldn't bear it any more. But before leaving, he put into my hands a photograph of my home when I was a child, and in my stupor I looked up and around like a real drunkard to see if anyone was in the place. Then I took the picture and suddenly I was myself, and in that drunken daze I cried hot tears. . . .

Noel Coward came over from London to Paris to hear me in *Resurrection*. When the performance was over he rushed up to my dressing-room and said:

'I've never seen anything in my life like that drunken girl, Mary. How did you ever get her into your mind? I could have sworn you were drunk yourself.'

'I don't know,' I said. 'I've only had two cocktails in my life, and then I never knew what was happening because I was carted away unconscious in an ambulance.'

And the simple truth is that I didn't know what I was throwing to the audience. I was just *living* Katusha at that moment. . . .

I find it so hard to discuss these things, sitting here in my bedroom, away from the lives and surroundings of those women. All I know is that I was never myself on the stage, except, in a certain sense, in *Louise*. That was modern. Louise lives to-day, and I could be myself in my own world, you might say. That was the only time they saw me as myself on the stage, till I returned as a lecturer. But in no other character was I Mary Garden. . . .

Perhaps 'creation' is the word. Somehow, instinctively, you know what is right. The next woman won't know. But *you* know; you have that divine something that makes you see and feel and live another woman. As I sang Salomé, I *was* in the court of Herod; I *was* living in those days. *Salomé*, incidentally, was the only opera I ever sang in that made me feel like a caged animal, before it started. I was just wild to go on before they opened the door to let me in.

*This was never a life of make-believe for me*. They were all real people who had lived, and I lived their lives again for them.

And then I went home and took a glass of milk and slept for nine hours. The next day I never thought of that strange thing of having lived another life the night before. I was just plain Mary Garden, and I never began thinking about that other woman until I got my foot on the stage again, and then I forgot there was anybody in the whole wide world who went by the name of Mary Garden.

People would meet me afterward and say, 'What a simple woman.' I suppose the contrast was very striking after me as Thaïs. We were worlds apart in the way we lived. And many would also remark, 'What a little woman.' And again they were right in being surprised. Because, you see, I'm only five feet four, and yet people got the idea that I was very tall, especially in *Thaïs*. Do you know why? From my toes to my waist I'm very long, and then my gestures were always very big, with my hands above my head—very high, very long, and very big. So they thought I was a tall woman, as they had thought I was a woman of lurid passions, and they were wrong again.

And I always knew how to shut the door on myself. My family never knew me when I acted. Once, after a performance of *Traviata*, my sister came to me in a paroxysm of grief.

'Mary,' she cried, 'I'm so glad you're alive'

If my own sister didn't know me on the stage, how could I know myself? There she stood, crying her heart out.

'My dear,' I said, 'stop being silly; I was only acting.'

But was I?

After a performance of Alfano's *Resurrection* she came into my dressing-room and again burst into tears.

'Mary,' she sobbed, 'are you sure you're all right?'

'I never felt better in my life; that was only Katusha, darling. This is me.'

I lived my rôles; I *was* the person. Perhaps that's why you can't give many of my rôles to-day. I don't find that complete obliteration of self that each of them requires. It wasn't anything cultivated. I never studied to achieve it. I found it the easiest and most natural thing in the world to do, so I suppose it was a gift from God. I must have been born with it.

The others 'acted' a rôle; I *was* the rôle. She who was Mary Garden died that it might live. That was my genius . . . and my sacrifice. It drained off so much of me that by comparison my private life was empty. I could not give myself completely twice.

Early in life I taught myself a very simple lesson—don't lean on anyone but yourself. I have always been independent in my work and in my life. I could never belong to anyone. I never needed anyone, and that was why I could give so much to my art. When I chose my career I resolved to crowd everything else out, and when I was in the theatre I was aware of nothing but my rôle.

I never let people interfere with my work or influence me. I had very few close friends during the thirty years of my career, for I wanted myself for myself and my work. Two months a year I had to be alone with nature, away from people. But that was solitude rather than loneliness. And from nature I drank in peace and health.

I believed in myself, and I never permitted anything or anybody to destroy that belief. My eye never wavered from the goal, and my whole life went into the operas I sang. I wanted liberty and I went my own way. Some called it a lonely way, but that wasn't true. I had myself and my music, and I was and am a happy person. I owe nothing to anyone but Mary Garden, and for that I paid the price of hard work. My help always came from myself, never from outside.

After one of my appearances, I was introduced to Governor Cox of Ohio, who had just written a book. Well, we sat down and talked about books and politics, and I said:

'Oh, Mr. Cox, I'm writing a book, too.'

'Why, that's fine, Miss Garden,' he said. 'What's it about?'

'It's all about me. But I'm worried about it.'

'Why is that?'

'My publishers tell me they want romance in it,' I said.

'I think they're perfectly right,' said Governor Cox.

'But that's my private life,' I protested. 'Why should I let the public in on it? It's none of their business.'

'That's quite true, Miss Garden,' he replied. 'But if your love helped a great man, I think that's a very interesting thing to tell the world.'

And that started me thinking, and I said to myself:

'Perhaps that would be a good subject to have in my book.'

Now, whether loving me helped any of the men whose stories I have told in this book I'm not at all sure. But I'm glad I was persuaded to put 'romance' into it, if only to show as forcefully and frankly as I know how that my music always came first, that I valued the men in my life only as they brought me companionship, and that the love and passion were on their side and never on mine. My passion was opera, and that was the only real 'romance' of my life.

# Index